Contents

Introduction: Moving to Learn and Learning to Move   v

Evridiki Zachopoulou   Ian Pickup
Alexander Technological Educational   Roehampton University, United Kingdom
Institute of Thessaloniki, Greece

Part I   Basics of an Early Childhood Physical Education Curriculum

Chapter 1   Early Childhood Physical Education in Europe   3

Arja Sääkslahti   Jarmo Liukkonen
University of Jyväskylä, Finland   University of Jyväskylä, Finland

Variations in Institutional Structures 4 • Physical Education in Early Childhood 4 • Societal and Environmental Challenges 6 • Conclusion 6 • References 7

Chapter 2   Teaching Methods   11

Ian Pickup
Roehampton University, United Kingdom

Need for Child-Centred Teaching Methods 12 • Starting From the Child 13 • Selecting What to Observe 14 • Acting on Observations 15 • Teaching Styles to Promote Learning 16 • Using Group Work 18 • References 18

Chapter 3   Teacher Behaviours   21

Niki Tsangaridou
University of Cyprus, Cyprus

Characteristics of Effective Teachers 22 • Essential Instructional Strategies for Teaching Physical Education 23 • Conclusion 28 • References 28

Chapter 4   Promoting Children's Sound Personality Development and Intrinsic Motivation Towards Physical Activity   31

Jarmo Liukkonen
University of Jyväskylä, Finland

Social Development Through Physical Education 33 • Development of Intrinsic Motivation Through Physical Education 34 • Motivational Climate in Physical Education 35 • References 37

Chapter 5   Early Steps Physical Education Curriculum Standards   41

Jarmo Liukkonen
University of Jyväskylä, Finland

Standard 1 43 • Standard 2 46 • References 50

Part II   Implementing the Early Steps Physical Education Curriculum

Chapter 6   Social Interaction Lesson Plans   57

Chapter 7   Healthy Behaviour Lesson Plans   125

Chapter 8   Evaluation Methods   189
Vasilis Grammatikopoulos
University of Thessaly, Greece

Evaluation in Education 190 • Evaluation in Early Childhood Education 190 • Evaluation Objects, Goals, and Criteria 191 • Programme Evaluation in Education 192 • Systems Approach Evaluation 192 • Practical Applications and Forms 193 • References 194

Appendix: Description of the Early Steps Project   195
Evridiki Zachopoulou
Alexander Technological Educational Institute of Thessaloniki, Greece

Index   219
About the Authors   222
About the Contributors   223

Moving to Learn and Learning to Move

Evridiki Zachopoulou, PhD
Alexander Technological Educational Institute of Thessaloniki, Greece

Ian Pickup
Roehampton University, United Kingdom

Early Steps Physical Education Curriculum: Theory and Practice for Children Under 8 offers both theory and practice for anyone who realises the value of movement in young children's lives and wishes to use movement as a learning tool for children under the age of 8. The main philosophy behind the Early Steps project is the use of movement to facilitate children's social interaction and to help them acquire the basic knowledge for maintaining a healthy, active lifestyle.

The child's body may be considered the primary learning centre when it comes to building the foundation for overall development and learning. It is important during the preschool and early elementary school years for children to have many opportunities for engaging in physical activities. Movement and use of the body have many meanings for the young child. Movement equates to discovery of the environment. It is an important ingredient in communication, it promotes acceptance, it is sheer enjoyment and sensuous pleasure, it means freedom, it means safety.

Movement games foster interpersonal skills and help children learn to cooperate with others. Through these experiences, children begin to find a place in the social world, while educators can capitalise on the cooperative aspects of partner games and foster sensitivity to and responsibility for one another. Movement experiences also give children an environment in which they can learn to play alone within a group. This not only fosters the ability to concentrate on one's own task while other activity is going on, but it also teaches the importance of allowing others to concentrate. This is an important form of self-discipline, which is a key to positive classroom behaviour and to individualised study later on.

This book has been designed as a resource for early childhood educators as they try to find the most appropriate way to facilitate children's socialisation while also helping them become familiar with aspects of a healthy lifestyle.

The term *healthy lifestyle* can be applied broadly to the behavioural choices people make in respect to activity levels, development of physical fitness, cardiorespiratory condition, emotional health and well-being, relationships, personal safety, smoking, alcohol consumption, drug abuse, and nutrition. These choices can be viewed as positive (i.e., a desire to be healthy) if they lower the risk of being seriously ill or dying early. A healthy lifestyle helps people enjoy more aspects of their lives for longer.

Some research shows that young people who engage in regular physical activity are more likely to make healthy lifestyle choices and that children who are regularly active have increased levels of concentration and higher academic attainment. These claims are difficult to substantiate, although most early childhood educators have anecdotal evidence supporting these claims. Regular physical activity helps children and young people build and maintain healthy bones, muscles, and joints; control body weight; reduce body fat; and develop cardiorespiratory function. It also helps to develop coordination and physical skills and control psychological feelings such as anxiety and depression. Physical activity has also been shown to promote greater energy and enable people to carry out daily tasks. Additionally, some theorists have suggested that the development of early motor patterns such as crawling and the fostering of core stability through activity are keys to children being able to access all learning in the classroom. The ability to sit up straight, to turn to look at the teacher, or to hold a pencil correctly all demand elements of stability and manipulation.

In early childhood, a learning focus on movement provides ample opportunity for children to become more physically competent *and* to learn in social, cognitive, and affective domains. Physical education has traditionally concentrated on learning in the physical domain that develops specific skills in certain activities. Although this is the distinctive ingredient of physical education, the parallel learning opportunities that enhance teamwork, self-esteem, and problem solving are just as important and for some children more meaningful in the interactive, dynamic, and challenging context that physical education provides. This is particularly so for young children, for whom play remains spontaneous, exciting, and central to the culture of childhood.

Early Steps Physical Education Curriculum: Theory and Practice for Children Under 8 is divided into two parts. Part I, Basics of an Early Childhood Physical Education Curriculum, focuses on the teaching approaches of a physical education curriculum for preschool-aged children. These chapters look at the teaching methods most often used in an early childhood curriculum, explain the ways the educator can promote children's learning, describe the teacher's role in enhancing children's intrinsic motivation towards physical activity, and present the standards on which the Early Steps Physical Education Curriculum (ESPEC) was based. Part I includes chapters 1 through 5.

Part II, Implementing the Early Steps Physical Education Curriculum, includes the 48 lesson plans of ESPEC. Each lesson plan has specific goals and objectives to be achieved. The descriptions contain detailed information for the activities and games of each lesson plan and include

specific points of emphasis that the early educator has to follow during implementation of the lessons. Part II includes chapters 6, 7, and 8.

Chapter 1 provides information on the role of physical education in the educational settings of various European countries. Chapter 2 focuses on the teaching methods most often used in an early childhood curriculum. A teaching method is a set of decisions made by the instructor to achieve the learning objectives of the lesson. Using a combination of teaching methods may help provide a structure for meaningful teacher intervention. The selection and use of teaching methods should be based on what the teacher knows about the learner's stage of motor development.

Chapter 3 covers the topic that is frequently the teacher's primary concern: teacher behaviour. The scientific analysis of teaching opened new horizons for educators. Today there is a body of knowledge about teaching that suggests how teachers can promote student learning. Research on teacher effectiveness has identified specific pedagogical patterns that increase student learning and positive attitudes. A brief review of the most significant findings regarding teacher behaviour and student learning, which constitute the pedagogical knowledge base of effective teaching, are briefly summarised in this chapter.

Chapter 4 describes the elements of physical education climates that increase children's intrinsic motivation towards physical activity. It also explains how children's perceptions of physical competence can be increased in an early childhood physical education class.

ESPEC was designed to develop children's social skills and to help children understand the importance of a healthy lifestyle. Chapter 5 includes a description of the two standards on which ESPEC was based, including their subgoals and objectives describing what children should have learned after the implementation of ESPEC lessons. Although the term *standard* has multiple meanings, it is most often associated with the quality of education. The quality of what children learn, the quality of the systems delivering education, the quality of teachers and their preparation, and the quality of curriculum content and its assessment are intended to be improved through the provision of standards.

Chapters 6 and 7 contain the 48 lesson plans of ESPEC. These plans offer educators detailed information on the lessons' activities, provide ideas for variations of the activities, and also deal with practical considerations such as planning and scheduling the lessons and using space and equipment.

Chapter 8 explains the methods of evaluation that educators could use and deals with practical evaluation considerations. This chapter provides information about evaluation theory and how it can form a solid foundation for every procedure. It might seem that this information could not offer much in the everyday praxis in preschool education. Yet, knowledge about evaluation procedures can lead to better understanding and communication between teachers and evalua-tors. It might also help educators to overcome the counteractive attitude that is often detected among teachers. Moreover, mastering basic evaluation skills could help teachers in independency, decentralisation, and the adoption of internal evaluation procedures.

The description of the Early Steps project is presented in the appendix, which looks at the theoretical background of the project and its main goals. It also describes the three phases of the project (the writing, training, and implementing phases), the activities of each year of the project, and the participants of each phase.

Early childhood education helps students develop physically, mentally, and socially.

Part I

Basics of an Early Childhood Physical Education Curriculum

The role of physical education for young children in the early 21st century is more important than ever before. Worldwide concerns regarding the health and body weight of children, the apparent growth of sedentary lifestyles, and the prevalence of a so-called toxic childhood (Palmer, 2006) point to the need for approaches that promote a lifelong love of physical activity and the parallel development of physical, social, cognitive, and affective skills. Such programmes must be well thought through and carefully considered to meet the developmental needs of the children and young people for whom they are designed.

In early childhood, children are predisposed to learning by using their bodies. Through play, young children learn about their own bodies, their physical and social environments, and how to become friends. After all, according to Bruner (1983), the culture of childhood is made up of movement, action, and play. In early childhood, movement is a key feature of learning within and beyond what could be termed *curriculum physical education*. Playground games, informal activities with friends and siblings, and physical education lessons have a natural connection to the culture of childhood and a role in facilitating a sense of delight and pleasure that may be missing from the rest of children's daily lives (Bailey, Doherty, & Pickup, 2007). Physical education in early childhood therefore has the opportunity to capitalise on this propensity for movement and to bridge the gap between play and the more formal approaches to learning seen in schools and sport settings.

Early childhood physical education curricula must therefore remain true to child-centred approaches to learning and teaching. Such approaches place the developmental and learning needs of children at the heart of the planning, teaching, and assessment processes; without starting from the child, the link to the culture of childhood is lost. Curricula must therefore be conceived with developmental goals in mind while maintaining a sense of flexibility for the teacher to change, omit, or add more relevant learning opportunities. A child-centred approach should not result in a backseat role for the teacher—the choice of behaviours and styles can have a significant impact on the ensuing learning. It is also important to consider how the curriculum will result in positive changes in interrelated developmental domains. For example, the development of movement skills should not be viewed in isolation from the development of social skills, self-esteem, problem-solving abilities, and so on. These transferable skills may hold the key to engagement with physical activity across the life span.

Early childhood physical education programmes have an opportunity to provide positive, motivational, fun, social, dynamic, and empowering experiences that stay with children throughout life, and the design and implementation of such curricula merit careful, considered action. These themes are explored and exemplified in the following chapters, and although contributions have been made by colleagues from across Europe operating in widely differing contexts, the principles of child-centred education remain at the heart of suggested practice. The reader is encouraged to reflect on the approaches advo-cated in this book, to take or adapt activities and methods to suit the specific context in which they are working, and to embrace the opportunity they have for making a difference to the lives of young children through physical education.

REFERENCES

Bailey, R., Doherty, J., & Pickup, I. (2007). Physical development and physical education. In J. Riley (Ed.), *Learning in the early years: A guide for teachers of children 3-7* (2nd ed.). London: Sage.

Bruner, J. (1983). *Child's talk—learning to use language.* Oxford: Oxford University Press.

Palmer, S. (2006). *Toxic childhood: How the modern world is damaging our children and what we can do about it.* London: Orion.

Chapter 1

Early Childhood Physical Education in Europe

Arja Sääkslahti
University of Jyväskylä, Finland

Jarmo Liukkonen
University of Jyväskylä, Finland

KEY POINTS

- Early childhood education refers to education for children younger than 8 years.
- The primary target for early childhood is to offer developmentally appropriate practice for young children.
- Quality education of early childhood educators strengthens the possibilities to realise new holistic, inclusive, and aligned pedagogical models in physical education.
- Each European country has its own governmental norms regulating kindergarten, preschool, and compulsory school physical education.

Physical education in kindergarten and preschool aims at offering children activities that support sound personality development and through which they develop intrinsic motivation towards physical activity. Early childhood education refers to education for children younger than 8 years. It considers all educational actions supporting young children's physical, social, emotional, and cognitive development. The primary goal of early childhood education is to offer developmentally appropriate practice for young children (Bredekamp & Copple, 1997; Gestwicki, 1999).

Variations in Institutional Structures

Institutional early childhood education is organised in various ways in European countries. There is thus a need for a short overlook of the educational systems in different countries. Plenty of variation is found in the ages of children starting school. School starts at the age of 5 years in Greece, the Netherlands, and the United Kingdom. In most European countries, such as Belgium, France, Germany, Italy, Portugal, and Spain, compulsory school begins at the age of 6 years. Children start school at the age of 7 years in Denmark, Finland, Hungary, Poland, and Sweden. Most European countries offer children and families an optional kindergarten education, generally starting from the age of 3 years. In some countries, only the last year before compulsory school is considered preschool, whereas in some countries preschool represents all age groups before compulsory school (e.g., from 3 to 5 years).

The percentage of 3- to 4-year-old children participating in kindergarten or preschool varies from 20% to 100% in European countries. In Belgium, Spain, France, and Italy the percentage is 100%, whereas the rate for Switzerland, Ireland, Greece, Poland, and the Netherlands is less than 40%. Other European countries have a participation rate between 40% and 80% (Organisation for Economic Co-operation and Development [OECD], 2006). In the vast majority of European countries, families are offered free participation in preschools. In the Scandinavian countries as well as some other countries, kindergarten is organised for children before they start preschool. For example, in Finland, Sweden, Norway, and Denmark, kindergarten is for children aged 1 year and older, and families have to pay for it according to their income level.

Every European country has its own governmental norms regulating kindergarten and preschool institutions (see table 1.1). Thus, there are cultural variations in facilities, such as the size of children's groups, the number of teachers and nurses in the groups, and the educational level of preschool personnel. There exist also a variety of differences in the circumstances for physical activity, such as the size of indoor and outdoor play facilities. Some preschools and schools have plenty of physical education equipment to use, but unfortunately, many preschools have a shortage of equipment. Many countries control the amount of physical education in kindergarten, preschools, and schools via curriculum regulations. However, it is typical that the amount of physical education is arranged systematically only in schools.

Research findings support the importance of the physical environment. Governments and communities should guarantee that there are appropriate and safe playgrounds for young children in neighborhoods as well as in kindergarten and schools (Fjørtoft & Gundersen, 2007; Powell & Ambardekar, 2005).

Physical Education in Early Childhood

Physical education in early childhood means promoting children's physical activity and overall development through developmentally appropriate practices (Gagen & Getchell, 2006; National Association for Sport and Physical Education [NASPE], 2002). The length of the day in kindergarten, preschool, and school varies, but in every European country the timetable includes both structured lessons and free play. These activities can be arranged both indoors and outdoors.

Structured indoor physical education lessons should facilitate a variety of content. Activities that focus on fine-motor skills increase children's attention (Stewart, Rule, & Giordano, 2007), but children also need possibilities for developmentally important exercise-play and rough-and-tumble play. Exercise-play is important for the development of strength and endurance, whereas rough-and-tumble play has distinctive social components (Pellegrini & Smith, 1998). Physical activities should begin with basic gross-motor skills and provide a flood of sensorimotor experiences. Children should be offered a variety of manipulative and obstacle-course activities

Table 1.1 Preschool Systems in Five European Countries

Country	Preschool availability	Age at which children participate in preschool	Number of children/ teacher	Required education of teachers	Physical education curriculum
Greece	98%	5 years	25 children/ 2 teachers	University bachelor level, 4 years	National curriculum (Ministry of Education)
Cyprus	100%	4.8-5.8 years	25 children/ teacher	University bachelor level, 4 years	National curriculum
Finland	100%	6 years	13 children/teacher 7 children/nurse	University bachelor level, 3 years	National curriculum Each city Each kindergarten and preschool
Italy	100%	5 years	25 children/teacher	University bachelor level, 4 years	National curriculum
United Kingdom	100%	5 years	13 children/teacher	University bachelor level, 4 years	National curriculum

(Gabbard, 1998). To develop children's intrinsic motivation towards physical activity, these activities should be based on children's enjoyment, perceived competence, and autonomy—that is, encouraging children to suggest their favourite play activities for the sake of pleasure and satisfaction (Deci & Ryan, 2002; Woods, Bolton, Graber, & Crull, 2007). Structured play lessons or programmes provide optimal motor stimulation and contribute more to health compared with free-play activities. Health benefits are received if heart rate is elevated to an appropriate level, which is 140 beats per minute (bpm) or above for small children (Pienaar & Badenhorst, 2001).

Indoor free-play activities are challenging because the unstructured nature of free play causes disturbing noise, and children need undisturbed time and space for intensive play in small groups and sometimes with the whole group. Free-play also affects working conditions for early childhood educators: Noise causes stress (Sandberg & Pramling-Samuelsson, 2005). For these reasons it is difficult for early educators to deal with free-play indoor activities; therefore, free-play activities are mostly allowed outdoors. However, there is a need for active, experimental free play to encourage children's creativity (Pienaar & Badenhorst, 2001), and most of all children need to feel that they are free to choose what to do rather than being forced to do certain activities (Taylor, Blair, Cummings, Wun, & Malina, 1999).

Facilities for structured outdoor physical education differ greatly even within one country. Many kindergarten, preschools, and schools have flat playgrounds with traditional equipment, such as climbing bars, swings, sandpits, seesaws, and slides. Unfortunately, there are also kindergartens, preschools, and schools without these possibilities. There is also a lot of variation in the size of playing areas. That is the reason why early educators usually organise structured lessons indoors and let children have free play outdoors. For the sake of children's developmental needs, it is necessary to organise structured physical education lessons that use outdoor facilities. Children's physical activity has been found to increase if playing areas are decorated, such as with colourful images that fascinate children's imaginations (Stratton & Leonard, 2002).

Especially in Scandinavian countries, kindergartens are built near forested areas. Green-profiled schoolyards encourage physical activity. Teachers use this opportunity of varied landscapes to stimulate children's functional play and development of motor skills (Fjørtoft, 2001). Complementing the rule-bound, competitive games supported by asphalt and turf playing fields, green playgrounds invite children to jump, climb, dig, lift, rake, build, role-play, and generally get moving in ways that nurture all aspects of their health and development. Through greening, school grounds diversify the play repertoire (Dyment & Bell, 2007).

However, in most European countries, play areas have asphalt surface. Studies have shown that hard playground surfaces are a significant predictor for higher physical activity levels in the case of boys compared with girls. Asphalt areas invite running and soccer play. Rural schoolyards afford playing in forested areas, which favour more physical activity in girls than in boys. Girls also seem to increase their physical activity under less supervision by teachers (Cardon, Van Cauwenberghe, Labarque, Haerens, & De Bourdeaudhuij, 2008; Fjørtoft, Kristoffersen, & Sageie, 2009). In the case of Norwegian 6-year-old schoolchildren, physical activity levels were similar for boys and girls in both asphalt and green schoolyards, but forest landscapes significantly determined higher activity levels in girls. The children were physically active in free play at moderate to vigorous levels for half of a recess of 40 minutes (Fjørtoft et al., 2009).

Societal and Environmental Challenges

During the last two decades, many researchers have pointed out health problems that decreasing physical activity and increasing sedentary behaviour (e.g., watching TV, playing electronic games, using the Internet) may cause in children (Jago, Baranowski, Thompson, Baranowski, & Greaves, 2005; Kelly et al., 2007). The most serious health problem relates to obesity. The number of overweight children is rapidly growing, leading to increases in diabetes and other problematic metabolic syndromes (Andersen et al., 2006; Pate et al., 2006). This is an alarming phenomenon because physical activity and sedentary behaviour are beginning from a very young age, often from 3 years onward. In other words, those 3-year-olds who are physically inactive also have a high risk of being inactive later in life (Kelly et al., 2007; Pate, Baranowski, Dowda, & Trost, 1996).

There is also evidence that physical activity has positive effects on children's bone health (i.e., stiffness of bones), cardiovascular disease risk factors (i.e., better levels of health-enhancing blood cholesterol, such as high-density lipoprotein [HDL], and lower total cholesterol), psychosocial health, cognitive functioning, and motor skills (Timmons, Naylor, & Pfeiffer, 2007).

It has been shown that the way children use their leisure time correlates with their well-being, including self-esteem and the acquisition of fundamental motor skills that are essential for functional capacity (Ben-Arieh & Ofir, 2002). When children are playing, they develop a positive body image, they learn to use their bodies, and they learn what they are able and unable to do. This helps children strengthen their self-esteem, which is highly correlated with positive mental health and well-being.

Fundamental motor skills are needed to manage everyday activities, and they are also prerequisites for participation in children's play and games (Gallahue & Cleland-Donnelly, 2003). Young children learn fundamental motor skills when they are playing outdoors (Sääkslahti et al., 1999) in versatile environments (Fjørtoft, 2001). That's why early childhood educators as well as parents of young children should encourage their children to play outdoors daily. Sound fundamental motor skills are associated with habitual physical activity (Fisher et al., 2005), and they are a predictor of physical activity later in life (Okely, Booth, & Patterson, 2001; Stodden et al., 2008). Therefore there is a need to provide opportunities for children to play actively both indoors and outdoors.

Conclusion

Many countries, such as Australia, Finland, the United Kingdom, and the United States, have published national recommendations for the physical activity of young children. This implies that people recognise the need to increase young children's physical activity and make sure that they have appropriate fundamental motor skills to manage independently in their everyday life and improve their health (Australian Government Department of Health and Ageing, 2004; Cavill, Biddle, & Sallis, 2001; Cardon & De Bourdeaudhuij, 2008; Gunner, Atkinson, Nichols, & Eissa, 2005; Ministry of Social Affairs and Health 2005; NASPE 2002).

National recommendations are a good start, although there is also a need to increase the amount and quality of physical education in teacher training. By teaching the importance of physical education and theories of motor skill development, as well as by giving concrete models for arranging developmentally appropriate physical education for young children, it is likely that the health and motor skills of children will improve (Gagen & Getchell, 2006). Quality

Physical activity helps children develop and strengthen a positive self-image.

education of early educators strengthens the possibilities to realise new holistic, inclusive, and aligned pedagogical models in kindergartens, preschools, and first years of schooling (Marsden & Weston, 2007).

REFERENCES

Andersen, L.B., Harro, M., Sardinha, L.B., Froberg, K., Ekelund, U., Brage, S., & Anderssen, A. (2006). Physical activity and clustered cardiovascular risk in children: A cross-sectional study (The European Youth Heart Study). *Lancet, 368,* 299-304.

Australian Government Department of Health and Ageing. (2004). *Australia's physical activity recommendations for 5-12-year olds.* Canberra: Commonwealth of Australia.

Ben-Arieh, A., & Ofir, A. (2002). Time for (more) time-use studies: Studying the daily activities of children. *Childhood, 9*(2), 225-248.

Bredekamp, S., & Copple, C. (1997). *Developmentally appropriate practice in early childhood programs.* Washington, DC: NAEYC.

Cardon, G.M., & De Bourdeaudhuij, I.M.M. (2008). Are preschool children active enough? Objectively measured physical activity levels. *Research Quarterly for Exercise and Sport, 79*(3), 326-332.

Cardon, G., Van Cauwenberghe, E., Labarque, V., Haerens, L., & De Bourdeaudhuij, I. (2008). The contribution of preschool playground factors in explaining children's physical activity during recess. *International Journal of Behavioral Nutrition and Physical Activity, 5*(11).

Cavill, N., Biddle, S., & Sallis, J.F. (2001). Health-enhancing physical activity for young people: Statement of the United Kingdom Expert Consensus Conference. *Pediatric Exercise Science, 13,* 12-25.

Deci, E.L., & Ryan, R.M. (2002). Self-determination research: Reflections and future directions. In E.L. Deci & R.M. Ryan (Eds.), *Handbook of self-determination research* (pp. 431-441). Rochester, NY: University of Rochester Press.

Dyment, J.E., & Bell, A.C. (2007). Grounds for movement: Green school grounds as sites for promoting physical activity. *Health Education Research.* Advance Access, 22, 2007.

Fisher, A., Reilly, J.J., Kelly, L.A., Montgomery, C., Williamson, A., Paton, J.Y., & Grant, S. (2005). Fundamental movement skills and habitual physical activity in young children. *Medicine and Science in Sports and Exercise, 37*(4), 684-688.

Fjørtoft, I. (2001). The natural environment as a playground for children: The impact of outdoor play activities in pre-primary school children. *Early Childhood Education Journal, 29*(2), 111-117.

Fjørtoft, I, & Gundersen, K.A. (2007). Promoting motor learning in young children through landscapes. In J. Liukkonen, Y.V. Auweele, D. Alfermann, B. Vereijken, & Y. Theodorakis, (Eds.), *Psychology for Physical Educators* (pp. 41-55). Champaign, IL: Human Kinetics.

Fjørtoft, I., Kristoffersen, B., & Sageie, J. (2009). Children in schoolyards: Tracking movement patterns and physical activity using global positioning system and heart rate monitoring. Landscape and Urban Planning. DOI.

Gabbard, C. (1998). Windows of opportunity for early brain and motor development. *JOPERD, 69*(8), 54-55, 61.

Gagen, L.M., & Getchell, N. (2006). Using "constraints" to design developmentally appropriate movement activities for early childhood education. *Early Childhood Education Journal, 34*(3), 227-232.

Gallahue, D., & Cleland-Donnelly, F. (2003). *Developmental physical education for all children* (4th ed.). Champaign, IL: Human Kinetics.

Gestwicki, C. (1999). *Developmentally appropriate practice curriculum and development in early education.* Albany, NY: Delmar.

Gunner, K.B., Atkinson, P.M., Nichols, J., & Eissa, M.A. (2005). Health promotion strategies to encourage physical activity in infants, toddlers, and preschoolers. *Journal of Pediatric Health Care, 19*(4), 253-258.

Jago, R., Baranowski, T., Thompson, D., Baranowski, J., & Greaves, K. (2005). Sedentary behaviour, not TV viewing, predicts physical activity among 3- to 7-year-old children. *Pediatric Exercise Science, 17,* 364-376.

Kelly, L.A., Reilly, J.J., Jackson, D.M., Montgomery, C., Grant, S., & Paton, J.Y. (2007). Tracking physical activity and sedentary behavior in young children. *Pediatric Exercise Science, 19,* 51-60.

Marsden, E., & Weston, C. (2007). Locating quality physical education in early years pedagogy. *Sport, Education and Society, 12*(4), 383-398.

Ministry of Social Affairs and Health. (2005). *Recommendations for physical activity in early childhood education.* Helsinki, Finland: Author.

National Association for Sport and Physical Education (NASPE). (2002). *Active start: A statement of physical activity guidelines for children from birth to five years.* New York: AAPHERD.

Okely, A.D., Booth, M.L., & Patterson, J.W. (2001). Relationship of physical activity to fundamental movement skills among adolescents. *Medicine and Science in Sports and Exercise, 33*(110), 1899-1904.

Organisation for Economic Co-operation and Development (OECD). (2006). *Education at a glance*: OECD Indicators 2006. Paris: Centre for Educational Research and Innovation.

Pate, R.R., Baranowski, T., Dowda, M., & Trost, S.G. (1996). Tracking of physical activity in young children. *Medicine and Science in Sports and Exercise, 28*(1), 92-96.

Pate, R.R., Davis, M.G., Robinson, T.N., Stone, E.J., McKenzie, T.L., & Young, J.C. (2006). Promoting physical activity in children and youth. *Circulation, 114,* 1214-1224.

Pellegrini, A.D., & Smith, P.K. (1998). Physical activity play: The nature and function of a neglected aspect of play. *Child Development, 69*(3), 577-598.

Pienaar, A.E., & Badenhorst, P. (2001). Physical activity levels and play preferences of pre-school children: recommendation for "appropriate" activities. *Journal of Human Movement Studies, 41,* 105-123.

Powell, E.C., & Ambardekar, E.J. (2005). Poor neighborhoods: Safe playgrounds. *Journal of Urban Health, 82*(3), 403-410.

Sääkslahti, A., Numminen, P., Niinikoski, H., Rask-Nissilä, L., Viikari, J., Tuominen, J., & Välimäki, I. (1999). Is physical activity related to body size, fundamental motor skills, and CHD risk factors in early childhood? *Pediatric Exercise Science, 11*(4), 327-340.

Sandberg, A., & Pramling-Samuelsson, I. (2005). An interview study of gender differences in preschool teachers' attitudes toward children's play. *Early Childhood Education Journal, 32*(5), 297-305.

Stewart, R., Rule, A., & Giordano, D. (2007). The effect of fine motor skill activities on kindergarten student attention. *Early Childhood Education Journal, 35*(2), 103-109.

Stodden, D., Goodway, J., Langendorfer, S., Roberton, M., Rudisill, M., Garzia, C., & Garzia, L. (2008). A developmental perspective on the role of the motor skill competence in physical activity: An emergent relationship. *Quest, 60,* 290-306.

Stratton, G., & Leonard, J. (2002). The effects of playground markings on the energy expenditure on 5- to 7-year-old school children. *Pediatric Exercise Science, 14*(2), 170-180.

Taylor, W.C., Blair, S.N., Cummings, S.S., Wun, C.C., & Malina, R.M. (1999). Childhood and adolescent physical activity patterns and adult physical activity. *Medicine and Science in Sports and Exercise, 31*(1), 118-123.

Timmons, B.W., Naylor, P-J., & Pfeiffer, K.A. (2007). Physical activity for preschool children—how much and how? *Applied Physiology, Nutrition and Metabolism, 32,* S122-S134.

Woods, A.M., Bolton, K.N., Graber, K.C., & Crull, G.S. (2007). Influences of perceived motor competence and motives on children's physical activity. *Journal of Teaching in Physical Education, 26,* 390-403.

RESOURCES

Following are some examples of national standards and curricula:

Finland

http://varttua.stakes.fi/NR/rdonlyres/78BC5411-F37C-494C-86FA-BE409294709B/0/e_vasu.pdf

Cyprus

www.moec.gov.cy

Greece

www.pi-schools.gr/programs/depps/index_eng.php

United Kingdom

http://curriculum.qca.org.uk/index.aspx\
www.standards.dcsf.gov.uk/eyfs/site/index.htm

Italy

www.pubblica.istruzione.it

Chapter 2

Teaching Methods

Ian Pickup
Roehampton University, United Kingdom

KEY POINTS

- Play and spontaneity are important building blocks from which to develop appropriate physical education teaching methods in early childhood.

- Educators should carefully design tasks that support each child's development and use skilful observation to assess learning and inform subsequent planning.

- Teaching methods used in physical education should be based on the same principles used in classroom settings.

- The role of educators is crucial, and they can influence the amount and rate of learning through the use of various teaching styles.

- Indirect teaching styles allow children to make decisions and solve problems and can be closely aligned with play experiences.

- Cooperative learning encourages interdependence among learners and fosters prosocial behaviours.

This chapter discusses possible teaching approaches for physical education in the early years and focuses on the role of the teacher in facilitating learning. With early childhood educators so keen to build on children's natural physical exuberance and to use play as a learning context, physical education is well placed to make a significant contribution to every child's development. Physical learning is the unique ingredient of lesson content, but the subject also provides a range of opportunities for learning in all developmental domains. Working in pairs and groups to solve problems and using the body as a tool for learning provides a unique context for the educator to interact with young children. It is vital therefore that such opportunity is not missed through the assumption that children will simply learn by carrying out prescribed tasks. The choice of teaching style and planned interaction of the educator with the children in physical education can influence the rate and amount of learning, and it is this process that lies at the heart of this chapter.

Need for Child-Centred Teaching Methods

The methods used by educators in early childhood have been the focus of considerable academic debate throughout the last century. Central to this debate has been the role of the teacher in bringing about learning and the extent to which learning is fully child-centred. Some theorists would argue that as soon as educators begin to plan learning, the focus of the lesson moves from being child-centred and spontaneous to one that is adult led and overstructured. This argument has come under sharp focus in recent years where physical education curricula have been designed to have an impact on the perceived obesity crisis and decreasing rates of physical activity among children. Such concerns, subject to significant media attention and policy rhetoric, together with a view that physical education is synonymous with sport, have led some theorists to question the underpinning rationale of physical education, particularly that which is delivered for young children. As Marsden and Weston (2007, p. 384) ask, "Should it not be the social, emotional, cultural and developmental needs of children themselves that provides the starting point from which to develop a philosophy for early year's physical education?"

All early childhood educators should therefore take some time to reflect on their own underpinning rationale for physical education and their starting points for planning lessons. Sport, with its adult-relevant rules and regulations, competitive structures, tactics, and coaching, is not the best vehicle for teaching young children. A better starting point may be to build on the broader role of movement in the lives of children, using play and the seemingly natural desire of young children to move within interactive, collaborative, physical, and multisensory approaches to learning (Pickup, Haydn-Davies, & Jess, 2007, p. 9). To most early childhood professionals, the role of play and spontaneity is central to the learning process and is nonnegotiable. This viewpoint has been popularised by educational theorists from the 1800s to the present day and is one that gives value to the educative role of movement in the lives of young children. It is generally accepted that movement helps young children to engage actively with experiences, to construct their own views of the world (Bruner and Haste, 1987), and to take an active, inventive role in reconstructing tasks through their own understanding (Smith, 1993). The educator must therefore aim to build on this and facilitate learning in physical education that

- is in keeping with a holistic and thematic approach to education;
- is developmentally appropriate for each child, taking account of social, physical, cognitive, and affective domains;
- allows for spontaneity and child-centred activity; and
- is not overly dependent on teacher intervention.

The skilful educator must develop a keen awareness of each child's learning needs and choose appropriate, relevant, and purposeful teaching methods to support learning. This is complex, not least because each child is unique and a variety of anatomical, physiological, psychological, sociological, and cultural dimensions can influence the learning process in physical education. The methods used by the educator will also be shaped by curriculum frameworks that for many years have assumed that children simply learn physical skills naturally through their play. This viewpoint, advocated by psychologists in the 1920s (see, for example, the work of Arnold Gessell, 1928), has since been criticised by observers who suggest that children

Educators must allow for the spontaneity and child-centred nature of play within their curriculum.

are simply not developing the range of physical skills required for lifelong involvement in physical activity (Jess, Dewar, & Fraser, 2004). Advocates of this lifelong approach to physical education stress the importance of developing a broad range of physical skills in childhood, allowing increased specificity and application to a wide range of activities across the life span. The early years are generally thought to be a critical time for the development of fundamental motor skills, and it would appear that for many children, the maturation and subsequent application of such skills is being left almost to chance.

As we have seen in chapter 1, approaches to early childhood physical education vary enormously from country to country and raise many questions regarding appropriate strategies for the teacher to employ. The approach advocated in this chapter builds on early childhood educators' existing knowledge and understanding, values the role of skilful observation and task design, and is based on methods that sit within holistic views of early childhood education. In particular, the methods discussed are strategies through which

the educator can ensure that learning in physical education remains in "the exploratory world of early childhood . . . allowing for the child to develop skills at their own pace through provision of opportunity" (Marsden & Weston, 2007, p. 390).

Starting From the Child

In building on naturally occurring and playful movements, the early childhood educator can take notice of Fisher's (2000) advice to start from the child and capitalise on what young learners are already doing. This should also include a willingness to value physical activity taking place in the home and community settings, and the educator should ensure that movement outside the classroom is brought into the learning experience (Bailey & Pickup, 2007). The bedrock of every early childhood educator's practice is skilful observation, whether this is within free play or a more structured environment. The observing educator seeks to reflect on existing attributes, knowledge and understanding, and levels of development in all domains. This observation is not merely a snapshot for formal records or for reports written for the benefit of parents. It is assessment for learning, designed to help the educator bring about further learning both at that specific moment in time and in subsequent learning episodes. Figure 2.1 shows that observation is a key part of the learning and teaching cycle.

In placing observation at the heart of the learning process, the educator must ask the following:

- What are the children already doing?
- How can I build on this to help move learning forward?
- What do I have to do and say now to facilitate learning?
- Should I offer feedback or facilitate learning in a more indirect way?
- How can subsequent sessions build on what I am seeing now?

Selecting What to Observe

A physical education class of 30 children who are 4 years old presents a dynamic, colourful, and exciting opportunity for observation. With a multiplicity of social interactions and behaviours, in addition to a range of performances of specific movement patterns, it is possible for the observer to find the opportunity a little overwhelming. Focused observation must therefore ensure that particular aspects of learning are addressed, with criteria for observation strongly linked to the intended learning outcomes of the activity. In most cases, the observer should also focus on a small number of children to ensure that sufficient detail can be gleaned. These areas for observation and assessment will be linked to broader curriculum objectives where developmental domains often make up stated areas of learning. Where observations are being carried out within unstructured contexts, the educator

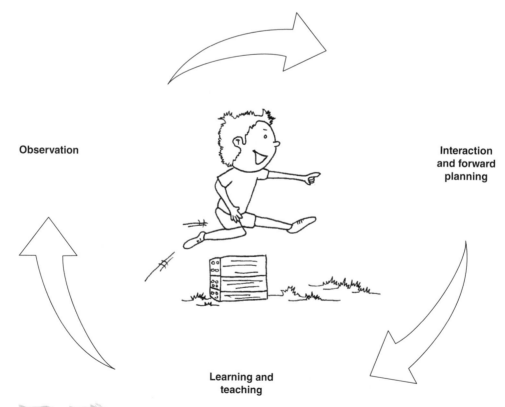

Observation

Interaction and forward planning

Learning and teaching

FIGURE 2.1 The observe-interact-learn cycle.

should have an eye for specific detail, but also keep an open mind for noting spontaneous and unexpected outcomes.

For the lessons contained in this book, observations will normally centre on the learning that is taking place through the planned physical activity, largely in the social domain. Children's understanding of healthy behaviours can also be noted, and the opportunity to observe this learning will not be limited solely to lesson time. Children's conversations, interactions during break time, and attitudes towards food at mealtimes all provide opportunities for ongoing observation and reflection. In this regard, educators should also build a positive relationship with parents and carers and build their own understanding of the social world in which the children live.

The observation of *physical learning* is perhaps more challenging for the early childhood educator more accustomed to observing learning in a classroom context. Knowing what to say in relation to physical skill learning and how to structure subsequent tasks does require subject-specific knowledge, particularly regarding motor development. The observation of movement and assessment of physical learning is not a skill that can be developed quickly, and early childhood educators should take some time to consider their own existing knowledge, particularly with regards to the development of fundamental movement skills (see, for example, Gallahue & Cleland-Donnelly, 2003; Pickup & Price, 2007). Such movement skills can be assessed through focused observation, and it is useful to consider breaking movements into parts. This can be done in two ways:

1. *Sequential movement analysis*—The observer considers the body actions during the phases of movement. This may relate to the starting position, preparation, execution, and follow-through.

2. *Segmental movement analysis*—The observer considers the physical actions according to body segments. For example, the position of the feet (stance), movement of the hands and arms, and position of the head and trunk are important in the execution of all physical skills.

In both cases, the observer can describe what the child is doing and seek to identify ways through which improvement can be fostered. The precise method through which this learning is taken forward is part of the educator's decision-making process, and a range of methods will be discussed later in this chapter. The key issue here is that observations help the educator decide what strategies are appropriate to bring about further learning.

Acting on Observations

Building on what children can already do is a useful motto to keep close to hand. In doing so, the educator is able to identify appropriate next steps in the learning experience. In this way, observation is an ongoing process, fused with intervention in a virtuous spiral (Papatheodorou, 2005). These next steps may be continued self-directed play or may involve various levels of interaction with the educator or other children. Many early childhood educators are skilful at knowing when and how to interact during classroom-based learning episodes, with practice commonly built on theories that link the development of cognition with socialisation. Lev Vygotsky's (1978) notion of scaffolding emphasises the importance of others in supporting learning, and the application of such principles should not cease on entry to a physical education environment.

Social learning theories acknowledge the critical role played by teachers in the learning process. This notion has sometimes been overlooked by advocates of child-centred education (Blenkin & Kelly, 1987), where observation of busy, happy, and well-behaved children engaged in a movement task may be wrongly construed as a context in which learning is taking place. Educators should not lose sight of the role that they can play in skilfully intervening to help move the children from the present level of attainment towards potential achievement. During learning episodes, then, educators should strive to enhance the role of the learners by

- highlighting the critical features of the activity,
- buffering the children's attention through distractions,
- channelling the children's activities to ensure success,
- using errors to encourage learning,
- enabling procedures to be commented upon and explained, and
- allowing responsibility for the activity to be gradually transferred to the learners contingent upon their success.

Adapted from Meadows, 1993.

All of this can be achieved through a variety of teaching methods that may differ from child to child and from task to task. This will be influenced too by the intended learning outcomes that the educator has planned for and the extent to which the activity is spontaneous or structured. In any case, it is desirable for the educator to promote learning by encouraging effort as well as achievement, but physical learning should also be afforded some attention within verbal feedback.

Effective observation should also lead to the design of subsequent tasks that are linked to previously observed learning. This should provide opportunities for children to explore new skills and behaviours in carefully designed learning environments, as well as provide opportunities for recently acquired knowledge and skills to be practised and reinforced. The tasks themselves should also be geared to learners' needs, and the educator should ensure that differentiation of task allows children to learn at their own pace. Where open-ended questions and instructions are used as a teaching strategy, differentiation will occur by outcome—in other words, children will respond to the task at their own level. A more focused approach would see each task carefully differentiated by adjusting the parameters of the task for specific reasons. Pickup and Price (2007, p.112) describe the STTEP principle of differentiation, providing educators with a useful acronym to guide alterations to task structure:

S: Manipulating **space** for the task that is bigger, smaller, or a different shape

T: Changing the **time** in which the task is performed (faster, slower)

T: Changing the requirements of the **task** completely

E: Using different kinds of **equipment**

P: Altering numbers and roles of the **people** involved

Reprinted, by permission, from I. Pickup and L. Price, 2007, *Teaching physical education in the primary school: A developmental approach* (London: Continuum), 112.

Teaching Styles to Promote Learning

It is widely acknowledged that children learn in different ways and that learning should be the key influence on teachers' decisions and task design. In recognising that all children learn in different ways and at different rates, it would not make sense for early childhood educators to use only one teaching method. Choice of teaching approach will depend on a range of factors related to the *learner* (stage of development, level of attainment, level of cognitive understanding, degree of physical development, common affective behaviours, motivation to learn), *environment* (facilities and equipment, time, safety considerations, weather, group numbers, number of educators), *task* (difficulty, complexity, risk factors associated), and *teacher* (underpinning philosophy, personality, subject knowledge, lesson objectives, ability to adapt, class control, confidence). Ultimately, the selection of teaching methods in physical education should be based on what we know about the learner's stage of development and an ultimate aim of providing an appropriate next step in the learning process.

Muska Mosston (1966) first introduced the term *spectrum of teaching styles* to describe a range of choices in relation to teacher behaviour. The term *teaching style* refers to methods governed by a pattern of decisions made in relation to the learner, the task, and the environment (Gallahue, 1996). Mosston's original spectrum of teaching styles has undergone a number of revisions, most recently including two clusters of styles—the first focused on the reproduction of past knowledge, and the second aiming to produce new knowledge. The key distinction when selecting a teaching style is the degree to which decision making is in the hands of the teacher or learner.

At one end of the spectrum lies command-style teaching, a direct approach that is highly structured, teacher centred, and controlled (Byra, 2006). At the opposite end of the spectrum lies guided-discovery teaching, with a focus on using questions to facilitate small discoveries by the learner. In the purest form of guided-discovery teaching, each question is designed to elicit a single, correct response by the learner, during which the teacher provides feedback and praise in response to the learner's discovery. The teacher's role is specifically geared to facilitating, shaping, and influencing movement outcomes and can result in children showing greater versatility, increased skilfulness, and clarity of intent and outcome (Davies, 2003).

A variation on the guided-discovery style is convergent discovery, where children are challenged to discover the solution to a movement task with the teacher simply providing feedback and clues without providing the solution. This style fosters a greater level of decision making among learners and a wider range of possible correct responses.

A final variation is the divergent production style, in which children are engaged in exploring a range of possible responses. The teacher presents movement challenges or questions that do not require one specific solution—any reasonable attempt at the task is seen as acceptable. This style is sometimes called *free exploration* and allows children to move in any way they wish. It focuses on the learning process itself and not on any specific product of learning.

Such discovery styles are based on a constructivist view of the learning and teaching process and are often closely aligned with the development of critical-thinking skills. Early childhood physical education teachers should err towards this group of indirect styles of teaching, especially where learning intentions are not solely centred on skill acquisition. The indirect styles of teaching facilitate the discovery of existing concepts, as well as the development of alternatives and new concepts (Gallahue & Cleland-Donnelly, 2003). The link between indirect styles of teaching physical education and child-centred strategies

common to the early years of schooling can be seen as a convergence of philosophies; furthermore, the process of learning is seen as equally important as the acquisition of a specific skill and ultimately more transferable beyond the physical education and sport setting.

Despite the advantages of indirect teaching styles, some educators appear reluctant or unable to use such approaches productively in physical education, perhaps hampered by a perceived lack of subject-specific knowledge or concern over the safety of children. Overdependence on direct styles may also prevail where the teacher is concerned about maintaining discipline or where the predominant learning intention is to develop technique. Though one doesn't doubt the difficulty of physical education that involves managing 30 children who are 4 years old, the design of tasks and choice of teaching method should not result in activities that are more appropriate for army recruits moving only when the sergeant says so! The focus of early childhood physical education should be on the learner, with the educator playing the role of skilful facilitator, guiding and shaping learning through a clearly thought-through range of approaches.

As a teacher, you can take a more indirect role with students while still guiding and shaping their learning.

The use of a combination of teaching styles may help to provide a focus for the educator's involvement in a learning episode, particularly in planning when to observe actions and when to provide specific feedback. Gallahue (1996) suggests a model in which teaching involves a combination of indirect and direct teaching styles that progress from free exploration at the start of the lesson to specific skill instruction later on. The funneling of activity in this way ensures that children are allowed time for free expression and the opportunity to solve problems themselves. In addition, specific feedback relevant to skill development is valued and physical learning outcomes are not lost.

This approach also has enormous potential for a cross-curricular focus. For example, children's stories can provide a rich stimulus for movement, and the words contained in stories can be used to promote early exploratory movements. As learning progresses, the educator may choose to focus on specific actions or learning outcomes and channel the children's attention to moving in specific ways.

Using Group Work

Advocates of collaborative approaches to learning value the role of group work in the educative process. Cooperative learning is a teaching structure where small groups of heterogeneous learners work together to complete an assigned task or project (Byra, 2006), and it is often used as a generic term for small-group interactive instructional procedures. In such approaches to learning, children work together on shared tasks to help themselves and their peers learn. In the early childhood context, such tasks see children sharing an activity area, such as a role-play activity, or working together in a movement task, sharing apparatuses and equipment. Broadhead and English (2005) suggest that children's play in the cooperative domain also represents significant cognitive challenge and that children demonstrate a high level of concentration and absorption during collaborative activity.

Cooperative learning simultaneously models interdependence and provides students with the experiences they need to understand the nature of cooperation (Johnson & Johnson, 1989). The two central conditions for collaborative learning are said to be positive independence and individual accountability (Johnson & Johnson,

1991). It is commonly thought that compared with competitive and individualistic efforts, cooperation results in higher achievement and greater productivity; more caring, supportive, and committed relationships between children; greater psychological health, social competence, and self-esteem; enhanced critical and creative thinking; and positive attitudes towards school. Grineski (1989) confirmed that young children learning cooperatively demonstrated more frequent prosocial interactions compared with children who were taught within competitive group games.

Wood, Bruner, and Ross' (1976) extension of Vygotsky's work on collaborative learning explained that children do not passively absorb the strategies of the adult but instead take an active inventive role, reconstructing tasks through their own understanding. The educator therefore needs to make a conscious, planned decision to design learning episodes that require children to share, discuss, rationalise, and find shared solutions.

REFERENCES

Bailey, R., & Pickup, I. (2007). Movement learning: Bringing movement into the classroom. In R. Austin (Ed.), *Letting the outside in: Developing teaching and learning beyond the early years classroom*. Stoke: Trentham Books.

Blenkin, G.M., & Kelly, A.V. (Eds.). (1987). *The early childhood education: A developmental curriculum*. London: Paul Chapman.

Broadhead, P., & English, C. (2005). Open-ended role play: Supporting creativity and developing identity. In J. Moyles (Ed.), *The excellence of play* (2nd ed.). Maidenhead: Open University Press.

Bruner, J., & Haste, H. (Eds.). (1987). *Making sense: The child's construction of the world*. London: Methuen.

Byra, M. (2006). Teaching styles and inclusive pedagogies. In D. Kirk, D. Macdonald, & M. O'Sullivan (Eds.), *The handbook of physical education* (p. 452). London: Sage.

Davies, M. (2003). *Movement and dance in early childhood* (2nd ed.). London: Paul Chapman.

Fisher, J. (2002). *Starting from the child, teaching and learning from 3 to 8* (2nd ed.). Buckingham: Open University Press.

Gallahue, D.L. (1996). *Developmental physical education for today's children*. Dubuque, IA: Brown & Benchmark.

Gallahue, D.L., & Cleland-Donnelly, F.C. (2003). *Developmental physical education for all children* (4th ed.). Champaign, IL: Human Kinetics.

Gessell, A. (1928). *Infancy and human growth.* New York: Macmillan.

Grineski, S. (1989). Children, games, and prosocial behavior—insights and connections. *Journal of Physical Education, Recreation and Dance, 60*(3), 20-35.

Jess, M., Dewar, K., & Fraser, G. (2004). Basic moves: Developing a foundation for lifelong physical activity. *British Journal of Teaching Physical Education, 35*(2), 24-27.

Johnson, D.W., & Johnson, R.T. (1989). *Cooperation and competition: Theory and research.* Edina, MN: Interaction Book Company.

Johnson, D.W., & Johnson, R.T. (1991). *Learning together and alone: Cooperative, competitive, and individualistic learning* (3rd ed.). Boston: Allyn & Bacon.

Marsden, E., & Weston, C. (2007). Locating quality physical education in early years pedagogy. *Sport, Education and Society, 12*(4), 383-398.

Meadows, S. (1993). *The child as thinker: The development and acquisition of cognition in childhood.* London: Routledge.

Mosston, M. (1966). *Teaching physical education.* Columbus, OH: Charles E. Merrill.

Papatheodorou, T. (2005). Play and special needs. In J. Moyles (Ed.), *The excellence of play* (2nd ed., p. 55). Maidenhead: Open University Press.

Pickup, I., Haydn-Davies, D., & Jess, M. (2007). The importance of primary physical education. *Physical Education Matters, 2*(1), 8-11.

Pickup, I., & Price, L. (2007). *Teaching physical education in the primary school: A developmental approach.* London: Continuum.

Smith, A.B. (1993). Early childhood educare: Seeking a theoretical framework in Vygotsky's work. *International Journal of Early Years Education, 1*(1).

Vygotsky, L.S. (1978). *Mind and society: The development of higher mental process.* Cambridge, MA: Harvard University Press.

Wood, D., Bruner, J.S., and Ross, G. (1976). The role of tutoring in problem solving. *Journal of Child Psychology and Psychiatry, 17*(2), 89-100.

Chapter 3

Teacher Behaviours

Niki Tsangaridou, PhD

University of Cyprus, Cyprus

KEY POINTS

- Findings from research on teacher effectiveness have revealed that effective teachers use specific pedagogical behaviours that facilitate student learning.

- Planning is an essential instructional strategy for physical education. It includes the organisation of content, selection and sequencing of learning activities, and student grouping, as well as consideration of student motivation, emotional well-being, and social interaction.

- Preventive class management refers to the proactive (rather than reactive) strategies and techniques that teachers use to establish a positive, on-task climate in which minimal time is allocated to managerial tasks (Siedentop & Tannehill, 2000).

- The key management behaviours that distinguish effective teachers are those that prevent misbehaviour by eliciting students' cooperation and involvement in assigned work.

This chapter analyses the research on teaching physical education and discusses the most significant findings that affect student learning. Some essential instructional strategies for teaching effectively in physical education are also presented. The chapter closes with a synopsis of the main findings of teachers' behaviours in physical education.

Characteristics of Effective Teachers

Many agree that the major aim of schools is to provide the best education to students and that teachers are the main players responsible for accomplishing this task (Floden, 2001; Kirk, 2005; Pangrazi, 2003; Rink, 2003; Siedentop 2005; van der Mars, 2006). Whether teachers have a positive influence on students' performance has been an enduring question in teaching research. Over the years educational researchers have attempted to find out what makes some teachers more effective than others (Hastie & Siedentop, 2006; Rink, 2006; Siedentop, 2005).

Early research on teaching (pre-1960s) failed to identify any conclusive findings regarding the characteristics and strategies of effective teachers (Campbell, Kyriakides, Muijs, & Robinson, 2003; Floden, 2001; Rink, 2003, 2006). As a result, many started to believe that teachers do not make a difference in students' learning. The enormous methodological improvements in educational research over the last decades have helped researchers study teacher and student behaviours during the interactive phase of instruction (Floden, 2001; van der Mars, 2006). A major conclusion is that teachers do make a difference in students' lives (Floden, 2001; Rink, 2003; Siedentop & Tannehill, 2000). This line of research, which is often called *process-product research*, attempts to explain between-class differences in achievement in terms of differences in teaching processes. The ultimate hope of this kind of analysis is a list of classroom characteristics known to affect the outcomes of teaching (Campbell et al., 2003; Rink, 2006).

Researchers have also named this line of research *teacher-effects research* because it deals with teachers' effects on their students (Floden, 2001; Rink, 2006). The most significant findings regarding teacher behaviours and student learning, which constitute the pedagogical knowledge base of effective teaching, are briefly summarised in this section.

Expectancy Effects

Effective teachers have high expectations for their students. These teachers not only believe that their students can learn but also that they can teach their students effectively. Effective teachers hold their students accountable for learning the curriculum. Research has indicated that it is important for teachers to believe that students are able to learn from instruction and to communicate this message to their students. Effective teachers expect all students to master the curriculum and devote most available time to academic activities. They have high performance expectations for their students and hold them accountable for achieving such expectations (Graber, 2001; Rink, 2006; Siedentop & Tannehill, 2000).

Content Covered and Academic Learning Time

Effective teachers provide opportunities for their students to learn, move the students briskly through the curriculum, and spend most of their time teaching the curriculum to their students. Findings indicate that the content covered and the time spent academically engaged have significant effects on student learning. The content covered and the academically engaged time have been found to provide the highest and most consistent correlations with gains in achievement (Rink, 2006; Siedentop, 2005; van der Mars, 2006). The message is clear: What is not taught and attended to in academic areas is not learned. Academic learning time (ALT), which refers to the allocated time in which students are engaged at a high success rate to activities or instructional materials related to the class objectives, has been found to have a positive influence on student achievement (Floden, 2001; Rink, 2003; Siedentop, 2005; van der Mars, 2006).

Effective Teachers Are Also Effective Managers

Effective teachers employ instructional procedures to cover specific academic content, motivate students, and facilitate student learning.

Managerial structures are intended to provide organisation and establish a purposeful lesson flow that maximises student learning. In other words, instructional and managerial procedures are prerequisite conditions to efficient learning (Rink, 2006; Siedentop & Tannehill, 2000).

Many studies have found that not all time allocated to academic activities is actually spent in these activities (van der Mars, 2006). Effective teachers, however, structure their classes in ways that maximise student engagement in academic activities and increase student learning. Research has showed that engagement time depends on the teacher's ability to manage and organise the classroom as an efficient learning environment where activities run smoothly, transitions are brief and orderly, and little time is spent getting organised or dealing with inattention or resistance (Graber, 2001; Rink, 2003; Siedentop, 2005). A word of caution is necessary here. It is true that effective teachers are also effective managers, but effective management alone does not make a teacher effective. Effective management is necessary but not sufficient for instruction to occur. Instruction should be sufficiently well constructed in itself to provide student learning (Siedentop & Tannehill, 2000).

Rules and Routines

Students gain in achievement when their teachers spend some time at the beginning of the school year teaching classroom rules and routines and providing opportunities for students to practise such rules and routines. Clear classroom rules, routines, and expectations should be established in every teaching situation (Graber, 2001; Graham, 1992; Rink, 2006). When a teacher creates a structure, the students immediately know what is expected of them and behave accordingly. Establishing these structures is extremely important in achieving and maintaining student learning. When teachers organise and manage their classrooms effectively, they can provide students with more engagement time in academic tasks and more opportunities to learn the academic content (Graber, 2001; Hastie & Martin, 2006; Rink, 2006; Sientenop & Tannehill, 2000).

Instructional Principles

Effective teachers incorporate effective instructional principles while delivering the curriculum. Research studies have also identified specific instructional behaviours that effective teachers use to increase student engagement and achievement. Effective teachers present the curriculum to their students in a clear and consistent way, provide opportunities for practice, and monitor and hold students accountable during the learning process (Graber, 2001; Rink, 2006; Siedentop & Tannehill, 2000).

The literature suggests that students learn better when their teachers (a) provide clear information and check for students' understanding during the initial presentation; (b) guide their students in practice, provide cues and prompts, check for understanding, provide corrections, provide specific feedback, provide reinforcement, provide sufficient repetition, and reteach if necessary; (c) move students to independent practice in order to learn how to perform the concepts or skills accurately and rapidly; and (d) actively supervise their students (monitor students' progress, provide help and feedback, ask questions, and give explanations) during independent practice (Graber, 2001; Hastie & Martin, 2006; Rink, 2006; Siedentop & Tannehill, 2000).

Essential Instructional Strategies for Teaching Physical Education

During the last few years, considerable attention has been focused on dimensions of instructional quality in early childhood pedagogy (Kirk, 2005; Marsden & Weston, 2007; Pangrazi, 2003; Sheridan, 2007; Siedentop, 2005). Research suggests that in order for children to receive quality instruction in their early years, there is a need for teachers to be highly prepared to do so (Kirk, 2005; Sheridan, 2007). One of the critical functions of quality pedagogy is the ability of teachers to plan in a way that facilitates learner engagement with the content (Rink, 2006). Another vital function of quality instruction is the teacher's capability to develop and maintain a managerial system that supports learning (Hastie & Siedentop, 2006). "Effective classroom management is the key to student success in the classroom. According to both research and practice, the inability to establish an orderly learning environment through effective classroom management clearly contributes to misbehavior and disruptions" (Freiberg,

1996, cited in Siedentop & Tannehill, 2000, p. 60). In every teaching situation, teachers are expected to plan both the content and the methods in order to provide quality education and meaningful experiences to children. A discussion of planning procedures and classroom management strategies follows.

Planning

Planning is an integral part of effective teaching and ensures that a sequential and progressive lesson is implemented (Graham, Hale, & Parker, 2001; Rink, 2006; Siedentop & Tannehill, 2000). "Planning is to teaching as writing music is to a symphonic performance. It's analogous to the notes, the scales, the written plan that the musicians follow. Without the written music, a symphony orchestra would be reduced to nothing more than discordant noise with no connection or purpose" (Graham, 1992, p. 13).

Effective planning includes the organisation of content, selection and sequencing of learning activities, student grouping, assignments, grading practices, and classroom management, as well as consideration of student motivation, emotional well-being, and social interaction (Rink, 2006; Siedentop & Tannehill, 2000). Most educators suggest that teachers' planning should be based on the linear rational model of planning (Tyler, 1950). In this model the relationship between planning and instruction is described in four logical steps: specify objectives, select learning activities, organise learning activities, and design evaluation procedures. A brief description of the four steps follows:

1. Specify objectives—An objective should describe what the students will be able to do when they demonstrate their achievement and how the teacher will know they are doing it. A good learning objective has three parts: an observable behaviour, the condition under which the behaviour will occur, and criteria for acceptable performance.

2. Select learning activities—After the objective has been specified, the teacher needs to find a way to help students reach the objective. This involves the selection and

Teachers must use managerial systems that enable students to focus while still being able to enjoy the activities and be active participants.

sequencing of learning activities (e.g., presenting or demonstrating a task, assigning a drill, applying a modified game).

3. Organise learning activities—Selecting learning activities is not enough. The activities should be sequenced from simple to complex and from concrete to abstract, which facilitates the learning process and enhances the students' motivation.

4. Design evaluation procedures—Set up evaluation procedures to determine the extent to which the learning has taken place. The assessment procedures and tools should be carefully selected, and teachers should base their decisions on the procedures in reporting students' progress.

Teachers plan to ensure progression during and between lessons, to use time effectively, to reduce anxiety and build confidence, and to fulfil professional responsibilities (Graham et al., 2001; Rink, 2006; Siedentop & Tannehill, 2000). There is no perfect structure or format for planning a lesson. As Siedentop and Tannehill (2000) indicated, "Our suggestion is to design a format that meets your needs and includes space for you to document and highlight information that will guide your teaching and student participation" (p. 251). However, good lesson plans generally include the following components:

- Task progressions with a time allotment for each task

- Task communication (descriptions for how each task will be communicated to students)

- Organisational arrangement for each task

- Teaching cues (such as critical elements of a skill)

- Reflection on teaching (what, when, why, or what might be changed)

Quality physical education is a worthy goal for all children, and planning is a critical part of quality physical education programmes. Successful teachers plan effective lessons that are interesting and exciting to students. "Plans are guides, not cast on stone" (Graham et al., 2001, p. 115). The school, the children, and the context of the teaching situation may require teachers to be flexible with their lesson planning. In other words, plans change when they need to be changed (Graham et al., 2001; Hastie & Martin, 2006; Rink, 2006; Siedentop & Tannehill, 2000).

Preventive Class Management

Preventive class management refers "to the proactive (rather than reactive) strategies teachers use to develop and maintain a positive, predictable, task-oriented class climate in which minimal time is devoted to managerial tasks and optimal time is therefore available for instructional tasks" (Siedentop & Tannehill, 2000, p. 61). Research has shown that successful teachers are, first of all, good managers. Effective teachers employ instructional procedures to cover specific academic content, motivate students, and facilitate student learning. To teach successfully, it is important to create an environment conducive to learning. Thus, an effective managerial system is a necessary precondition for meaningful learning (Rink, 2006).

Managerial structures are intended to provide organisation and establish a purposeful lesson flow that maximises student learning (Hastie & Siedentop, 2006). As Doyle (1986) suggests, "Teaching has two major task structures organized around the problems of (a) learning and (b) order. Learning is served by the instructional function. . . . Order is served by the managerial function" (p. 395). In other words, instructional and managerial procedures are prerequisite conditions to efficient learning.

Many studies have found that not all time allocated to academic activities is actually spent in these activities (van der Mars, 2006). Effective teachers, however, structure their classes in ways that maximise student engagement in academic activities and increase student learning. Findings have shown that engagement time depends on the teacher's ability to organise and manage the classroom as an efficient learning environment where tasks run smoothly, transitions are brief and orderly, and little time is spent getting organised or dealing with interruptions (Rink, 2006). As Siedentop and Tannehill (2000) pointed out, effective teachers manage student behaviour and direct learning tasks without controlling student thinking. Teachers create a positive atmosphere by managing and organising the learning environment to reinforce a feeling of safety and stability for children. An effective managerial system also generates structures through which the physical education class becomes predictable and operates smoothly. It establishes the limits for behaviour and the teacher's expectations for the students. An inadequate class management system tends to increase discipline problems and reduce the time that can be used for learning (Hastie & Martin, 2006; Rink, 2006; Siedentop & Tannehill, 2000).

Rules and Routines

A successful managerial system begins with the development and establishment of class rules and routines (Siedentop & Tannehill, 2000). In planning rules and routines, teachers should consider the needs of their students and the physical environment of their classrooms. The literature indicates that it is crucial for teachers to establish an appropriate learning environment in the first days of the school year. It is also suggested that teachers need to explicitly teach rules and routines and then constantly monitor the rules and routines once they have been implemented (Rink, 2006; Siedentop & Tannehill, 2000).

Rules refer to general expectations for behaviours in a specific setting (Rink, 2006). They "identify appropriate and inappropriate behaviors and the situations within certain behaviors are acceptable or unacceptable" (Siedentop & Tannehill, 2000, p. 64). *Routines* are procedures that the class follows in its daily activities. In particular, routines refer to specific procedures for performing tasks within the class. Teachers should establish routines for frequently occurring tasks so that more time can be dedicated to substantial parts of the lesson (Rink, 2006).

Teaching Rules

Rules help children learn the behaviours needed to work cooperatively with others. Rules are learned through continual examples of appropriate and inappropriate responses to rules (Graham et al., 2001). For rules to be effective, they need to be clearly stated and enforced fairly and consistently. Rink (2006) suggests that teachers can follow these guidelines in preparing rules:

- Rules should be developed cooperatively with students when possible.
- Rules should be communicated in language that is age appropriate.
- Rules should be few (four to seven) so students will remember them.
- State rules positively and provide both positive and negative examples.
- Rules must be consistent with school rules.
- Develop the consequences and clearly identify their relationship to rule violations.
- Reinforce the rules consistently and fairly.
- Make sure that the students understand the rules.

Siedentop and Tannehill (2000) have suggested that rules for physical education should cover behaviour in the following categories:

- Safety
- Respect for others
- Respect for the learning environment
- Support for others' learning
- Trying hard

Physical education classes share many of the rules established in a regular classroom setting. In addition, the unique physical education context requires additional rules for meaningful and positive learning. According to Rink (2006, p. 143), the following rules are commonly acknowledged as fundamental to a positive and safe environment in physical education:

- When others are talking, we try not to talk.
- We are supportive of our classmates' efforts.
- We respect the rights of others.
- We take care of equipment.
- We try our best.

Teaching Routines

As mentioned, routines are procedures for completing specific tasks or duties within a class. "They are different than rules in that they usually refer to specific activities and they are usually aimed at accomplishing tasks rather than forbidding behaviors" (Graham et al., 2001, p. 121). Routines should also be taught at the beginning of the year. Young children will need more practice of the routines and constant reinforcement. The literature indicates that the most important factor affecting the establishment of routines in a class is the degree to which the teacher consistently reinforces those routines. If a teacher teaches a routine and then does not act in response when routines are not followed, it is unlikely that the routine will be established (Rink, 2006). Research also suggests that routines need to be taught as specifically as one would teach content, such as how to dribble or pass. Teaching a routine means that the teacher should use explanations, demonstrations, practice with feedback, and all other elements related to learning. In other words, the keys to teaching routines effectively are no different than the keys to teaching sport skills (Rink, 2006; Siedentop & Tannehill, 2000). Siedentop

Classroom rules will help students learn to be respectful of each other and their surroundings.

and Tannehill (2000) provided the following teaching strategies in establishing routines:

- Explain and show. Describe the procedure in language that is age specific, and show students how it looks.

- Show nonexamples. Demonstrate the wrong way to do something in addition to showing the right way.

- Rehearse. Provide opportunities for practicing the procedure.

- Expect perfection, reward direction. You should expect perfection and support children as they gradually get better and better.

- Use positive models. When students or groups perform the procedure successfully, indicate it to the rest of the class.

- Provide frequent feedback. Reinforce success and improvement and provide behaviour-specific feedback rather than general feedback.

- Use activities to practise routines. Use several activities that allow children to practise the specific routines.

- Check for children's understanding. Ask them to describe the procedure and why it is significant to do it properly.

Routines should be taught for all procedural aspects of lessons. For example, children should know what to do when the teacher gives a signal for attention or how to return to the classroom. The literature indicates that successful teachers must establish routines for events that commonly occur in a physical education lesson (Graham et al., 2001; Hastie & Martin, 2006; Rink, 2006). Siedentop and Tannehill (2000) suggest that to run a lesson smoothly and efficiently, routines should be established for the following events:

- Entering the gymnasium
- Getting equipment
- Gathering
- Gaining attention
- Choosing partners
- Getting water
- Establishing boundaries
- Finishing
- Leaving

Children need to know the appropriate procedure for dealing with these class events. When teachers have established routines for these events, students know what the expected behaviour is and are more likely to behave appropriately (Rink, 2006).

Conclusion

Findings from research on teacher effectiveness have revealed that effective teachers use specific pedagogical behaviours that facilitate student learning. They have high performance expectations and hold their students accountable for learning. They provide appropriate feedback to their students, ask appropriate questions, and give clear instructions, explanations, and demonstrations. Contextual variables such as grade level, socioeconomic status, and aptitude of learners are always considered by effective teachers during instructional time. Furthermore, effective teachers provide optimal coverage of appropriately sequenced content and maximise academic learning time by actively engaging all students in productive and meaningful work (Graber, 2001; Hastie & Siedentop, 2006; Rink, 2003, 2006; Siedentop, 2005; Siedentop & Tannehill, 2000; van der Mars, 2006).

Planning is an essential instructional strategy for teaching physical education. It includes the organisation of content, the selection and sequencing of learning activities, and student grouping, as well as consideration of student motivation, emotional well-being, and social interaction. Planning provides emotional security to teachers and organises instruction into teachable segments. Effective teachers plan for instruction. In contrast with previous findings, which suggested that physical education teachers plan for keeping students "busy, happy, and good" (Placek, 1983), recent results indicate that effective teachers are concerned with students' learning and plan their lessons in such a way that learning can occur. As Rink (2003) pointed out, effective teachers plan for students to achieve specific goals and objectives, and they hold students accountable for achieving them.

Preventive class management refers to the proactive (rather than reactive) strategies and techniques that teachers use to establish a positive, on-task climate in which minimal time is allocated to managerial tasks (Siedentop & Tannehill, 2000). This includes routines, school and classroom rules, and instruction that promote a climate conducive to student learning. Research indicates that preventive management is more important than remedial management. The key management behaviours that distinguish effective teachers are those that prevent misbehaviour by eliciting students' cooperation and involvement in assigned work (Rink, 2003, 2006; Siedentop & Tannehill, 2000). The literature emphasises that effective teachers know how to organise their instructional activities and classrooms so that students are always engaged in productive work, thus preventing inappropriate or undesirable behaviours in the first place. As Siedentop and Tannehill (2000) point out, the key to successful management is the teacher's understanding of the possible formation of events in a physical education context and the teacher's skilfulness in monitoring and guiding activities based on this information.

Research on teaching in physical education has shown clearly that teachers can make a difference. Effective teachers are those who have a positive, proactive attitude towards their instruction, plan thoroughly for student learning, and monitor students' behaviours. Teachers who care about student learning use essential teaching behaviours that result in increased student learning.

REFERENCES

Campbell, R.J., Kyriakides, L., Muijs, R.D., & Robinson, W. (2003). *Assessing teacher effectiveness: A differentiated model.* London: RoutledgeFalmer.

Doyle, W. (1986). Classroom organization and management. In M.C. Wittrock (Ed.), *Handbook of research on teaching* (3rd ed., pp. 392-431). New York: Macmillan.

Floden, R. (2001). Research on effects of teaching: A continuing model for research on teaching. In V. Richardson (Ed.), *Handbook of research on teaching* (4th ed., pp. 3-16). New York: Macmillan.

Graber, K. (2001). Research on teaching in physical education. In V. Richardson (Ed.), *Handbook of research in teaching* (4th ed., pp. 491-519). Washington, DC: American Educational Research Association.

Graham, G. (1992). *Teaching children physical education: Becoming a master teacher.* Champaign, IL: Human Kinetics.

Graham, G., Hale, S., & Parker, M. (2001). *Children moving: A reflective approach to teaching physical education* (5th ed.). Mountain View, CA: Mayfield.

Hastie, P., & Martin, E. (2006). *Teaching elementary physical education: Strategies for the classroom teacher.* San Francisco: Pearson Benjamin Cummings.

Hastie, P., & Siedentop, D. (2006). The classroom ecology paradigm. In D. Kirk, D. Macdonald, & M. O'Sullivan (Eds.), *The handbook of physical education* (pp. 214-225). London: Sage.

Kirk, D. (2005). Physical education, youth sport and lifelong participation: The importance of early learning experiences. *European Physical Education Review, 11*(3), 239-255.

Marsden, E., & Weston, C. (2007). Locating quality physical education in early years pedagogy. *Sport, Education and Society, 12*(4), 383-398.

Pangrazi, R. (2003). Physical education K-12: "All for one and one for all". *Quest, 55,* 105-117.

Placek, J. (1983). Conceptions of success in teaching: Busy, happy, and good? In T.J. Templin & J.K. Olson (Eds.), *Teaching in physical education* (pp. 46-56). Champaign, IL: Human Kinetics.

Rink, J. (2003). Effective instruction in physical education. In S. Silverman & C. Ennis (Eds.), *Student learning in physical education: Applying research to enhance instruction* (2nd ed., pp. 165-186). Champaign, IL: Human Kinetics.

Rink, J. (2006). *Teaching physical education for learning* (5th ed.). New York, NY: McGraw-Hill.

Sheridan, S. (2007). Dimensions of pedagogical quality in preschool. *International Journal of Early Years Education, 15*(2), 197-217.

Siedentop, D. (2005). The effective physical educator: Then and now avec les hommages de l'auteur á Maurice. In F. Carreiro da Costa, M. Cloes, & M. Gongalez (Eds.), *The art and science of teaching in physical education and sport* (pp. 89-104). Lisbon: MH Faculdade de Motricidada Humana.

Siedentop, D., & Tannehill, D. (2000). *Developing teaching skills in physical education* (4th ed.). Mountain View, CA: Mayfield.

Tyler, R. (1950). *Basic principles of curriculum and instruction.* Chicago: University of Chicago Press.

van der Mars, H. (2006). Time and learning in physical education. In D. Kirk, D. Macdonal, & M. O'Sullivan (Eds.), *The handbook of physical education* (pp.191-213). London: Sage.

Promoting Children's Sound Personality Development and Intrinsic Motivation Towards Physical Activity

Jarmo Liukkonen

University of Jyväskylä, Finland

KEY POINTS

- Early childhood physical education plays an important role in the socialisation process that leads to a physically active lifestyle.

- Children's intrinsic motivation towards physical activity increases if they perceive competence, autonomy, and social relatedness in physical education.

- Intra-individual, self-referenced, task-involving motivational climates should be fostered and normative, other-referenced, ego-involving motivational climates should be avoided in physical education if children's motivation and enjoyment are desired.

A convincing body of evidence shows the importance of physical activity in health promotion (Cavill, Biddle, & Sallis, 2001; Corbin & Pangrazi, 1999; Malina, Bouchard, & Bar-Or, 2004). Research has shown that participation in physical education may affect students' motivation to engage in physical activity because physical education has the potential to provide positive experiences for students (Hagger, Chatzisarantis, Culverhouse, & Biddle, 2003; McKenzie, 2007; Pratt, Macera, & Blanton, 1999). When children and adolescents experience positive outcomes from their involvement in physical activity, they can also be expected to remain involved in physical activity in adulthood (Sallis, Prochaska, & Taylor, 2000; Telama et al., 2005; Vlachopoulos, Biddle, & Fox, 1996). Although studies have shown that physical activity in childhood is associated with physical activity in adulthood (Malina, 2001; Pate, Baranowski, Dowda, & Trost, 1995; Telama et al., 2005), the role of intrapersonal, social, and environmental factors underlying the stability of a physically active lifestyle is largely unclear (Malina, 1990; Sallis et al., 2000).

Motivation is a key factor for physical activity in accordance with environmental support in the form of sport, exercise, and play facilities (Vallerand, 2001). Intrinsic motivation and self-determination have been found to be related to persistence in physical activity (Fortier & Grenier, 1999; Pelletier, Fortier, Vallerand, & Brière, 2001). Intrinsic motivation is associated with positive cognitive, affective, and behavioural consequences (Deci & Ryan, 1991, 2000). Evidence supporting this proposition has shown that self-determined forms of motivation correlate positively with many desirable responses towards engagement in physical activity, such as high effort (Goudas, Biddle, & Underwood, 1995; Ntoumanis, 2001), increased interest (Goudas, Biddle, & Fox, 1994), high levels of positive affect (Ntoumanis, 2005), increased enjoyment (Goudas et al., 1995), preference for attempting challenging tasks (Standage, Duda, & Pensgaard, 2005), and intention to be physically active in leisure time (Hagger et al., 2003; Ntoumanis, 2001; Standage, Duda, & Ntoumanis, 2003). Additionally, nonautonomous forms of motivation in physical education have been shown to be related to negative outcomes, such as boredom and unhappiness (Ntoumanis, 2002; Standage et al., 2005). Overall, research has shown that autonomous motives strongly influence children's attitudes towards physical activity and other desirable motivational indices. In contrast, nonautonomous motivation has been shown to correlate negatively with positive outcomes and to undermine children's adaptive responses.

Early childhood physical education plays an important role in the socialisation process that leads to a physically active lifestyle because of its potential to provide positive physical activity experiences to a large number of children. When children have positive cognitive and affective experiences from their involvement in physical activity, they are more likely to become involved in physical activities later as adults (Haywood, 1991; Vlachopoulos et al., 1996). Therefore it is important to discover cognitive, affective, and motivational mechanisms that determine whether children perceive early childhood physical education as enjoyable or as anxiety provoking. Enjoyment and passion in physical activity seem to be linked with sport and exercise involvement of children (Liukkonen, 1998; Sallis et al., 2000; Vallerand et al., 2006). In addition to positive affect, perceived physical competence is associated with continued physical activity.

In line with the suggestions of Martens (1978), differences in the subjective social-emotional environment of physical education settings, which is created primarily by teachers, lead to variability in the psychological consequences of activity involvement for children. Based on the evidence of Smoll, Smith, Barnett, and Everett (1993) that coaching behaviours and leadership styles can be modified by training, the awareness of the early childhood teachers concerning their students' perceptions of the climate in physical education classes may be increased by teacher education (Jaakkola, 2002).

It is generally believed that physical education in itself has a positive influence on children's personality development. Although physical educators have been able to demonstrate the role of organised physical activity in the development of positive self-concept, self-esteem, and self-realisation, they have been a little vague in terms of definitions and a little short on empirical support. In spite of the general belief that sport has a positive influence on personality development, research has in some amount also shown negative effects on prosocial behaviour (Telama & Polvi, 2007). What appears to be essential is how or in what way physical education and sport activities are carried out. The particular characteristics of physical activity and its emphasis on action, the close interaction between teachers and children, and the wealth and versatility of experiences offer good opportunities for teachers to create a favourable environment for the personality development of children.

Social Development Through Physical Education

Physical education is an important psychosocial context for the development of peer status, peer acceptance, and self-worth (Hovelynck, Auweele, & Mouratidis, 2007; Stiller & Alfermann, 2007). It can also play an important role in solving developmental crises of competence and identity in the psychosocial phases of youth. Enjoyment has emerged as one of the major constructs for understanding the experiences and motivation of people who participate in sport and exercise. Accordingly, various theoretical models have been developed to explain the concept of enjoyment. Enjoyment is an important predictor of sport commitment and, correspondingly, the lack of enjoyment and perception of anxiety decrease commitment to physical activity and early childhood physical education (Scanlan & Simons, 1992).

Sociability, which at its highest level can be seen as prosocial behaviour in activities, is an important dimension of both personality development and moral development, from heteronymous morality to moral autonomy. To be morally independent, children need to be able to realise the consequences of their behaviour (Telama & Polvi, 2007).

Through situations that arise in physical education, a child can easily internalise the line between right and wrong through the principle of fair play. Teachers and children should continually discuss situations where moral conflicts occur. If following rules is controlled by adults, it may create situations of double standards or compromised ethics. For example, children may learn that when the teacher is not present or does not see what happens, it is justifiable to break the rules or to behave in a way that harms others. Breaking rules and cheating may decrease if children are involved in the process of both defining and observing the rules. In addition, the teacher's own example is important for the spirit of sportspersonship. The fairness of the teacher in controlling the rules and decisions in conflict situations offers a model for fair treatment and taking everybody's equal rights into account.

Prosocial behaviour includes positive social behaviour, such as consideration of others, willingness to initiate cooperation with others, altruistic feelings, and manifestations of helping

Physical education can provide the environment and opportunity for children to develop their social and emotional skills.

behaviour. It also refers to a lack of negative social behaviour, such as violence and bullying. Empathetic ability is crucial for altruistic behaviour, which is a central form of prosocial behaviour. Altruistic behaviour has an unselfish purpose, and it reflects empathy and the voluntary nature of activity as well as helping others. Helping behaviour is usually associated with cooperating, sharing, giving, taking care, encouraging, correcting mistakes, and strengthening. In modern educational programs, cultivating altruism and prosocial behaviour may be considered fundamental goals. It is desirable for adults to be concerned not only for their own well-being but also for the welfare of others (Telama & Polvi, 2007).

Development of Intrinsic Motivation Through Physical Education

Intrinsic motivation is an important determinant of persistence in physical activity. Thus, reliable knowledge is needed about the motivating role of physical education for children. Differences

in the subjective social environment operating in physical education settings—created by significant others, primarily the teachers—can lead to variability in the psychological consequences of physical activity for children.

Through education, we can expect to increase teachers' awareness of the psychological and motivational climate in physical education classes. Because the training process in physical education classes is often evaluative, participation in physical education can be associated with social pressure. Competitive and normative evaluation create worries about one's level of competence, especially among boys, for whom it is often important to be physically able (Roberts, 1984). Physical education can be considered more or less an outcome-oriented activity in which the goal is often defined in terms of success and failure. For example, failure when performing a difficult task in front of classmates and the teacher might raise negative affective responses. Furthermore, a less skilled student will also experience negative affect when asked to perform a task in front of others. The possibility of demonstrating low competence, the perceived importance of being competent in the tasks of the lesson, and peer and group evaluation are important factors that can

Failure in a physical education setting can lead to a negative experience for a child. The teacher should help children to focus on personal goals that can be worked toward and achieved.

trigger negative affect, such as anxiety, in physical education classes (Barkoukis, 2007).

Achievement goal theory is a social-cognitive framework for understanding motivational processes in achievement settings (Nicholls, 1989). Although research on children's achievement motivation has yielded several important motivational factors, the two goal perspectives dominant in performance settings are task (self-referenced) and ego (other-referenced) goal orientations. These orientations refer to how success is perceived and how competence is evaluated. Past experience in predominantly task- or ego-involving contexts relates to the development of a personal disposition towards mastery (task-involving) or social comparison–based (ego-involving) goals (Ames, 1992; Nicholls, 1989; Roberts, 2001). These two motivational perspectives have an orthogonal relationship, which means that a child can have a high or low level of both orientations or have a high level in one orientation and a low level in the other (Liukkonen, 1998). Thus, children may have different combinations of task and ego orientation (high task orientation and high ego orientation, high task orientation and low ego orientation, low task orientation and high ego orientation, or low task orientation and low ego orientation).

It is expected that when a child focuses on task-involving goals, more favourable motivation-related outcomes will result, regardless of whether the child has a high or low perception of competence. Such outcomes are cognitive (e.g., values and expectations towards physical activity, perceptions of high physical competence, intention to participate in physical activities), affective (e.g., enjoyment), and behavioural (e.g., continued participation in physical activity, putting effort on physical activities). It is also hypothesised that children will not experience motivational problems when ego-involving goals are emphasised as long as the children are confident in their physical ability. Maladaptive motivational patterns result when children have adopted ego-involving goals but have doubts about the adequacy of their competence to meet the task at hand (Roberts, 2001). A task-oriented goal perspective has been associated with increased enjoyment and intrinsic motivation in physical activity, regardless of the level of physical competence (Duda & Whitehead, 1998; Fox, Goudas, Biddle, Duda, & Armstrong, 1994; Liukkonen, 1998). Task orientation has also been found to be associated with continued participation in sport (Fox et al., 1994). In addition, task orientation is linked with intention to be

physically active (Biddle, Soos, & Chatzisarantis, 1999; Sarrazin, Vallerand, Guillet, Pelletier, & Cury, 2002) and with self-reported physical activity (Dempsey, Kimiecik, & Horn, 1993; Kimiecik, Horn, & Shurin, 1996). Early childhood educators should help children focus on learning, personal development, and effort, and they should decrease focus on normative evaluation. Educators play an important role in creating a favourable social-emotional climate that supports the development of children's task involvement.

Motivational Climate in Physical Education

Motivational climate refers to a situational psychological perception of the activity that directs the goals of action (Ames, 1992; Ames & Archer, 1988; Dweck & Leggett, 1988; Nicholls, 1984, 1989). Motivational climate in early childhood physical education affects children's self-experiences and attitudes towards physical activity. In the achievement goal orientation approach, the motivational climate has two perspectives, namely a task-involving and an ego-involving climate. An ego-involving climate stresses performance outcomes and social comparison between children. This leads to increased external motivation and anxiety, as well as decreased interest. In a task-involving climate, children connect their performance to their personal development, are rewarded for effort, and set their personal goals themselves. A task-involving climate is created if the teacher's pedagogical and didactical solutions support the development of children's task orientation. A largely applied presentation of task- and ego-involving motivational climate is Epstein's (1989) TARGET model of education (see table 4.1). TARGET is an acronym formulated from six elements in teaching: task, authority, rewards, grouping, evaluation, and timing.

Within the educational domain, perceptions of a task-involving climate have been found to be related to a pattern of cognitions and affective responses that is likely to enhance children's involvement in learning (Ames 1992). A task-involving motivational climate has been associated with adaptive affective responses, including enjoyment (Kavussanu & Roberts, 1996; Liukkonen, 1998; Seifriz, Duda, & Chi, 1992), satisfaction (Carpenter & Morgan, 1999; Walling, Duda, & Chi, 1993), intrinsic interest (Cury et al., 1996),

Table 4.1 TARGET Principles in Physical Education

TARGET principles	Description of principle	How to support a task-involving climate	What should be avoided
Tasks	Design of learning activities and assignments	• Include variety, challenge, and purpose for each activity. • Give students the opportunity to choose from a variety of tasks. • Encourage students to set their own goals.	Basing task goals on who will be first, who will score the most points, and so on
Authority	Students' opportunities to develop a sense of personal control, independence, and participation in the instructional process	• Foster active participation and a sense of autonomy. • Use questioning skills. • Give students the opportunity to choose (within the assigned content framework). • Involve students in decision making during teaching (e.g., how to complete tasks, which materials to use, and so on).	• Assuming all the responsibility as the teacher • Giving students orders and no choices
Rewards	• Formal and informal use of incentives and praise • Reasons for recognition	• Focus on individual progress and improvement. • Recognition of students' accomplishments is kept private and rewards are given for improvement.	Recognising students' accomplishments in public and giving rewards in comparison with others
Grouping	• Manner and frequency of students working together • Arrangements in classroom that allow students to master course content	• Use individual and cooperative learning. • Students work on individualised tasks, in dyads, or in small cooperative groups. • Grouping is flexible and heterogeneous.	Basing grouping in ability
Evaluation	• Methods used to assess and monitor learning • Standards for performance and feedback	• Evaluation is self-referenced and private. • Give opportunities to improve. • Use diverse methods. • Progress is judged on the basis of individual objectives, participation, effort, and improvement. • Students are encouraged to evaluate their own performances.	Basing evaluation on norms and comparison with others
Time	Includes workload, pace of instruction, and learning	• Allow students to participate in scheduling. • Time limits for task completion are flexible. • Students help schedule timelines for improvement.	Not allowing time limits to be flexible

Reprinted, by permission, from J. Liukkonen et al., 2007, *Psychology for physical educators* (Champaign, IL: Human Kinetics), 5.

effort (Kavussanu & Roberts, 1996), and lowered tension (Carpenter & Morgan, 1999; Kavussanu & Roberts, 1996; Ommundsen, Roberts, & Kavussanu, 1997). Ego-involving motivational climate has been associated with worrying (Walling et al., 1993); tension, anxiety, and pressure (Ntoumanis & Biddle, 1998; Seifriz et al., 1992; Walling et al., 1993); and lowered effort (Yoo, 1997).

Research has consistently demonstrated low or negligible correlations between the dimensions of task-involving and ego-involving climates (e.g., Barkoukis, Thøgersen-Ntoumani, Ntoumanis, & Nikitaras, 2007; Liukkonen, Telama, & Biddle, 1998; Ommundsen & Kvalø, 2007). These results highlight the independence of the two factors.

In addition to achievement goal theory, self-determination theory (Deci & Ryan 2000, 2002) has been a prevailing approach in studying human motivation, particularly in achievement and participation contexts. The major concept of the theory is self-determination, which means "a quality of human functioning that involves the experience of choice, in other words, the experience of an internal perceived locus of causality" (Deci & Ryan, 1985, 38). Self-determination is the capacity to choose and to have those choices—rather than reinforcement contingencies, drives, or any other forces or pressures—be the determinants of one's actions. Self-determination is an innate need more than a capacity.

Perception of self-determination leads to intrinsic motivation. Research has shown that children who are self-determined in their behaviour are more persistent in their physical activities (Hagger et al., 2003; Ommundsen, 2005). Children may feel intrinsic motivation if they perceive competence, autonomy, and social relatedness in an activity. Thus, events or behaviours that increase competence, autonomy, and relatedness enhance intrinsic motivation. Conversely, events that decrease these three perceptions diminish intrinsic motivation.

Perceived autonomy means the chance to affect one's own behaviour. If the action is regulated externally or controlled by a person not involved in it, the interest towards the task will decrease (Deci & Ryan, 2000). When children are playing, they often concentrate on the activity and their own roles so completely that they exclude most external stimuli from their consciousness. When rules created by adults start regulating children's play, their interest in it will decrease. The same mechanism is also present in pedagogical situations. Strong perceptions of autonomy in physical education classes have been found to increase physical activity not only during class but also during leisure time (Hagger et al., 2003).

Social relatedness is a natural need by human beings to belong to a group, be accepted, and feel positive emotions while acting as a group member (Deci & Ryan, 2000). Children can play games until exhaustion day after day. They enjoy action and voluntarily come back to the game again and again. If the same game—and the energy and time committed to it—were executed in another group defined by an adult or someone else, the eagerness and level of participation would probably be remarkably lower.

REFERENCES

Ames, C. (1992). The relationship of achievement goals to student motivation in classroom settings. In G. Roberts (Ed.), *Motivation in sport and exercise* (pp. 161-176). Champaign, IL: Human Kinetics.

Ames, C., & Archer, J. (1988). Achievement goals in the classroom: Students' learning strategies and motivation processes. *Journal of Educational Psychology, 80,* 260-267.

Barkoukis, V. (2007). Experience of state anxiety in physical education. In J. Liukkonen, Y. Auweele, D. Alfermann, B. Vereijken, & Y. Theodorakis (Eds.), *Psychology for physical education: Student in focus* (pp. 57-72). Champaign, IL: Human Kinetics.

Barkoukis, V., Thøgersen-Ntoumani, C., Ntoumanis, N., & Nikitaras, N. (2007). Achievement goals in physical education: Examining the predictive ability of five different dimensions of motivational climate. *European Physical Education Review, 13,* 267–285.

Biddle, S.J.H., Soos, I., & Chatzisarantis, N. (1999). Predicting physical activity intentions using a goal perspectives and self-determination theory approach: A study of Hungarian youth. *Scandinavian Journal of Medicine & Science in Sports, 9,* 353-357.

Carpenter, P., & Morgan, K. (1999). Motivational climate, personal goal perspectives, and cognitive and affective responses in physical education classes. *European Journal of Physical Education, 19,* 302-312.

Cavill, N., Biddle, S., & Sallis, J. (2001). Health-enhancing physical activity for young people: Statement to the United Kingdom Expert Consensus Conference. *Pediatric Exercise Science, 13,* 12–25.

Corbin, C., & Pangrazi, R.P. (1999). *Toward a better understanding of physical fitness and activity.* Scottsdale, AZ: Holcomb Hathaway.

Cury, F., Biddle, S.J.H., Famose, J.P., Goudas, M., Sarrazin, P., & Durand, M. (1996). Personal and situational factors influencing intrinsic interest of adolescent girls in school physical education: A structural equation modeling analysis. *Educational Psychology, 16*, 305-315.

Deci, E.L., & Ryan, R.M. (1985). *Intrinsic motivation and self-determination in human behavior*. New York: Plenum Press.

Deci, E.L., & Ryan, R.M. (1991). A motivational approach to self: Integration in personality. In R. Dienstbier (Ed.), *Nebraska symposium on motivation: Perspectives on motivation* (pp. 237-288). Lincoln, NE: University of Nebraska Press.

Deci, E.L., & Ryan, R.M. (2000). The "what" and "why" of goal pursuits: Human needs and the self-determination of behavior. *Psychological Inquiry, 11*, 227-268.

Deci, E.L., & Ryan, R.M. (2002). Self-determination research: Reflections and future directions. In E.L. Deci & R.M. Ryan (Eds.), *Handbook of self-determination research* (pp. 431-441). Rochester, NY: University of Rochester Press.

Dempsey, J.M., Kimiecik, J.C., & Horn, T.S. (1993). Parental influence on children's moderate to vigorous physical activity participation: An expectancy-value approach. *Pediatric Exercise Science, 5*, 151-167.

Duda, J.L., & Whitehead, J. (1998). Measurement of goal perspectives in the physical domain. In J.L. Duda (Ed.), *Advances in sport and exercise: Psychology measurement* (pp. 21-48). Morgantown, WV: Fitness Information Technology.

Dweck, C.S., & Leggett, E.L. (1988). A social-cognitive approach to motivation and personality. *Psychological Review, 95*, 256-273.

Epstein, J.L. (1989). Family structures and student motivation: A developmental perspective. In C. Ames & R. Ames (Eds.), *Research on motivation in education* (pp. 259-295). San Diego: Academic Press.

Fortier, M.S., & Grenier, M.N. (1999). Les determinants personnels et situationnels de l'adherence a l'exercice: Une etude prospective. *STAPS: Revue des Sciences et Techniques des Activites Physiques et Sportives hiver, 20*, 25-37.

Fox, K.R., Goudas, M., Biddle, S.J.H., Duda, J.L., & Armstrong, N. (1994). Children's task and ego profiles in sport. *British Journal of Educational Psychology, 64*, 253-261.

Goudas, M., Biddle, S.J.H., & Fox, K. (1994). Perceived locus of causality, goal orientations, and perceived competence in school physical education classes. *British Journal of Educational Psychology, 64*, 453-463.

Goudas, M., Biddle, S.J.H., & Underwood, M. (1995). A prospective study of the relationships between motivational orientations and perceived competence with intrinsic motivation and achievement in teachers' education course. *Educational Psychology, 15*, 89-96.

Hagger, M., Chatzisarantis, N., Culverhouse, T., & Biddle, S.J.H. (2003). The processes which perceived autonomy support in physical education promotes leisure-time physical activity intentions and behaviour: A trans-contextual model. *Journal of Educational Psychology, 95*, 784-795.

Haywood, K.M. (1991). The role of physical education in the development of active lifestyles. *Research Quarterly for Exercise and Sport, 62*, 151-156.

Hovelynck, J., Auweele, Y., & Mouratidis, T. (2007). Group development in the physical education class. In J. Liukkonen, Y. Auweele, D. Alfermann, B. Vereijken, & Y. Theodorakis (Eds.), *Psychology for physical education: Student in focus* (pp. 101-119). Champaign, IL: Human Kinetics.

Jaakkola, T. (2002). *Changes in students' exercise motivation, goal orientation, and sport competence as result of modifications in school physical education teaching practices.* Research Reports on Sport and Health Sciences. LIKES, Research Center for Sport and Health Sciences. University of Jyväskylä, Finland.

Kavussanu, M., & Roberts, G.C. (1996). Motivation in physical activity contexts: The relationship of perceived motivational climate to intrinsic motivation and self-efficacy. *Journal of Sport and Exercise Psychology, 18*, 264-280.

Kimiecik, J., Horn, T.S., & Shurin, C.S. (1996). Relationships among children's beliefs, perception of their parents' beliefs and their moderate-to-vigorous physical activity. *Research Quarterly for Exercise and Sport, 67*, 324-336.

Liukkonen, J. (1998). *Enjoyment in youth sports: A goal perspectives approach.* Research Reports on Sport and Health Sciences. LIKES, Research Center for Sport and Health Sciences. University of Jyväskylä, Finland.

Liukkonen, J., Telama, R., & Biddle, S. (1998). Enjoyment in youth sports: A goal perspectives approach. *European Yearbook of Sport Psychology, 2*, 1-19.

Malina, R. (1990). Growth, exercise, fitness, and later outcomes. In C. Bouchard, R.J. Shephard, T. Stephens, J.R. Sutton, & B.D. McPherson (Eds.), *Exercise, fitness and health: A consensus of current knowledge* (pp. 637-653). Champaign, IL: Human Kinetics.

Malina, R. (2001). Adherence to physical activity from childhood to adulthood: A perspective from tracking studies. *Quest, 53*, 346-355.

Malina, R.M., Bouchard, C., & Bar-Or, O. (2004). *Growth, maturation, and physical activity* (2nd ed.). Champaign, IL: Human Kinetics.

Martens, R. (1978). *Joy and sadness in children's sports*. Champaign, IL: Human Kinetics.

McKenzie, T.L. (2007). The preparation of physical educators: A public health perspective. *Quest, 59*, 346-357.

Nicholls, J.G. (1984). Conceptions of ability and achievement motivation. In R. Ames & C. Ames (Eds.), *Research on motivation in education: Student motivation* (pp. 39-73). New York: Academic Press.

Nicholls, J.G. (1989). *The competitive ethos and democratic education.* Cambridge, MA: Harvard University Press.

Ntoumanis, N. (2001). Empirical links between achievement goal theory and self-determination theory in sport. *Journal of Sport Sciences, 19,* 397-409.

Ntoumanis, N. (2002). Motivational clusters in a sample of British physical education classes. *Psychology of Sport and Exercise, 3,* 177-194.

Ntoumanis, N. (2005). A prospective study of participation in optional school physical education based on self-determination theory. *Journal of Educational Psychology, 97,* 444-453.

Ntoumanis, N., & Biddle, S. (1998). The relationship between competitive anxiety, achievement goals, and motivational climates. *Research Quarterly for Exercise and Sport, 69,* 176-187.

Ommundsen, Y. (2005). Motivation and affect in physical education classes: A self-determination perspective. Active lifestyles: The impact of education and sport. *AIESEP World Congress.* Abstracts Book, 192.

Ommundsen, Y., & Kvalø, E. S. (2007). Autonomy-mastery, supportive or performance focused? Different teacher behaviours and pupils' outcomes in physical education. *Scandinavian Journal of Educational Research, 51,* 385-413.

Ommundsen, Y., Roberts, G.C., & Kavussanu, M. (1997). Perceived motivational climate and cognitive and affective correlates among Norwegian athletes. In R. Lidor & M. Bar-Eli (Eds.), *Innovations in sport psychology: Linking theory into practice* (pp. 522-524). Proceedings of the 9th World Congress of Sport Psychology: International Society of Sport Psychology.

Pate, R., Baranowski, T., Dowda, M., & Trost, S. (1996). Tracking of physical activity in young children. *Medicine & Science in Sports & Exercise, 28*(1), 92-96.

Pelletier, L., Fortier, M., Vallerand, R., & Brière, N. (2001). Associations among perceived autonomy support, forms of self-regulation, and persistence: A prospective study. *Motivation and Emotion, 25,* 279-306.

Pratt, M., Macera, C.A., & Blanton, C. (1999). Levels of physical activity and inactivity in children and adults in the United States: Current evidence and research issues. *Medicine & Science in Sports & Exercise, 31,* 526-533.

Roberts, G.C. (1984). Achievement motivation in children's sport. In J. Nicholls (Ed.), *Advances in motivation and achievement: The development of achievement motivation* (pp. 251-281). Greenwich, CT: JAI Press.

Roberts, G.C. (2001). Understanding the dynamics of motivation in physical activity: The influence of achievement goals, personal agency beliefs, and the motivational climate. In G.C. Roberts (Ed.), *Advances in motivation in sport and exercise* (pp. 1-50). Champaign, IL: Human Kinetics.

Sallis, J.F., Prochaska, J.J., & Taylor, W.C. (2000). A review of correlates of physical activity of children and adolescents. *Medicine and Science in Sports and Exercise, 32,* 963-975.

Sarrazin, P., Vallerand, R., Guillet, E., Pelletier, L., & Cury, F. (2002). Motivation and dropout in female handballers: A 21-month prospective study. *European Journal of Social Psychology, 32,* 395-418.

Scanlan, T.K., & Simons, J.P. (1992). The construct of sport enjoyment. In G.C. Roberts (Ed.), *Motivation in sport and exercise* (pp. 199-215). Champaign, IL: Human Kinetics.

Seifriz, J., Duda, J.L., & Chi, L. (1992). The relationship of perceived motivational climate to intrinsic motivation and beliefs about success in basketball. *Journal of Sport and Exercise Psychology, 14,* 375-391.

Smoll, F.L., Smith, R.E., Barnett, N.P., & Everett, J.J. (1993). Enhancement of children's self-esteem through social support training for youth sport coaches. *Journal of Applied Psychology, 78,* 602-610.

Standage, M., Duda, J.L., & Ntoumanis, N. (2003). A model of contextual motivation in physical education: An integration of self-determination and goal perspective theories in predicting leisure-time exercise intentions. *Journal of Educational Psychology, 95,* 97-110.

Standage, M., Duda, J.L., & Pensgaard, A.M. (2005). The effect of competitive outcome and the motivational climate on the psychological well-being of individuals engaged in a coordination task. *Motivation and Emotion, 29,* 41-68.

Stiller, J., & Alfermann, D. (2007). Promotion of a healthy self-concept. In J. Liukkonen, Y. Auweele, D. Alfermann, B. Vereijken, & Y. Theodorakis (Eds.), *Psychology for physical education: Student in focus* (pp. 123-140). Champaign, IL: Human Kinetics.

Telama, R., & Polvi, S. (2007). Facilitating prosocial behaviour in physical education. In J. Liukkonen, Y. Auweele, D. Alfermann, B. Vereijken, & Y. Theodorakis (Eds.), *Psychology for physical education: Student in focus* (pp. 85-99). Champaign, IL: Human Kinetics.

Telama, R., Yang, X., Viikari, J., Välimäki, I., Wanne, O., & Raitakari, O. (2005). Physical activity from childhood to adulthood: A 21-year tracking study. *American Journal of Preventive Medicine, 28,* 267-273.

Vallerand, R.J. (2001). A hierarchical model of intrinsic and extrinsic motivation in sport and exercise. In G.C. Roberts (Ed.), *Advances in motivation in sport and exercise* (pp. 263-319). Champaign, IL: Human Kinetics.

Vallerand, R.J., Rousseau, F.L., Grouzet, F., Dumais, A., Grenier, S., & Blanchard, C. (2006). Passion in sport: A look at determinants and affective experiences. *Journal of Sport and Exercise Psychology, 28,* 454-478.

Vlachopoulos, S., Biddle, S.J.H., & Fox, K. (1996). A social-cognitive investigation into the mechanisms of affect generation in children's physical activity. *Journal of Sport and Exercise Psychology, 18,* 174-193.

Walling, M.D., Duda, J.L., & Chi, L. (1993). The perceived motivational climate in sport questionnaire: Construct and predictive validity. *Journal of Sport and Exercise Psychology, 2,* 172-183.

Yoo, J. (1997). Motivational and behavioural concomitants of goal orientation and motivational climate in the physical education context. In R. Lidor & M. Bar-Eli (Eds.), *Innovations in sport psychology: Linking theory into practice* (pp. 773-775). Proceedings of the 9th World Congress in Sport Psychology: International Society of Sport Psychology.

Chapter 5

Early Steps Physical Education Curriculum Standards

Jarmo Liukkonen
University of Jyväskylä, Finland

KEY POINTS

- The basis for children's social development is recognising the diversity among children.
- Fundamental motor skills are the foundation for future motor development and physical activity.
- Health maintenance is based on participation in physical activities and on healthy eating habits.

The importance of physical education in schools is recognised worldwide due to its remarkable role in promoting children's physical activity and health. In Britain, for example, the 1988 Education Reform Act included physical education as one of the foundation subjects in the national curriculum (Ntoumanis, 2001). In the United States, Sallis and McKenzie (1991) reported that prominent professional organisations, such as the American Academy of Kinesiology and Physical Education and the American Academy of Pediatrics Committees on Sports Medicine and School Health, have made strong arguments in favor of physical education programmes and have emphasised the role of these programmes in public health. Sallis and McKenzie (1991) argued that positive experiences in children's physical education promote physically active lifestyles later in adulthood.

Today's early childhood physical education focuses on the learning and psychological experiences of the child, keeping in mind the two major goals of physical education: learning *in* and learning *through* physical activities (Council of Physical Education for Children [COPEC], 1992; Liukkonen, Auweele, Alfermann, Vereijken, & Theodorakis, 2007; Mosston & Ashworth, 2002; National Association for Sport and Physical Education [NASPE], 1995; Physical Best, 2004; Siedentop, Hastie, & Mars, 2004).

STANDARD 1   Through physical activities, children will be able to cooperate with others and respect individual differences.

   Goal 1.1 Interact positively with group members.

   Objective 1.1.1 Children will be able to work in groups.

   Objective 1.1.2 Children will be able to share the place and resources with others.

   Objective 1.1.3 Children will be able to participate in activities without disturbing others.

   Objective 1.1.4 Children will be able to share ideas and roles.

   Goal 1.2 Recognise and respect individual differences.

   Objective 1.2.1 Children will be able to appreciate their own work and that of others.

   Objective 1.2.2 Children will be able to help others.

STANDARD 2   Through the acquisition and development of motor skills, children will have a desire to be involved in a healthy lifestyle.

   Goal 2.1 Be involved in a variety of physical activities.

   Objective 2.1.1 Children will be able to travel in many ways showing variations in direction, level, and speed.

   Objective 2.1.2 Children will be able to participate in balancing activities.

   Objective 2.1.3 Children will be able to send and receive a variety of objects in many ways.

   Goal 2.2 Recognise changes in body functions during physical activities.

   Objective 2.2.1 Children will be able to identify changes in heart rate.

   Objective 2.2.2 Children will be able to identify changes in breathing.

   Objective 2.2.3 Children will be able to identify changes in body temperature.

   Goal 2.3 Become aware of healthy lifestyle activities.

   Objective 2.3.1 Children will be able to enjoy moving in a variety of ways.

   Objective 2.3.2 Children will be able to identify healthy foods.

   Objective 2.3.3 Children will be able to understand the need for rest and recovery.

The Early Steps Physical Education Curriculum (ESPEC) is designed to develop children's social skills and to help children understand the importance of a healthy lifestyle. The programme is based on two standards with subgoals and specific objectives describing what children have learned after participating in ESPEC with twice-weekly physical education lessons during 9 months. These standards are based on the idea that all children have two basic needs: They have to feel at home in their own bodies (and thus they must gain body mastery), and they need to be able to form relationships (Sherborne, 1993). The fulfilment of these needs—relating to oneself and to other people—can be achieved through physical education.

Standard 1

Through physical activities, children will be able to cooperate with others and respect individual differences.

Development of social skills is a basic curriculum goal of physical education because modern life places a premium on the ability to relate well to others, to work effectively in groups, and to deal with interpersonal conflicts and tensions (Telama & Polvi, 2007). Preschools have an increased responsibility for helping children learn the basic skills needed to cope with these life challenges. A class characterised by mutual support and trust contains opportunities for constructive peer feedback and feelings of acceptance. These positive relationships that are learned and experienced during the preschool and school years play an important role in developing social resilience in adult life, whereas poor school relationships lead to social vulnerability.

A second justification of including social skill development as a curriculum goal is the important part social processes play in the creation of a supportive emotional and motivational climate. Such a climate can facilitate the implementation of the other major curriculum goals: development of a mature self-concept, acquisition of motor skills, and development of the right attitude in children to enable them to develop and maintain an active and healthy lifestyle. Physical education will benefit from relational issues being settled to some degree (e.g., it is hard to focus on learning when one feels rejected by peers).

Supportive emotional climate, positive experiences, and enjoyment are important goals—and means—in physical education. They provide children with a foundation for lifelong exercise activity. The teaching and use of social and emotional skills help achieve a supportive learning atmosphere. Social and emotional skills include intrapersonal skills and the skills of being in relationships with others. The skills taught to children are the basic counselling skills, such as active listening; clear expression of feelings, beliefs, and thoughts; and problem-solving skills. Similar to motor skills, practice is an important part of learning these skills. Child-centred, action-oriented teaching methods are essential. Also, theory and research about training of children's social skills indicate that learning is more likely to occur when evidence-based training approaches are used (Durlak & Weissberg, 2007).

The basis for children's social development is recognising the diversity among children. Children learn to form pairs and small groups with all members of the class. Participation in group activities stimulates children to respond to others' approaches during play, to accept the ideas of other children and to share their own, and to assume leadership roles or follow other leaders when playing (Hellison, 1995; Hovelynck, Auweele, & Mouratidis, 2007; Schmuck & Schmuck, 2001).

Goal 1.1

Interact positively with group members.

Prosocial skills, such as helping behaviour, are learned similarly to any other skills. What is provided is a teaching methodology focusing on social interaction and cooperation among children. An important fact from the viewpoint of everyday life in early childhood is that learning prosocial skills does not require a special time that would reduce the time spent on other skills (e.g., motor skills). Helping behaviour is learned in activity that may be, among other things, training motor skills or fitness. Teachers need to take into account prosocial goals in their behaviour and methods used. The main methods for promoting prosocial behaviour are using a reciprocal teaching style, encouraging social behaviour in teacher feedback, and solving conflict between students through dialogue and discussion.

The components of prosocial behaviour include respect (courteousness, acceptance,

Working in pairs or small groups will help students learn to cooperate with others and learn to respect individual differences.

tolerance, diversity), responsibility (reliability, commitment, self-discipline, dependability), trustworthiness (honesty, integrity, truthfulness, loyalty), caring (thoughtfulness, empathy, compassion, friendliness), fairness (leadership, involvement, tradition, vision), and citizenship (equality, harmony, justice, democracy) (Collaborative for Academic, Social, and Emotional Learning [CASEL], 2008; Payton et al., 2000).

It has been found that in the majority of physical education in schools, very little real cooperative work between students (e.g., helping each other) is evident (Varstala, Paukku, & Telama, 1983). In youth sport, the situation is the same (Liukkonen, Laakso, & Telama, 1996). There are many reasons for this, one of which is the old belief that physical activity and sport promote prosocial behaviour and therefore it is not necessary to pay attention to social issues in teaching. Another reason may be that physical education has been seen as pronouncedly physical because it is the only school subject where the

body and its functions are the focus of teaching. It also has often been forgotten that physiological responses and bodily functions do not prevent taking account of social-psychological aspects of physical activities. One reason for the poor implementation of prosocial goals may be a perceived difficulty of teaching prosocial skills, which may be connected to the lack of proper definition of prosocial educational goals in physical education curricula for early childhood.

Prosocial behaviour means positive social behaviour—that is, consideration of others, willingness to genuinely cooperate with others, altruistic feelings, and manifestation of helping behaviour. It also means there is a lack of negative social behaviour, such as violence and bullying. We have to give up the old belief that physical activity in itself develops people ethically and socially. However, it remains a fact that physical activity and physical education share features that lend themselves to such development. In physical activity, there are plenty of opportunities for creating genuine interactive relations in the form of observing, giving feedback, supporting, and helping others. Physical activity also contains conflict situations that provide the opportunity for solving conflicts through dialogue and discussion.

To be successful, the teaching of prosocial behaviour should be based on an ethical approach to teaching physical education. This concerns both teachers and students. Teachers should understand that the things they say and do have ethical implications.

A physical education class, similar to any other class or group, is more than a mere collection of students, and it develops, as people do, during an academic year. Second, the group processes within a class can enhance the social development of students. Third, the social experiences that students acquire as their class develops are also a learning experience. Fourth, a well-developed classroom, in which students feel competent in dealing with their academic tasks and their interpersonal relations, constitutes an appropriate learning environment. Students in a safe environment, where issues concerning relationships have been settled, will encourage the class as a whole to work more efficiently and to successfully fulfil the major educational objectives. Besides, peer relationships have an indirect effect on prosocial behaviour of students, which in turn affects their academic achievement.

At the core of group development theory lies the assumption that the interactions that take place among group members are the driving force of class development, and that in each stage, students have certain needs that should be met for them to become more mature and productive both at an individual and at a class level. However, because neither an individual student nor a class develop automatically towards a more mature stage, it is necessary to look for strategies to influence this development.

Goal 1.1 Objective 1

Children will be able to work in groups.

In early childhood education, children work in groups, often small groups consisting of five to seven children but also often in bigger groups. Group activities require cooperation skills, but working in groups also serves as a good learning opportunity for social skills. Early educators should use physical education in developing children's social skills because physical activities include plenty of socially challenging situations.

Goal 1.1 Objective 2

Children will be able to share the place and resources with others.

Children learn to share places and equipment with others if teachers pay attention to situations where conflicts may occur during physical activities, play, and games.

Goal 1.1 Objective 3

Children will be able to participate in activities without disturbing others.

It is important to teach children to participate in physical activities without disturbing others. Disturbing others happens often in the form of being noisy, taking space and resources from others, and being selfish in play. Teachers should pay attention to such situations and pedagogically utilise possible conflicts in discussions with the individual child and the whole group.

Goal 1.1 Objective 4

Children will be able to share ideas and roles.

If the teacher plans, organises, and runs all physical activities, it has a negative effect on children's initiative and creativity. As a result, children may learn helplessness. Children should be involved in planning, organising, and running activities. They can suggest games, ways of executing lessons, or ways to move. Children can also be given the chance to plan activities in small groups, exchanging ideas with themselves and with the teacher.

Goal 1.2

Recognise and respect individual differences.

All children are different. Children can help each other become aware of their positive features, ways of behaviour, qualities, and characteristics. When negative evaluation of others occurs, teachers should intervene and use them pedagogically in discussions of diversity and the need to accept and understand the richness of differences.

Goal 1.2 Objective 1

Children will be able to appreciate their own work and that of others.

When teachers praise children for their outcomes, effort, and good behaviour, the children learn to encourage and give positive feedback to others. This is especially important for children with low skill levels or other weaknesses.

Goal 1.2 Objective 2

Children will be able to help others.

Small-group activities create situations where children need to help each other, especially games with two or more teams competing and challenging team tasks that help children develop their helping skills. Helping others should also be a reason for encouragement and positive feedback.

Standard 2

Through the acquisition and development of motor skills, children will have a desire to be involved in a healthy lifestyle.

With today's lifestyle, children do not engage in as many interactive and active neighbourhood games and outdoor activities as they once did. Passive television viewing and time spent with video games seem to have replaced children's natural play. Physical education contributes, primarily through movement experiences, to the total growth and development of all children. Children have opportunities to gain knowledge, skills, and attitudes that promote physical activity as part of their everyday lives. For preschoolers, whose bodies continue to serve as the primary learning centre, participation in physical activities is essential for their motor, social, affective, and cognitive development.

Fundamental motor skills are the basis for a physically active lifestyle and physical well-being throughout the life span. By following a curriculum consisting of various motor activities, early childhood educators may help children develop a desire to be involved in physical activities. Through physical education activities, including discussions, play, and other pedagogical elements of health promotion, children may adopt a healthy lifestyle.

Goal 2.1

Be involved in a variety of physical activities.

Everything we discover about life, we discover through movement (Hodgson, 2001). Our body is also our language, and we have to cultivate it (Holm, 1980). All movement, however small, is a means of expressing and communicating. Early childhood educators have seen children engage in movements of an expressive nature along the following lines: jumping for joy, shaking with excitement, hitting out in anger, bursting with pride, digging in their heels, throwing themselves wholeheartedly—or whole-bodily—into the game, and so on (Davies, 2003). Teaching movement skills is the central task for physical educators. For preschool children, this includes not only teaching traditional sport skills but also basic motor skills, such as general body control and coordination, balance, flexibility, and adaptability (McCall & Craft, 2004; SportFun, 2001).

Physical education for children focuses on teaching basic motor skills to facilitate physical and functional development. Motor skills are necessary in everyday life, and they are critical to the later learning of complex movement skills. Once learned, these skills are retained for a lifetime.

Preschool children present special challenges to physical educators. They have quickly changing bodily characteristics and abilities, and their rapid development calls for a different approach compared with adults or adolescents. At the same time, they have an enormous capacity for acquiring new skills. This places more demands and responsibilities on physical educators. The main focus in preschool physical education should be the organisation and adaptation of the teaching process so that children learn motor skills in a natural way rather than through traditional instructional teaching (Fjørtoft & Gundersen, 2007). The theoretical framework is formed by the dynamic systems approach (Haywood & Getchell, 2001; Thelen & Smith, 1994; Vereijken & Bongaardt, 1999), which puts attention on the total development of motor abilities. That includes the biological ability of the child to learn motor skills, the tasks to learn, and the environment in which the child learns and develops (Newell, 1986). A complex learning environment may provide children with diverse tasks that challenge the selection, coupling, and exploitation of degrees of freedom that will promote motor skills in young children (Fjørtoft & Gundersen, 2007).

Motor learning can be considered the most fundamental of all learning by children. Children learn movements and have bodily experiences by exploring their environments, which develops their quality of movements in the form of speed, agility, force, and weight (Haywood & Getchell, 2001; Sheet-Johnstone, 1999). Motor learning is not only a result of maturation but also a process of learning through experiences (Malina, Bouchard, & Bar-Or, 2004). Motor learning is also important for other areas of development, such as cognition, socialisation, and emotional and psychological competence (Hopkins & Butterworth, 1997; Thelen & Smith, 1994).

The skill themes include stability, locomotor and nonlocomotor, and manipulative skills. These skills are critical to the later learning of complex, or specialised, movement skills—they serve as the basis for what goes beyond (Gallahue & Donnelly, 2003).

Goal 2.1 Objective 1

Children will be able to travel in many ways showing variations in direction, level, and speed.

Fundamental locomotor and nonlocomotor skills are developed through a variety of movement experiences. Total-body movements in which the body is propelled in an upright posture from one point to another in a roughly horizontal or vertical direction are called *locomotor skills*. The components of locomotor skills include activities such as running, leaping, horizontal jumping, vertical jumping, jumping from a height, hopping, skipping, sliding, and galloping.

The components of nonlocomotor skills include activities such as bending, stretching, twisting, curling, and swinging (Gallahue & Donnelly, 2003). These actions do not travel through space but are performed within one's personal space at a high, medium, or low level. Locomotor and nonlocomotor skills are necessary for purposeful and controlled movement through the environment and are basic to numerous specific skills needed for games, dance, and other physical activities.

Summary of Locomotor Skill Components

- Running
- Leaping
- Horizontal jumping
- Vertical jumping
- Jumping from height
- Hopping
- Skipping
- Sliding
- Galloping

Motor learning is a fundamental goal for all students.

Summary of Nonlocomotor Skill Components

- Bending
- Stretching
- Twisting
- Curling
- Swinging

Goal 2.1 Objective 2

Children will be able to participate in balancing activities.

Stability, which is required in all human balancing activities, is the most basic of the three categories of fundamental movement skills because there is an element of stability in all locomotor and manipulative movements. Balance is a complex activity, a core element of movement activity drawing upon visual, tactile, and vestibular factors. It plays a significant role in the early years because it is fundamental to many skills (Magill, 1998). Stability is the ability to sense a shift in the relationship of the body parts that alter one's balance, as well as the ability to adjust rapidly and accurately to these changes with appropriate compensating movements (Gallahue & Donnelly, 2003). Stability encompasses axial movements (such as bending, stretching, twisting, turning, reaching, lifting, and falling), springing movements (such as vertical jumping skills, springboard skills, trampoline skills, and inverted springing skills), upright supports (such as individual stunts, partner stunts, balance-board skills, balance-block skills, and balance-beam skills), and inverted supports (such as headstand skills, cartwheel skills, and handstand skills), all of which involve static or dynamic balance.

Summary of Stability Skill Components

- Axial movements
  - Bending
  - Stretching
  - Twisting
  - Turning
  - Reaching
  - Lifting
  - Falling
- Springing movements
  - Vertical jumping skills
  - Springboard skills
  - Trampoline skills
  - Inverted springing skills
- Upright supports
  - Individual stunts
  - Partner stunts
  - Balance-board skills
  - Balance-block skills
  - Balance-beam skills
- Inverted supports
  - Headstand skills
  - Cartwheel skills
  - Handstand skills

Goal 2.1 Objective 3

Children will be able to send and receive a variety of objects in many ways.

Fundamental manipulative skills may be developed and refined through a skill theme approach using movement experiences that are both individually appropriate and age-group appropriate. Manipulative movements, such as throwing, overhand throwing, catching, kicking, trapping, dribbling, striking, volleying, bouncing, and ball rolling, are generally considered to be fundamental manipulative skills (Gallahue & Donnelly, 2003).

Summary of Manipulative Skill Components

- Throwing (overhand throwing)
- Catching
- Kicking
- Trapping
- Dribbling
- Ball bouncing
- Ball rolling
- Striking
- Volleying

Goal 2.2

Recognise changes in body functions during physical activities.

To become aware of physiological responses to health-promoting physical activity, children should recognise changes in heart and breathing rates and in body temperature. This awareness helps children recognise activities that are intensive enough to have a positive effect on health. Thus, these changes in their body can be a motivating stimulus towards physical activity. It is important for children to understand that their changed bodily functions following physical effort are normal and even healthy physiological responses. Understanding physiological responses to effort in physical activity also helps children build their body image or self-image, which involves the body and emotions. Body image is directly related to how children feel about themselves on both physiological and emotional levels.

Goal 2.2 Objective 1

Children will be able to identify changes in heart rate.

Children easily learn how physical activity affects the heart muscle. When they measure their heart rates, they become aware that running, playing, games, and other activities make their hearts bump. This motivates them to be physically active. Children can be taught to measure heart rates from different points of the body, such as the wrist, neck, or breast, or after an intensive activity they may feel the heart bumps just by listening to their body in a silent environment. If the heart rate is not high, it is more difficult to measure it. Children soon learn that the more physical effort they exert, the higher their heart rate elevates. This observation initiates various creative ways to use the measurement of heart rates as a pedagogical, motivating tool and offer moments of excitement to them. Sometimes using heart rate monitors may offer a special experience for children.

Goal 2.2 Objective 2

Children will be able to identify changes in breathing.

Children also should be taught to understand and analyse changes in breathing as a response to physical activity. They will learn the role of breathing in energy production—specifically that they breathe in oxygen, which burns the nutrition in the body, thus freeing energy that they can use for physical load. The function of a car burning fuel to formulate energy for moving can be used as an example. Children can be taught to feel their breathing at rest, at moderate activity, and at fast exercise. They can also count the number of breaths in a given time frame and after activities of various intensities, which is a good method to increase concentration and perceptions of tranquillity. Discussions about changes

in breathing help children understand that for healthy purposes they need daily activity, in the form of play and games, which makes them feel out of breath.

Goal 2.2 Objective 3

Children will be able to identify changes in body temperature.

Body temperature can be explained to children as the central heating system of the body. When we move, our central heating system activates and starts to produce energy, which enables movement. This energy, in the form of heat, is transported to our skin, where it cools down. This release of heat keeps the body from becoming too hot, which is dangerous for our cells. When we have a fever, we all understand that it is not good for our functioning. Children can be asked to monitor changes in body temperature. For some, it means red faces and other parts of the body; for others it means sweating. In analysing these symptoms, children become aware of their bodies, and they learn not to be afraid of such responses. Instead, they learn that it is healthy to put effort into physical activities, play, and games up to the limit where bodily functions start to change.

Goal 2.3

Become aware of healthy lifestyle activities.

The majority of health problems in adulthood result from sedentary activities and unhealthy nutrition. The accumulated evidence suggests that children who are physically active stand to gain enormous health benefits (U.S. Department of Health and Human Services [USDHHS] 1996). According to the Centers for Disease Control and Prevention in the United States (2006), among states participating in the Behavioral Risk Factor Surveillance System in 1990, 10 states had a prevalence of obesity less than 10% and no states had prevalence equal to or greater than 15%. By 1998, no state had prevalence of obesity less than 10%, 7 states had prevalence between 20% and 24%, and no state had prevalence equal to or greater than 25%. In 2006, only 4 states had a prevalence of obesity less than 20%, 22 states had prevalence equal or greater than 25%, and 2 states had prevalence equal to or greater than 30%. In Finland during 1984, 7% of 13-year-old boys and 6% of girls were overweight, whereas in 2002 the obesity percentages were 17% for boys and 12% for girls. The same figures for 15-year-olds in 1984 were 8% for boys and 3% for girls, whereas in 2002 the percentages were 18% for boys and 9% for girls (Kannas et al., 2004). The same tendency regarding the increase of obesity levels in both children and adults in Western countries is largely accepted as fact.

The physical education activities described in the lesson plans of the Early Steps project are designed to help children understand and value physical fitness and healthy food for their contribution to a healthy lifestyle.

Goal 2.3 Objective 1

Children will be able to enjoy moving in a variety of ways.

Understanding the elements of movement helps children identify their body parts, explore and recognise space elements (personal and general space, levels, directions, pathways), understand spatial relations with objects (up, behind, between), and express rhythm elements through movement. Children have an innate need to be moving. Thus, they normally enjoy physical activities when they have an open space and some stimulating equipment. The more versatile the environment is, the more possibilities children have to find enjoyable activities.

Goal 2.3 Objective 2

Children will be able to identify healthy foods.

Through specific physical activities, children can be taught in a fun way to differentiate between healthy and unhealthy foods. For example, each child can be labelled as a food, such as carrots, potatoes, milk, blueberries, yoghurt, or hamburger. They can be asked to find other children labelled as the same food, as healthy or unhealthy food, and so on. Children may then change roles so that everyone will become familiar with various foods. Through discussions during and after activities, early educators may help children understand the importance of proper eating habits and recognising healthy and unhealthy food.

Goal 2.3 Objective 3

Children will be able to understand the need for rest and recovery.

When children get exhausted during intensive play, they enjoy having breaks, during which they can monitor bodily symptoms and relax. Moments of relaxation are recommended in early childhood physical education. Children will learn the importance of breaks and relaxation for physiological and mental recovery in relation to physical load. Breaks and moments of recovery also develop children's concentration skills. After relaxation, children are more concentrated and less restless, which helps them in active learning tasks.

REFERENCES

Centers for Disease Control and Prevention (CDC). (2006). State-specific prevalence of obesity among adults—United States. *Morbidity and Mortality Weekly Report, 55,* 985–988.

Collaborative for Academic, Social, and Emotional Learning (CASEL). (2008). http://www.casel.org/basics/definition.php.

Council of Physical Education for Children (COPEC). (1992). Developmentally appropriate physical education practices for children: A position statement of the Council on Physical Education for Children. Reston, VA: National Association for Sport and Physical Education.

Davies, M. (2003). *Movement and dance in early childhood.* London: Sage.

Durlak, J.A., & Weissberg, R.P. (2007). The impact of after-school programs that promote personal and social skills. Chicago: CASEL.

Fjørtoft, I., & Gundersen, K.A. (2007). Promoting motor learning in young children through landscapes. In J. Liukkonen, Y. Auweele, D. Alfermann, B. Vereijken, & Y. Theodorakis (Eds.), *Psychology for physical educators: Student in focus* (pp. 201-218). Champaign, IL: Human Kinetics.

Gallahue, D., & Donnelly, F. (2003). *Developmental physical education for all children.* Champaign, IL: Human Kinetics.

Haywood, K., & Getchell, N. (2001). *Life span motor development.* Champaign, IL: Human Kinetics.

Hellison, D. (1995). *Teaching responsibility through physical activity.* Champaign, IL: Human Kinetics.

Hodgson, J. (2001). *Mastering movement.* London: Methuen.

Holm, H. (1980). Hanya speaks. In J.M. Brown (Ed.), *The vision of modern dance.* London: Dance Books.

Hopkins, B., & Butterworth, G. (1997). Dynamical systems approaches to the development of action. In G. Bremner, A. Slater, & G. Butterworth (Eds.), *Infant development: Recent advances* (75-100). East Sussex: Psychology Press.

Hovelynck, J., Auweele, Y., & Mouratidis, T. (2007). Group development in the physical education class. In J. Liukkonen, Y. Auweele, D. Alfermann, B. Vereijken, & Y. Theodorakis (Eds.), *Psychology for physical educators: Student in focus* (pp. 101-119). Champaign, IL: Human Kinetics.

Kannas, L. et al. (Eds.). (2004). Students' health and health behaviour in change. *WHO-School student research 20 years.* University of Jyväskylä, Department of Health Sciences. Publications no 2.

Liukkonen, J., Auweele, Y., Alfermann, D., Vereijken, B., & Theodorakis, Y. (Eds.). (2007). *Psychology for physical educators: Student in focus.* Champaign, IL: Human Kinetics.

Liukkonen, J., Laakso, L., & Telama, R. (1996). Educational perspectives of youth sport coaches: Analysis of observed coaching behaviours. *International Journal of Sport Psychology, 27*(4), 439-453.

Magill, R. (1998). *Motor learning: Concepts and applications.* New York: McGraw-Hill.

Malina, R., Bouchard, C., & Bar-Or, O. (2004). *Growth, maturation, and physical activity.* Champaign, IL: Human Kinetics.

McCall, R., & Craft, D. (2004). *Purposeful play: Early childhood movement activities on a budget.* Champaign, IL: Human Kinetics.

Mosston, M., & Ashworth, S. (2002). *Teaching physical education.* New York: Benjamin Cummings.

National Association for Sport and Physical Education (NASPE). (1995). *Moving into the future: National standards for physical education.* St. Louis: Mosby.

Newell, K.M. (1986). Constraints on the development of coordination. In M.G. Wade & H.T.A. Whiting (Eds.), *Motor development in children: Aspects of coordination and control* (pp. 341-360). Dordrecht: Martinus Nijhof.

Ntoumanis, N. (2001). A self-determination approach to the understanding of motivation in physical education. *British Journal of Educational Psychology, 71*, 225-242.

Payton, J., Wardlaw, D., Graczyk, P., Bloodworth, M., Tompsett, C., & Weissberg, R. (2000). Social and emotional learning: A framework for promoting mental health and reducing risk behaviour in children and youth. *Journal of School Health, 70*, 179-185.

Physical Best. (2004). *Physical education for lifelong fitness: The Physical Best teacher's guide.* Champaign, IL: Human Kinetics.

Sallis, J.F., & McKenzie, T.L. 1991. Physical education's role in public health. *Research Quarterly for Exercise and Sport, 62*, 124-137.

Schmuck, R., & Schmuck, P. (2001). *Group processes in the classroom.* New York: McGraw Hill.

Sheet-Johnstone, M. (1999). *The primacy of movement.* Amsterdam: John Benjamin.

Sherborne, V. (1993). *Developmental movement for children.* New York: Cambridge University Press.

Siedentop, D., Hastie, P., & Mars, H. (2004). *Complete guide to sport education.* Champaign, IL: Human Kinetics.

SportFun. (2001). *Developmentally appropriate movement skill activities for 3- to 5-year-olds.* Champaign, IL: Human Kinetics.

Telama, R., & Polvi, S. (2007). Facilitating prosocial behaviour in physical education. In J. Liukkonen, Y. Auweele, D. Alfermann, B. Vereijken, & Y. Theodorakis (Eds.), *Psychology for physical educators: Student in focus* (pp. 85-99). Champaign, IL: Human Kinetics.

Thelen, E., & Smith, L.B. (1994). *A dynamic systems approach to the development of condition and action.* Cambridge, MA: MIT Press.

U.S. Department of Health and Human Services (USDHHS). (1996). *Physical activity and health: A report of the Surgeon General.* Atlanta: USDHHS, CDC.

Varstala, V., Paukku, P., & Telama, R. (1993). Teacher and pupil behaviour in P.E. classes. In R. Telama et al. (Eds.), *Research in school physical education* (pp. 38, 47-57). Jyväskylä: Reports of Physical Culture and Health.

Vereijken, B., & Bongaardt, R. (1999). Complex motor skill acquisition. In Y. Auweele, F. Bakker, S. Biddle, M. Durand, & R. Seiler (Eds.), *Psychology for physical educators.* Champaign, IL: Human Kinetics.

Part II

Implementing the Early Steps Physical Education Curriculum

The activities included in the Early Steps Physical Education Curriculum (ESPEC) use movement to help children achieve the standards and objectives of the curriculum. Children can achieve these by doing, meaning that children learn through active involvement with people and objects.

Standards

The lesson plans of ESPEC are based on two specific standards. The purpose of developing standards is to better serve schools, educators, and local communities in the process of curriculum planning. Standards also provide a framework for curriculum and assessment design. Standards are statements that define what students should know and be able to do upon completion of specific levels of instruction. Standards serve as a gauge for excellence and are differentiated from minimum competencies because they describe the challenging goals for improving education that we aspire to achieve.

ESPEC was designed to help children understand the importance of a healthy lifestyle and to develop their social skills. It includes 24 lesson plans for each specific standard, resulting in a total of 48 physical education lesson plans. The lesson plans are based on two standards with subgoals and objectives:

- Standard 1—Through physical activities, children will be able to cooperate with others and respect individual differences.

- Standard 2—Through the acquisition and development of motor skills, children will have a desire to be involved in a healthy lifestyle.

STANDARD 1 Through physical activities, children will be able to cooperate with others and respect individual differences (lesson plans 1-24).

Goal 1.1 Interact positively with group members.

Objective 1.1.1 Children will be able to work in groups.

Objective 1.1.2 Children will be able to share the place and resources with others.

Objective 1.1.3 Children will be able to participate in activities without disturbing others.

Objective 1.1.4 Children will be able to share ideas and roles.

Goal 1.2 Recognise and respect individual differences.

Objective 1.2.1 Children will be able to appreciate their own work and that of others.

Objective 1.2.2 Children will be able to help others.

STANDARD 2 Through the acquisition and development of motor skills, children will have a desire to be involved in a healthy lifestyle (lesson plans 25-48).

Goal 2.1 Be involved in a variety of physical activities.

Objective 2.1.1 Children will be able to travel in many ways showing variations in direction, level, and speed.

Objective 2.1.2 Children will be able to participate in balancing activities.

Objective 2.1.3 Children will be able to send and receive a variety of objects in many ways.

Goal 2.2 Recognise changes in body functions during physical activities.

Objective 2.2.1 Children will be able to identify changes in heart rate.

Objective 2.2.2 Children will be able to identify changes in breathing.

Objective 2.2.3 Children will be able to identify changes in body temperature.

Goal 2.3 Become aware of healthy lifestyle activities.

Objective 2.3.1 Children will be able to enjoy moving in a variety of ways.

Objective 2.3.2 Children will be able to identify healthy foods.

Objective 2.3.3 Children will be able to understand the need for rest and recovery.

Lesson Format

The duration of the lesson plans, with a few exceptions, is 40 to 45 minutes. The proposed activities of ESPEC are organised in a specific lesson format that includes information for their best clarification and application. The detailed description of each activity is followed by helpful teaching tools, such as points of emphasis and variations, to help educators implement the activity effectively for all preschool-aged children, regardless of their abilities.

- Objectives—Each lesson plan is based on one main objective and two or three related subobjectives.

- Equipment—A list of the suggested equipment for organising the activities is provided. Adequate teaching supplies are essential for children to accomplish the learning tasks planned for them. Much of the equipment is common in preschool centres, but there are also materials that educators could make or improvise by themselves or with children.

- Evaluation—Describes what children will have learned after participating in the specific lesson plan and lets you know what to watch for as the lesson progresses.

- Introduction—Includes one activity or game, usually lasting 5 to 8 minutes. Its purpose is to create a positive environment, and it helps children become familiar with the issues the specific lesson plan is going to deal with.

- Main lesson—Usually lasts 15 to 25 minutes and is based on a specific goal. Its organisation provides the most active participation possible for every child and a variety of structured activities. Some of these activities are skill related; that is, they are intended to challenge children with tasks at or slightly beyond their current level of ability. In other activities, children discover a theme through movement exploration and experimentation. The main lesson usually includes four or five activities aiming to achieve the specific objective and its subobjectives.

- Points of emphasis—These include a few keywords or phrases that refer mainly to the way of teaching. They suggest teaching cues for the most effective implementation of the activity.

- Variations—These comprise modifications and extensions of specific activities. The variations help educators modify an activity for the number of children and the available space.

- Conclusion—Lasts from 7 to 10 minutes. This final part of the lesson plan reviews the issues that were developed through the activities of the main part.

The learning needs of young children are not uniform. Thus, educators will need to use their own assessments, observations, and knowledge to plan activities that specifically meet the learning needs of the children. The lesson plans that follow should be used with this in mind, and adaptations, alterations, and variations are encouraged. In addition, educators are responsible for ensuring that activities comply with acknowledged safe practice guidelines (which differ from country to country) and that links are sought to the wider curriculum where possible.

Chapter 6

Social Interaction Lesson Plans

Reprinted in part from E. Zachopoulou, N. Tsangaridou, J. Liukkonen, I. Pickup, P. Innila, E. Konstantinidou, A.M. Pontinen, A. Saarikangas, E. Trevlas and P. Valkama, 2007, Early Steps Physical Education Curriculum (ESPEC) — Lesson plans. In *Early Steps: Promoting healthy lifestyle and social interaction through physical education activities during preschool years* (Thessaloniki, Greece: Xristodoulidi Publications), 47-143. Early Steps project funded by a grant from the European Commission Socrates Programme, Comenius 2.1 Action, Project number: 118192-CP-1-GR-COMENIUS-C21.

Lesson 1

Work in Groups
STANDARD 1, GOAL 1

OBJECTIVES

At the end of the lesson, children will be able to

- share the place and resources with others,
- walk and kick a stationary ball,
- run and kick a stationary ball,
- kick a ball that is rolling,
- kick a ball to a target, and
- play small soccer games.

EQUIPMENT

1 large ball per child

EVALUATION

1. On an evaluative sheet, record how successful each child is while kicking a ball to a target.
2. Observe and record how cooperative each child is in a small soccer game.

INTRODUCTION

Chasing Games (6 minutes)

Setup and Description

1. Divide the children into groups of four. Give each group a different vest or other item to identify teams. One child chases the other three. When the chasing person tags someone, that child becomes the chasing person.
2. All four members of a group chase the children in the other groups. Ask the children to count how many others they tag. The teams who tag the most children win. Change the chasing team so that all teams have the chance to chase the other teams.

Points of Emphasis

- Remind the children to be careful during the game.
- The children should not push each other.

MAIN LESSON: INDIVIDUAL, PARTNER, GROUP, AND GAME ACTIVITIES (32 MINUTES)

Individual Activity (6 minutes)

Setup and Description

1. The children each take a ball and line up facing one way, practicing kicking a stationary ball forwards. On your signal, they collect the balls. Repeat three to four times.
2. The children put the ball on the ground and walk and kick the ball. On your signal, they collect the balls. Repeat three or four times.
3. The children put the ball on the ground and run and kick the ball. On your signal, they collect the balls. Repeat three or four times.

Points of Emphasis

- Encourage children to keep their eyes on the ball as they kick it.
- Tell them to put their nonkicking foot alongside the ball and use the instep of the foot to kick the ball.
- Ask them to try to make the instep face in the direction in which the ball is intended to travel.

Partner Activity (8 minutes)

Setup and Description

1. Ask the children to choose a partner and start kicking a stationary ball to the partner. The partner returns the ball in the same way.
2. The children put the ball on the ground and walk and kick the ball to the partner. The partner returns the ball in the same way.
3. The children put the ball on the ground and run and kick the ball to the partner. The partner returns the ball in the same way.
4. The partner rolls the ball and the other student kicks the moving ball back to the partner.

Point of Emphasis   Ask the children to turn their foot so the inside of their foot faces the ball and their partner.

Group Activity (9 minutes)

Setup and Description   Organise the targets on the wall and arrange the cones or boxes and goals for each team.

1. In groups of four, the children practise kicking the ball at targets on a wall. Ask them to count how many successful efforts they had as a team.
2. In groups of four, the children practicing kicking the ball to hit an object such as a cone, small cardboard box, or milk carton. Ask them to count how many successful efforts they had as a team.
3. In groups of four, the children practise kicking the ball to score goals. Ask them to count how many successful efforts they had as a team.

Points of Emphasis

- Ask the children to try to be accurate when they kick the balls.
- Remind children to point their kicking foot towards the target to help send the ball straight to it.
- Ask the children to bend the knee of their kicking leg just before they kick to give them a stronger kick. Ask them to point their kicking foot towards the target as they kick.

Game Activity (9 minutes)

Setup and Description   Divide the space into small soccer courts and put out goals for each game.

1. Ask the children to practise their soccer skills in a 2v2 game.
2. Have the children play a 4v4 soccer game.

Points of Emphasis

- Ask the children to play as a team.
- Ask them to count how many goals they make.

CONCLUSION (2 MINUTES)

Discuss the main emphasis of the lesson. Remind the children how important is to learn to work cooperatively with each other, especially in a game such as soccer.

Lesson 2

Work in Groups
STANDARD 1, GOAL 1

OBJECTIVES
At the end of the lesson, children will be able to
- share the place and resources with others,
- show improved sending skills, and
- show improved receiving skills.

EQUIPMENT
Beanbags, soccer or plastic balls, tennis or ping pong balls, ropes, hoops, bats, sticks, and cones for each child

EVALUATION
- Observe how well the children are able to perform their activities.
- Observe how well they cooperate with their partner.
- Observe how accurate and consistent they are while sending the ball to their partner.

INTRODUCTION (10 MINUTES)

Four Countries

Setup and Description   Arrange the equipment (beanbags, balls, ropes, and so on) around the four corners of the working area.
1. Start the lesson with a game of Four Countries. Have the children spread out in the room. Each corner of the room has the name of a country. When you announce the name of a country, the children run as quickly as possible to the appropriate corner.
2. Place several pieces of equipment in the room. Divide the children into four groups. Each group gets the name of a particular country and goes to the appropriate corner. In each corner there is a big, empty box. On your signal ("Go"), the children try to collect as many items as possible and put them in their box. On your signal ("Stop"), the children stop collecting equipment. The country that has the most equipment in its box wins.

Points of Emphasis
- Encourage the children to run to the appropriate corner only when they hear your signal.
- Remind them that they should pick up and place in the box as many equipment items as possible.
- Remind them that each member of the group should contribute to this effort.
- Encourage them to work as a team.

MAIN LESSON: FOUR STATION ACTIVITIES (24 MINUTES)
Each country corner represents a station. In each station, children practise each activity for approximately 6 minutes and then rotate, moving to the next station and leaving the equipment ready for the following group.

Station 1 (6 minutes)

Setup and Description
1. Children send a ball to a partner with their hands, taking five turns each.
2. Each pair sets a hoop on the floor in the middle of the room. One partner then sends a ball to the other partner (using hands) by having the ball bounce in the hoop before it gets to the partner. Take five turns each.

Points of Emphasis
- Challenge the children to be accurate when they send the ball.
- Remind them that the ball should bounce in the hoop before it goes to the partner.

Station 2 (6 minutes)
Setup and Description
1. The children send a ball to a partner by kicking it, taking five turns each.
2. Each pair puts two cones in the middle of the room. One partner sends a ball to the other by kicking it through the cones. Take five turns each.

Points of Emphasis
- Challenge the children to be accurate when they kick the ball.
- Remind them that they should kick the ball by kicking it through the cones.

Station 3 (6 minutes)
Setup and Description
1. The children send a ball to a partner by striking it with a bat, taking five turns each.
2. Each pair puts a rope on the ground in the middle of the room. One partner sends a ball to the other by striking it with a bat and passing the ball over a rope (located on the ground). Take five turns each.

Points of Emphasis
- The children should strike the ball with the bat and make an effort to reach their partner.
- Remind them that the ball must pass over the rope.

Station 4 (6 minutes)
Setup and Description
1. The children send a ball to a partner using a stick, taking five turns each.
2. Each pair puts two cones in the middle of the work space. One partner sends a ball to the other using a stick, dribbling the ball through the two cones. Take five turns each.

Points of Emphasis
- Challenge children for accuracy while striking the ball.
- Remind them that they should dribble the ball through the cones.

CONCLUSION (6 MINUTES)
- Ask the children to discuss and reflect on the skills they have been practicing.
- Ask for difficulties in skill improvement or in working cooperatively with their partners.
- Discuss the importance of finding ways to work cooperatively with others.

Lesson 3

Work in Groups
STANDARD 1, GOAL 1

OBJECTIVES

At the end of the lesson, children will be able to

- share the place and resources with others,
- show improved dribble skills,
- show improved sending and receiving skills, and
- observe other children and give them feedback.

EQUIPMENT

- Music player and music
- Beanbags, balls, and cones for each child
- Hula hoops

EVALUATION

Observe children's small games and assess their skill development and team spirit.

INTRODUCTION (10 MINUTES)

Setup and Description

1. Children work in pairs. One of the pair is the tagger ("it") and chases their partner, tagging him or her by touching them when close by. The children then swap roles and repeat for a few minutes.
2. Ask the children to choose a different partner and play the same game, this time with skipping. The game is repeated for a few minutes. You can also choose to play music.

Point of Emphasis   Remind the children that they have to be conscious of others as they move around the space.

MAIN LESSON: PAIR AND GAME ACTIVITIES (26 MINUTES)

Dribbling a Ball in Pairs (16 minutes)

Setup and Description

1. In pairs, one child is dribbling the ball with feet around the markers and the other is observing and giving feedback. Change roles and repeat.
2. Partners do the same activity with an emphasis on using both the outside and inside of the feet. Change roles and repeat.
3. In pairs, one child is dribbling the ball with hands around the markers and the other is observing and giving feedback. Change roles and repeat.
4. Partners do the same activity with an emphasis on using both hands (right and left). Change roles and repeat.

Points of Emphasis

- Remind the children that they must try to keep the ball as close to their feet as possible.
- Remind them that they must try to use both the outside and inside of their feet.
- The children should push the ball hard into the ground.
- They should use their fingers to control the ball.

Game (10 minutes)

Setup and Description

1. The children form groups of four, and each group forms two pairs. The pairs play a basketball game (2v2). Work in a grid with hoops as the goals. The team of two aims to pass the ball to each other and to bounce the ball in the nearest hoop to score a goal. They should pass the ball at least twice before bouncing the ball into the hoop.

2. In fours, three children play a basketball game (2v1) and one observes (referee). Work in a grid with hoops as the goals. The team of two aims to pass the ball to each other and to bounce the ball in the nearest hoop to score a goal. The defender cannot touch the other two players. After two goals, swap roles. Each child should take a turn at being a defender and the observer.

Points of Emphasis

- Remind the children to pass the ball to their partner.
- They should dribble the ball close to the body.
- They should push the ball hard into the ground, using their fingers to control it.
- Remind them to work as a team.

CONCLUSION (2 MINUTES)

- Discuss the importance of dribbling, sending, and receiving skills in team games.
- Ask the children to reflect on their teamwork and observation experience.

Lesson 4

Work in Groups
STANDARD 1, GOAL 1

OBJECTIVES
At the end of the lesson, children will be able to

- share the place and resources with others,
- practise manipulative skills in a team formation,
- practise locomotor skills in a team formation, and
- work cooperatively in game situations.

EQUIPMENT
Cones, balls, beanbags, and hoops for each child

EVALUATION
- Observe and record how well the children are able to use manipulative and locomotor skills in a team formation.
- Observe and record whether they are able to cooperative effectively in game situations.

INTRODUCTION (6 MINUTES)
Statues Game
Setup and Description

1. Children form pairs, one person named *A* and the other *B*. All of the *A* children stand still while all of the *B* children run to find a new spot.
2. On your signal, *B* children stand still, look for their partner, and find the quickest way to get back to their partner.
3. Change roles and repeat the game.

Point of Emphasis   Ask the children to be aware of the rest of the class and to be careful when moving around the space.

MAIN LESSON: FOUR RELAY GAMES (36 MINUTES)
Arrange the class into groups of five, each assigned a different colour and standing one behind the other.

Zigzag Relay (8 minutes)
Setup and Description   Place six cones in front of each group.

1. The children run in between the cones, starting behind the line and finishing over the same line.
2. Do the same activity with hopping.
3. Do the same activity with skipping.
4. Do the same activity while carrying a ball.
5. Do the same activity while dribbling a ball.
6. Do the same activity while carrying a beanbag.

Point of Emphasis
Work as a team!

Ball Relay 1 (8 minutes)

Setup and Description

1. The first person in each line (group) gets a large ball or beanbag and passes it with both hands to the next person. The last person to receive the ball runs with it to the front of the line. Repeat until everyone has had a turn at the front of the line.
2. Use the same formation. The children stand with their legs apart, bend down, and look through their legs. They pass the ball between their legs to the person behind.
3. Use the same formation. The children pass the ball over their head to the person behind.

Point of Emphasis   Remind the children to be careful not to drop the ball or beanbag.

Out-and-Back Relay (8 minutes)

Setup and Description

1. Starting behind the line, the children run out around the marker cone and return to their team.
2. Do the same activity with hopping.
3. Do the same activity with skipping.
4. Do the same activity while carrying a ball.
5. Do the same activity while dribbling a ball.
6. Do the same activity while carrying a beanbag.

Point of Emphasis   Remind the children to be careful not to knock down the cones.

Ball Relay 2 (6 minutes)

Setup and Description

1. The first child faces the other four, who stand one behind the other in a line, their legs wide apart.
2. The first child rolls the ball through the legs of the second, third, and fourth children.
3. The fifth child picks up the ball and runs to the front of the line.
4. Keep going until everyone has had a turn. Repeat the activity twice.

Point of Emphasis   Encourage the children to roll the ball as quickly as possible.

Hoops Relay (6 minutes)

Setup and Description   Place five or six hoops in front of each group in a snake shape.

1. Starting behind the line, the children run in and out of the hoops carrying a ball and then return to their team.
2. Do the same activity with skipping.
3. Do the same activity while dribbling a ball.

Point of Emphasis   Encourage the children as they go through the snake.

CONCLUSION (5 MINUTES)

- Ask the children to shake hands and congratulate each member of each team.
- Ask them to tell you three reasons why they must always work cooperatively with others.

Lesson 5

Share the Place and Resources With Others
STANDARD 1, GOAL 1

OBJECTIVES
At the end of the lesson, children will be able to

- share the place and resources with others,
- show improved spatial awareness skills,
- show improved travelling skills, and
- work with a partner.

EQUIPMENT
Traffic cones or milk cartons, foam balls, and beanbags for each child

EVALUATION
Observe and record in a recording sheet how well each child shares the place with others.

INTRODUCTION (10 MINUTES)

Numbers Game

Setup and Description

1. Start the lesson with the Numbers Game, with the children spread throughout the room.
2. Shout out various numbers and ask the children to respond with the agreed-upon response. For example, *one* means travel (walk or run) forwards, *two* means stop, *three* means travel sideways, and so on.
3. Repeat the game using various travelling skills such as skipping, hopping, and galloping.
4. Ask the children to choose a partner and repeat the game.

Points of Emphasis

- Encourage the children to move in all general space.
- Ask them to show you how they can travel forwards using their skipping abilities.
- Can they and their partner travel sideways using their hopping abilities?

MAIN LESSON (20 MINUTES)

Forest Trip

Setup and Description

1. Explain to the children that they will play the Forest Trip game. Tell them that they are in a big forest and they have been assigned the task of planting more trees in the forest.
2. Ask the children to plant trees throughout the space (use traffic cones or milk cartons to represent trees).
3. Ask the children to walk around the trees in the forest. If they bump into a tree, they replant the tree and continue moving.
4. Challenge the children to run, skip, hop, gallop, and march around the trees.
5. Challenge the children to use the same movements in a zigzag pathway around the trees.

Points of Emphasis

- Encourage the children to watch carefully where they are moving and to be careful not to knock any trees over.
- Ask them to show you how fast they can walk or run around the trees.
- Ask them to show you if they can walk backwards around the trees.

- Can they gallop around the trees without knocking any trees over?
- Can they travel around the trees in a zigzag pattern without knocking the trees over?

CONCLUSION (10 MINUTES)

Setup and Description

1. Ask the children to find creative ways to cut the trees down (they can kick them or knock them with their hands).
2. Ask the children to replant the trees and cut them down once more, this time throwing foam balls or beanbags to cut them down.
3. After the trees have been cut down twice, ask the children to put the trees away.

Points of Emphasis

- Ask the children to show you different ways of cutting down trees. Encourage them to be creative.
- Ask the children to throw the ball to cut the trees.

Lesson 6

Share the Place and Resources With Others
STANDARD 1, GOAL 1

OBJECTIVES

At the end of the lesson, children will be able to

- share the place and resources with others,
- show improved travelling and stopping skills,
- perform animal-like movements,
- understand the meaning of personal and general space, and
- understand the meaning of section places.

EQUIPMENT

Variety of small equipment items (6 individual ropes, 6 balls, 6 beanbags, and so on) placed in 4 boxes

EVALUATION

Observe and record on a recording sheet to what degree each child understands the meaning of section places.

INTRODUCTION (10 MINUTES)

Setup and Description

1. Organise the children into four groups and divide the space into four sections. Call them *section places* or ask the children to give them names. Inform the children that on your command ("Go"), the children in section 1 must walk quickly without touching anyone or anything and find their own space in the room. Wait a couple of minutes and then call sections 2, 3, and 4.
2. Repeat the activity.
3. Ask all four groups to move at the same time and on your signal to find their own section places.

Points of Emphasis

- Encourage the children to walk correctly as fast as they can.
- Remind the children that they must be careful not to touch anyone.

MAIN LESSON: ANIMAL AND MECHANICAL MOVEMENTS AND PLAYING WITH EQUIPMENT AND SHARING WITH OTHERS (20 MINUTES)

Animal and Mechanical Movements (6 minutes)

Setup and Description

1. Choose two or three children to demonstrate the movement to the class. Then ask all of the children to move (e.g., walk, run, jump) while performing animal (e.g., elephant) or mechanical (e.g., robot) movements.
2. Continue this challenge, changing animals or mechanical movements.

Points of Emphasis

- Ask if the children can walk like giants around their section place without touching anyone.
- Ask if they can move like robots.

Playing With Equipment and Sharing With Others (14 minutes)

Setup and Description   Set boxes of equipment in four corners.

1. Inform children that on your signal, they can go to the box near their section space, pick up an equipment item, and play with it in their own space.

2. Ask the children to find a partner, exchange their equipment, and play together in their section space.

3. Ask the children to form groups of four and play with equipment in designated spaces.

Points of Emphasis

- The children should play with the equipment without bothering anyone.
- Remind them to use a variety of movements while playing with their partner.
- They should play all together with their equipment.
- Remind children to stay in their designated space and not move around the room.

CONCLUSION (10 MINUTES)

Automobiles

Setup and Description

1. Holding one piece of equipment, the children run in a designated direction, pretending to be automobiles and passing others. On your signal, everyone must stop. Automobiles who fail to stop or who bump into another automobile lose a point.

2. Perform the same activity. On your signal, the children must stop and exchange equipment with the person next to them.

3. Discuss the importance of sharing the place and resources with others.

Points of Emphasis

- Remind the children to be careful not to hit other cars.
- Remind them to stop immediately after the signal.
- The children should share their equipment with the person next to them. They should not move to find a friend to exchange equipment with.

Lesson 7

Share the Place and Resources With Others
STANDARD 1, GOAL 1

OBJECTIVES
At the end of the lesson, children will be able to

- share the place and resources with others,
- show improved manipulative skills,
- show improved travelling skills, and
- work with a partner.

EQUIPMENT

- 1 hoop per student
- 1 medium ball per student
- 32 cones or milk cartons
- Music player and music

EVALUATION
Observe and record on a recording sheet to what degree each child shares the place and resources with others.

INTRODUCTION (6 MINUTES)

Hoops Game

Setup and Description   Spread out the hoops in the room, using one less hoop than the number of the children in class. You can play music during the game.

1. The children run quickly anywhere in the room but do not touch the hoops or step inside them.
2. On your signal, the children try to stand inside a hoop, one child in each hoop.
3. The child without a hoop is out of the game.
4. Repeat the game, taking out one hoop every round.

Point of Emphasis   Inform the children that they should not stay near one hoop while they are supposed to be running.

MAIN LESSON: HOOP, BALL, AND PARTNER ACTIVITIES (26 MINUTES)

Hoop Activities (8 minutes)

Setup and Description   Place one hoop per child in the play area.

1. The children walk around their hoops.
2. They skip in the spaces around the hoops, and on your signal they return to their hoops.
3. They bowl the hoop along the ground.
4. They try to spin the hoop on the ground.

Points of Emphasis

- Children should skip nicely around the hoops.
- Remind them to practise without touching anyone.
- See who can spin the hoop for the longest time.

Ball Activities (8 minutes)

Setup and Description   Keep the hoops from the hoop activities scattered on the floor in the room.

1. The children travel while carrying a ball in their hands, avoiding the obstacles (hoops).
2. They travel with the ball using other body parts, avoiding the obstacles (hoops).

Points of Emphasis

- Remind children to be careful not to touch any obstacles.
- Remind them to use different body parts when travelling around the room.

Partner Activities (10 minutes)

Setup and Description

1. Have the children work with a partner, with one hoop on the floor between the two children. They challenge each other to a skill: jumping in the hoop, skipping around the hoop, rolling the hoop, and so on.
2. Partners challenge each other to dribble a ball inside the hoop and around the hoop.
3. Partners practise various ways of sending the ball to the each other without touching the hoop.
4. Partners send the ball to each other, making sure that the ball bounces in the hoop.
5. Partners dribble the ball with their hands in and out of obstacles (hoops).

Points of Emphasis

- Ask the children to show you how they can jump and skip around the hoop with their partner.
- Have the children send the ball to their partner using creative ways.
- Have them use both hands, then the right hand only, and then the left hand only. Which is the best way?

CONCLUSION (6 MINUTES)

Setup and Description   Set up eight cones in front of each group.

1. Organise the children into groups of four. Each group works in a designated space.
2. Each child stands at the starting line (1.5 m away from the cones) and tries to hit the cones with a ball. Each child has five attempts to hit as many cones as possible.
3. Each cone counts for 1 point. The group with the most points wins the game.

Points of Emphasis

- Remind the children to be accurate when sending the ball.
- They should try to hit as many cones as they can.
- They should encourage their team to get the most points.

Lesson 8

Share the Place and Resources With Others
STANDARD 1, GOAL 1

OBJECTIVES

At the end of the lesson, children will be able to

- share the place and resources with others,
- explore various ways of throwing an object,
- explore various ways of catching an object,
- balance an object on their body, and
- create a game.

EQUIPMENT

Beanbags, hoops, scarves, small balls, medium balls, and cones for each child

EVALUATION

Observe and record on a recording sheet how well each child shares the place and resources with others and to what degree the child respects and appreciates the ideas and work of others. (You may want to base your evaluation on the children's creative games.)

INTRODUCTION (10 MINUTES)

Tails

Setup and Description

1. Have the children find partners. One child in each pair has a colourful scarf tucked in back of the waistband. On your signal, the other partner chases the child around the entire space, trying to grasp the tail (scarf). Change roles and continue the game.
2. Do the same procedure with galloping or skipping.

Points of Emphasis

- Remind the children to be careful when grasping tails.
- They should not push other children.
- Have them show you their best galloping and skipping skills.

MAIN LESSON: ACTIVITIES WITH BEANBAGS, BEANBAGS AND HOOPS, AND CREATIVE GAMES (25 MINUTES)

Activities With Beanbags (8 minutes)

Setup and Description

1. Have the children take one beanbag and walk around the space carrying (or balancing) the beanbag on their elbow, head, back, and so on (wait a few seconds for each body part).
2. Repeat with running, skipping, sliding, or galloping.
3. Ask the children to balance the beanbag on one knee, toss it into the air from the knee, and catch it.
4. Ask them to explore other ways of throwing and catching the beanbag.

Points of Emphasis

- Ask the children to move around the working area and show you how they can balance their beanbag on their head, back, and so on.
- Have them think of several ways of throwing and catching the beanbag.

Activities With Beanbags and Hoops (8 minutes)

Setup and Description

1. Have the children hold a beanbag and stand 2 metres away from a hoop. Ask them to count how many times they can throw their beanbag in the hoop in 1 minute.
2. Ask the children to throw the beanbag in the hoop using various ways (two hands, one hand, and so on).
3. Ask the children to sit and throw their beanbag into the hoop in various ways.
4. Ask the children to use other parts of the body (lying on side, kneeling, and so on) while throwing the beanbag into the hoop.

Point of Emphasis   Have the children count how many times they were successful.

Creative Games (9 minutes)

Setup and Description

1. Organise the children into small groups. They select small equipment and play a throwing and catching game in a designated space.
2. Ask the children to choose equipment and play a different game. They can use goals if they want.
3. Ask each group to demonstrate their new game to the whole class.

Points of Emphasis

- All members of the team should share their ideas in creating the game.
- The children should not move to other spaces.
- Have them carefully observe the other teams and see how similar or different the games are to theirs.

CONCLUSION (5 MINUTES)

Setup and Description

1. Divide the class into three circles and give the children in each circle numbers.
2. Number 1 gives the beanbag to number 2, who runs around the outside of the circle and then gives the bag to number 3. Continue until the last child has finished.
3. The first circle to finish is the winner.

Point of Emphasis   Children should run as quickly as possible.

Variation   Specify the ways of sending and receiving that the circles have to use.

Lesson 9

Participate in Activities Without Disturbing Others
STANDARD 1, GOAL 1

OBJECTIVES
At the end of the lesson, children will be able to

- share ideas and roles;
- travel in different levels, directions, and speeds;
- respond to a range of verbal, auditory, and visual stimuli;
- work safely and effectively on their own;
- identify and work in their own space; and
- work with partners and in small groups.

EQUIPMENT
- Tambourine or similar percussion instrument
- Movement vocabulary cards (with words *fast, slow, high, low*)
- Animal picture cards showing a variety of young animals
- Music ranging from fast to slow
- Music player
- 1 piece of cloth per four children (to make puppy tails)
- 1 hoop per child

EVALUATION
Ask the children to circle the face that describes how they worked in today's lesson.

1. I have listened well and followed instructions.
    a. ☺
    b. ☺
    c. ☹
2. I have worked safely on my own.
    a. ☺
    b. ☺
    c. ☹
3. I have worked with different people today.
    a. ☺
    b. ☺
    c. ☹

INTRODUCTION: MAGIC SPOT, MOVE LIKE ME AND RHYTHMICAL NAMES, AND GROWING AND MOVING ACTIVITIES (16 MINUTES)

Magic Spot (3 minutes)
Setup and Description

1. Explain to the children that as soon as they arrive, you want them to find and stand in their own space—on a magic spot. This should result in an even spread across the space with children facing you so that they can see you. This magic spot idea will be used in other lessons.
2. Ask the children to show you their best standing and to remember where their magic spot is. This is the place they will return to during the lesson.

Points of Emphasis

- Ask the children to avoid others and think about their own space.
- *Best standing* refers to upright posture with shoulders back—standing proud like toy soldiers.

Move Like Me, and Rhythmical Names (8 minutes)

Setup and Description

1. Ask the children to move by copying your actions. Use these words: "I wiggle my fingers, wiggle my toes, wiggle my hips, and touch my nose!" Ask the children to copy you and repeat your words.
2. Ask the children to stretch up tall (as tall as a house!), to make themselves small (as small as a mouse!), to stretch wide (as wide as a gate!), and to make themselves narrow (as thin as a pin!).
3. Now lead a shape-making and stretching activity. Ask the children to copy your movements and to make the same shapes as you.
4. After a short while, clap a rhythm for the children to move to. The rhythm can be based on words that the children know, such as their own names. Ask the children to move in time to the words, showing variation in speed, level, and direction.

Points of Emphasis

- Ask the children to copy you and to identify parts of the body by pointing to them.
- Emphasise different shapes by moving limbs in different ways, at different levels, and at different speeds.

Growing and Moving (5 minutes)

Setup and Description

1. Ask the children to make themselves as small as they can on their magic spot.
2. Use the tambourine as a symbol for them to grow by extending their bodies slowly each time they hear the tambourine.
3. Once they are as big as they can be, ask the children to move in the space in response to the percussion (you can vary the tempo from slow to fast).

Points of Emphasis

- Ask for tucked shapes, stretching gradually in response to the percussion—listen.
- Slow movements should increase speed and show contrast. Children respond to different percussion tempos with different speeds of actions.

Variations

- For each of these games, children can be chosen to be the leader and to give instructions.
- Make task cards with words and pictures that provide various stimuli for the children to respond to.
- Ask the children to hold hands with a partner and respond to the same commands.
- Ask the children to think of their own favourite action rhymes.

MAIN LESSON: PUPPY MOVES, FOLLOW THE LEADER, AND CATCH THE PUPPY'S TAIL ACTIVITIES (17 MINUTES)

Puppy Moves (8 minutes)

Setup and Description

1. Ask the children to start on their magic spots and return to the spot when they hear these instructions: "Puppies return to your magic spot in 5, 4, 3, 2, 1, stop."
2. Show the children picture cards of young animals—puppies, kittens, chicks, and so on. Ask the children to think of how the animals move and to move as if they were the animal.

> continued

3. Encourage the children to work at various levels and speeds based on the animal they are imitating.

4. Ask the children to show their movements to a partner.

5. Ask the children to vary the way in which they are moving, imagining that the animals are happy, sad, energetic, tired, and so on.

Points of Emphasis

- Encourage the children to think about directions, levels, and speeds, as well as ways of travelling—skipping, hopping, galloping, sliding, and so on.

- Movement should be haphazard and in irregular pathways—no straight lines—to encourage weaving in and out among each other.

- Ask the children to evade each other and avoid bumping into each other, always recognising space. Can they get to all the corners, sides, and middle of the space? Can they avoid others through changing direction, stopping, dodging, and turning?

- Have the children change the way in which their animal moves to express moods and feelings. They will alter the time, weight, space, and flow of their actions.

Follow the Leader (5 minutes)

Setup and Description

1. Ask the children to form pairs with the child nearest to their magic spot.

2. One child is the leader and the other follows, moving around the space in a variety of ways. Encourage the children to maintain safe use of space and avoid others.

3. Ask the leader and follower to swap roles on the signal (percussion or word from you).

Points of Emphasis

- The children should take turns being the leader and follower, all the while looking for safe space and avoiding others as they show variety in their actions.

- They should vary their movements and actions and respond by copying the leader.

Catch the Puppy Tail (4 minutes)

Setup and Description

1. Ask pairs of children to join to make groups of four. The children form a linked chain, holding onto each other with hands placed around the waist.

2. The child at the back of the line has a piece of cloth tucked into the waistband as a tail. The child at the front of the line has to try to grab the tail.

3. Repeat, changing positions in the line to ensure that each child has the chance to be at the front and rear of the line.

Points of Emphasis

- The children must work cooperatively to keep the line intact.

- They need strong grips to keep the line intact.

Variation   This game can be varied so that three children hold hands in a circle and the chaser is on the outside. The circle moves around to avoid being tagged.

CONCLUSION: SLOW MOTION AND PUPPY'S BEDTIME ACTIVITIES (10 MINUTES)

Slow Motion (5 minutes)

Setup and Description

1. Ask the children to return to their magic spots.

2. Play music that starts fast and then progressively gets slower. Ask the children to move as the animal of their choice until the music stops.

3. Ask the children to freeze when the music stops and stay still like a statue.

4. When the music starts again, ask the children move again, this time like a different animal. Repeat several times.

Points of Emphasis
- Remind the children about safe use of space and avoiding others.
- The children should use several ways of travelling.
- Can the children react quickly to the stop in music?
- Can they show a variety of statue shapes when they freeze?

Variation   Give the children verbal commands while they are moving, using words similar those used on a DVD player: *play, fast-forward, rewind, slow motion, pause,* and *eject. (Eject* means to stop and jump in the air.)

Puppy's Bedtime (5 minutes)

Setup and Description
1. Ask the children to each collect a hoop and place the hoop on the floor.
2. Ask the children to imagine that they are tired puppies who are ready for bed.
3. The hoop is the puppy's bed. Ask the children to travel slowly around the hoop and then make themselves into a small, comfortable shape inside the hoop.
4. When everyone is quiet and still, tap each child in turn on the shoulder and ask the child to line up at the door, ready to return to the classroom.

Points of Emphasis
- The children cool down and relax in readiness for return to classroom.
- Ask the children to self-evaluate through questions and answers at this time.

Variations
- Have the children share their hoop with others.
- Ask them to link together before settling at a low level.
- Ask them to work side by side, back to back, or facing towards or away from their partner.

Lesson 10

Participate in Activities Without Disturbing Others
STANDARD 1, GOAL 1

OBJECTIVES

At the end of the lesson, children will be able to

- refine and practise movement skills,
- work as an individual without disturbing others,
- help to develop a simple game with a partner or small group,
- share ideas and roles,
- appreciate their own work and that of others, and
- send and receive a variety of objects in many ways.

EQUIPMENT

- Hoops, balls (various colours and sizes), beanbags, and other implements that can be thrown safely
- Song sheet
- Cards with key words such as *near, far, away from, and towards*
- Percussion instruments (e.g., drum, bell)

EVALUATION

Ask the children to circle the face that describes how they worked in today's lesson.

1. I have practised my skills.
    a. ☺
    b. ☺
    c. ☹
2. I have worked with different people.
    a. ☺
    b. ☺
    c. ☹
3. I have shared ideas and roles.
    a. ☺
    b. ☺
    c. ☹

INTRODUCTION: BEST STANDING, HEAD AND SHOULDERS, AND MOVE LIKE ME ACTIVITIES (8 MINUTES)

Best Standing (1 minute)

Setup and Description

1. Children enter the space and move to a magic spot (encourage them to begin in a different spot than in the previous lesson).
2. Tell the children, "Show me your best standing on your magic spot."

Points of Emphasis

- Emphasise recognition of and safe use of space.
- For best standing, check for good posture and readiness to listen to instructions.

Head and Shoulders (3 minutes)

Setup and Description

1. Ensure that the children familiarise themselves with the space by entering quietly and moving to magic spots. The children need to be in enough space to move without disturbing others. Make sure you can be seen and heard by all.

2. Lead an action song. Choose a traditional rhyme or song that incorporates actions and parts of the body. Ask the children to join in by singing and copying your actions.

Points of Emphasis

- Encourage the children to copy your instructions accurately.
- Some children will begin to anticipate actions once they learn the song.

Variations

- Ask some children to be the leader.
- Use a variety of rhymes and action songs.
- Extend the activity to lead and copy or to a mirroring activity in pairs or small groups.

Move Like Me (4 minutes)

Setup and Description

1. Ask the children to form pairs. One is the leader and the other is the follower. The children decide who will take which role first.

2. Instruct the pair to move around the space as a mirror image facing each other, copying actions and body dynamics.

3. Ask the children change roles on your signal (e.g., percussion, voice, physical signal).

4. Ask the children to change partners on a different signal (e.g., drum could mean change partners, bell could mean change roles).

5. Repeat so that the children have the opportunity to play with a number of others.

Points of Emphasis

- Ask the children to think about what *mirror image* means. Discuss the difference between mirroring movements and performing opposite movements.
- Explain that now that there are two of them, they need to be even more careful in the space. If necessary, they should slow down or stop to avoid collisions.
- Ask the children to think about using dodging and swerving.

Variations

- Children could be encouraged to shake the follower off their tail by changing directions, turning, dodging, and so on.
- Increase the group size to three and then four.
- Alter the size of the space to make the activity easier (more space) or more difficult (less space).

MAIN LESSON: BEANBAG SEND AND EXPLORATION AND PARTNER SEND ACTIVITIES (22 MINUTES)

Beanbag Send and Exploration (14 minutes)

Setup and Description   Set out all equipment in advance of the lesson, positioning it in piles at a variety of points around the space that allow ease of access for each group. The equipment bases will include a range of balls, hoops, skipping ropes, and so on. Because the children will be allocated to groups, group different-coloured equipment accordingly for easy recognition.

> *continued*

1. Ask the children to collect a beanbag each. While standing on their magic spot, they send the beanbag into a new space (e.g., sliding, pushing, underarm throw, kicking), travel to collect the beanbag (in a way of their choice), pick it up, and repeat, having identified new space. You will need to demonstrate this first, or ask a child to demonstrate to the rest of the group.

2. Give a signal for the children to hold their beanbag in two hands and return to their magic spot, showing their best standing. This signal could be a percussion instrument, a key word, or a clap (your choice).

3. Ask the children to return their beanbags to the base and then choose another piece of equipment (allow open choice of which equipment they use).

4. Give open-ended instruction and foster guided discovery:

    a. Show me how many ways you can use your equipment.

    b. Can you send your equipment in different ways?

      • Near your magic spot

      • Far away from your magic spot

      • Towards your magic spot

      • Over your magic spot

Points of Emphasis

• Remind the children to aim their beanbag into a safe space, avoiding others. They should look to where they would like the beanbag to go and if another child is in the way, they must wait until the space is free.

• Emphasise quality of ways of travelling—time, weight, space, and flow. Even with variety in pathway, they must always avoid other children.

• Praise the efforts of all children and refer to the key language introduced. You might say, for example, "Well done for waiting before you threw the beanbag", or praise a more technical emphasis about aiming and body actions.

Variations

• Differentiation of task is possible through equipment allocation, and you can influence this. For example, have the blue group use large balls or balloons, have the yellow group choose a hoop or a rope, and so on.

• Discuss ways of moving.

Partner Send (8 minutes)

Setup and Description

1. Ask the children to find a partner, suggesting somebody they haven't yet worked with.

2. Instruct the partners to work with a hoop and a beanbag or ball each. The children decide on the amount of space they would like to use. One of each pair stands in the hoop. Can the partner outside the hoop get the beanbag to the partner in the hoop without handing it over directly? Try near and far away, high and low, along the ground, and so on. How many ways can they send and receive? For each time the beanbag reaches the partner in the hoop, the pair scores a point.

3. After six tries, change roles. Can the children help each other come up with new ways of sending the beanbag?

4. Ask who scored some points.

Variation   Introduce a barrier between the sender and the receiver. This could be a bench, a rope, or a line of cones. Can they send the ball over, across, or under the barrier?

CONCLUSION (10 MINUTES)

Our Game

Setup and Description

1. Give the children an open-ended task: Partners must think of their own game that both of them can play at the same time.

2. Some children will need more guidance than others, but allow their imagination to work before you give them too many ideas. Support those who struggle for ideas.

3. Allow the children time to practise and encourage them to experiment.

4. Identify some of the children's new games to demonstrate to the whole class, saying things like "Can we all see how X is . . ." to emphasise good points. Ask, "What do we like about what we see? What could we improve in our games for next time?"

5. Ask the children to put the equipment away and return to their magic spots.

Points of Emphasis

- Emphasise participating well and evaluating and praising other children's work.
- Highlight good cooperative games and demonstrate with children who have cooperated well with each other.

Variations

- Ask the children to work in small groups with different equipment in different spaces.
- Specify which ways of sending and receiving they have to use in their games.

Lesson 11

Participate in Activities Without Disturbing Others
STANDARD 1, GOAL 1

OBJECTIVES

At the end of the lesson, children will be able to

- recognise good individual space,
- share ideas and roles,
- respond to a range of instructions and stimuli,
- send and receive a variety of objects in many ways,
- work cooperatively with a partner, and
- appreciate their own work and that of others.

EQUIPMENT

- Balls in a variety of colours, sizes, textures, and weights, 1 per child
- Skittles, hoops, baskets, boxes, and other objects to aim at
- 1 skipping rope per child
- Percussion instrument (e.g., drum or similar)

EVALUATION

Ask the children to circle the face that describes how they worked in today's lesson.

1. I can send and receive objects in different ways.

   a. ☺

   b. ☺

   c. ☹

2. I have worked well with a partner.

   a. ☺

   b. ☺

   c. ☹

3. I have listened well to instructions.

   a. ☺

   b. ☺

   c. ☹

INTRODUCTION: SIMON SAYS AND CHILD SAYS ACTIVITIES (8 MINUTES)

Simon Says (3 minutes)

Setup and Description

1. Ask the children to move to an individual space, using magic spots as in the previous lesson.

2. Lead a game of Simon Says: "Simon says touch your nose", "Simon says jump up and down three times", and so on. Instructions without "Simon says", such as "Jump up in the air three times", shouldn't be responded to and children should remain still. As with previous lessons, ensure that the children are spaced evenly across the space. It is important for children to recognise space for themselves without too much support from you.

3. Lead the initial activity to encourage children to move in response to the instructions.

4. Start with simple actions and then link two actions together (e.g., travel and jump).

Points of Emphasis

- To begin with, look for good identification of space by all, with children spread evenly across the space and with ample space in between.
- The children will begin to copy actions accurately with increasing confidence and skill.

Child Says (5 minutes)

Setup and Description

1. Ask the children to work in groups of three or four.
2. Ask each child to take turns being Simon, with the other three children responding to the commands.

Point of Emphasis   Emphasise that the children must work well together by taking turns and responding to the leader.

Variations

- Increase the numbers in the group.
- Change the amount of space the children work in.
- Ask the children to include specific actions.

MAIN LESSON: TRUCK AND TRAILER, SENDING FOR ACCURACY, AND ROB THE NEST ACTIVITIES (22 MINUTES)

Truck and Trailer (6 minutes)

Setup and Description   Place large balls, beanbags, and small balls at four points outside the space. Remain vigilant to ensure that the size and type of equipment chosen is suitable for the children's age and stage of development.

1. Ask the children to work with a partner. In pairs, they collect a piece of equipment and stand one behind the other in their space. Pairs agree on which equipment they would like to play with.
2. The children will be moving in haphazard pathways again and need to avoid others. The child with the ball is at the front.
3. Ask the children to move around the space, staying close to each other. When you give the prearranged signal (e.g., percussion, word, flash card, hand signal), the leader hands or sends the ball to the follower. This child now travels in front with the other child behind.
4. On a separate command, ask the children to find a new partner. Encourage the children to work with a new person.

Points of Emphasis

- Ask the children to think about working together safely in the space.
- Encourage the children to look for safe space and travel to it.
- Encourage the children to change ways of travelling.
- Encourage the children to change ways of sending the object to their partner.
- Remind the children to reach both hands towards the object when they are the receiver and to say "Thank you!"
- Remind the children to check to make sure that their partner is ready before sending. (They will be looking towards you and asking for the ball.)

Variation   Vary ways of travelling, using specific skills to send and receive equipment.

> continued

Sending for Accuracy (8 minutes)

Setup and Description   Place a variety of objects around the space.

1. Ask the children to help their partner aim balls or beanbags at targets (objects) at various distances and heights.

3. Encourage accuracy by awarding 1 point for getting the beanbag inside the target or knocking down a skittle.

4. Ask the children what they think they have to do to change the trajectory of the implement. What do they have to do to aim their ball or beanbag higher, lower, farther, nearer, and so on?

Points of Emphasis

- Observe actions carefully and offer constructive feedback.
- Encourage careful aiming, and look at each aspect of the child's throw—look, aim, and release.
- Remind the children to point to where they would like the object to go.
- Praise effort and cooperation with partners and others, as well as skill and accuracy.
- If a ball goes into another pair's area, children must only collect when it is safe to do so—look and ask!

Variations

- Ask the children to select another piece of equipment (e.g., basket, hoop) to use as the target in their game. Ensure that each pair has sufficient space.
- Ask the children to first aim at their own target and then to consider other targets at various heights and distances.
- Encourage the children to try different equipment.
- Ask them in what other ways they can send the equipment.

Rob the Nest (8 minutes)

Setup and Description   Mark a circle in the middle of the space using rope, chalk, or a hoop.

1. Ask the children to place all the equipment inside the circle.

2. Divide the children into groups of four. Each team is given a space that is a base for the team (bases also can be marked on the floor).

3. The children have to work as a team to collect as much equipment as possible from the middle of the space and return it to their base.

4. If necessary, set up three or more concurrent games so that not all children are going for the same equipment.

5. Once all equipment is gone from the middle, children can steal equipment from other groups' bases! You can set a time limit for this.

Point of Emphasis   Emphasise effective cooperation with others to allow the game to flow.

Variations

- Extensions include more teams and bases in the same game.
- Develop the game so that one child sends equipment from the middle to a receiving partner.
- Introduce an interceptor to try to prevent the equipment from being stolen from the base.
- Extend the game so that groups are aiming over or under a barrier.

CONCLUSION (10 MINUTES)

Rabbits and Burrows

Setup and Description

1. Ask the children to return their equipment to the piles, each collect a hoop, and stand inside it.

2. Ensure that hoops are spread evenly across the space. The hoop is the burrow and the child inside is the rabbit.

3. Ask the children to move around the space as if they were rabbits. When they hear the farmer coming (e.g., use percussion such as wooden blocks or a drum to signify steps), the children have to return to their burrows and make themselves as small and quiet as possible.

4. Develop the game so that some children can be the farmer and tag the rabbits that aren't in their burrows.

5. After a few rounds, once all the rabbits are safely home, ask the groups in turn to line up at the door, ready to head back to the classroom.

Points of Emphasis

- Tell the children to move like rabbits by jumping and taking weight on the feet as well as on the hands.
- Emphasise light jumps and soft, quiet landings.

Variations

- Remove a number of hoops so that children have to share burrows.
- Change the size of the space.

Lesson 12

Participate in Activities Without Disturbing Others
STANDARD 1, GOAL 1

OBJECTIVES

At the end of the lesson, children will be able to

- share ideas and roles;
- enjoy moving in a variety of ways;
- understand how to move quietly and carefully;
- travel in many ways showing variations in direction, level, and speed;
- understand how feelings can be shown through movement; and
- respond to a range of stimuli.

EQUIPMENT

- 1 animal mask per child
- Pictures of jungle animals
- Music player
- Music that exemplifies happy or sad moods
- Drum or other percussion instrument
- Objects to place in the space—mats, cones, benches, skittles, hoops

EVALUATION

Ask the children to circle the face that describes how they worked in today's lesson.

1. I moved quietly and carefully.
   a. ☺
   b. ☺
   c. ☹
2. I moved in lots of ways.
   a. ☺
   b. ☺
   c. ☹
3. I have listened well to instructions.
   a. ☺
   b. ☺
   c. ☹

INTRODUCTION: JUNGLE ADVENTURE AND TRACKING THE ELEPHANT ACTIVITIES (8 MINUTES)

Jungle Adventure (3 minutes)

Setup and Description Place a number of objects and obstacles around the space. These can be mats, benches, hoops, skittles, and so on.

1. Before entering the play space, ask the children to think about the jungle. Tell the children that today's lesson is about a jungle and the animals that live there.
2. Emphasise the need to be quiet—otherwise they will wake up the monkeys, snakes, and lions.
3. On entering the space, encourage the children to tiptoe ever so carefully, making sure they explore the whole area.

Points of Emphasis

- Remind the children to stay on their toes, moving as carefully and quietly as mice.
- Encourage them to be aware of their careful movements and to show control.
- Encourage safe use of space, working skilfully to avoid the objects placed in the space.
- The children should consider working low to the ground.

Variation   Encourage the children to explore ways of moving over, around, under, or through the obstacles.

Tracking the Elephant (5 minutes)

Setup and Description

1. The teacher is the elephant and the children are the trackers! Turn your back to the class. Move around the space slowly and ask the children to follow behind ever so quietly.
2. When you turn around, the children have to freeze and hold their positions as if they were statues so that the elephant doesn't see them.
3. Develop the game so that children have the chance to be the elephant in smaller groups. Children work in groups of six and take turns being the elephant and the trackers. Each child should be given a chance to try both roles.

Points of Emphasis

- Emphasise staying on the toes, moving as carefully and quietly as mice.
- Encourage the children to be aware of their careful movements and to show control.
- Encourage safe use of space, working skilfully to avoid the obstacles.
- The children must work quietly to avoid being caught.
- Have the children consider working low to the ground.

Variations

- Have the children change the shape they make each time the elephant turns around.
- Can they make themselves look like a tree, a snake close to the ground, or a rock?

MAIN LESSON: ANIMAL MAGIC, HAPPY ELEPHANT, AND TRUNK BY TRUNK ACTIVITIES (22 MINUTES)

Activity 1: Animal Magic (6 minutes)

Setup and Description

1. Have the children act like a jungle animal, giving them a free choice from a range of animals. Ask them to travel around the space as though they were elephants, tigers, lions, monkeys, giraffes, snakes, and so on.
2. Ask the children to change animals when they hear the percussion signal.
3. Show the children pictures of jungle animals. Can the children think how each animal moves?
4. Ask the children to move like the animal in the picture.

Points of Emphasis

- Can the children think of the ways in which different animals move?
- Can they show variation in the time, space, weight, and flow of their movements? Can they alter pathways?

Variations

- Use music to suggest actions—small, quick, fast, light, heavy, and so on.
- Give the children masks to wear to symbolise the animals (these could be made in an art activity).
- Ask the children to think of an animal that is high in the air or low to the ground.

> continued

Happy Elephant (10 minutes)
Setup and Description

1. Show the children a picture of an elephant, discussing its characteristics. How might it move?
2. Ask the children to move in their space like elephants.
3. Ask the children to think about how an elephant would move differently if it were happy, sad, angry, tired, and so on.

Points of Emphasis

- Encourage the children to respond accurately to the stimuli (some auditory and some pictorial).
- Encourage children to think about heavy, slow, direct, or restricted movements.
- Can the elephants work at high levels by reaching high with their trunks?
- Can they work at low levels to roll in the mud?

Variation   Play music to signify happiness, sadness, or other moods. Can the elephants change the way they move?

Trunk by Trunk (6 minutes)
Setup and Description

1. In groups of six, ask the children to form trains of elephants trunk by trunk. This is done by the child in front reaching through her legs to hold hands with the child behind, who does the same with his other hand. Choose one group to demonstrate how to form the train.
2. Ask the children to move around the space in their trains. Keeping the trunks linked, the children move around the space, avoiding the other trains of elephants.
3. Give a signal to change directions or to reorganise the lines.

Points of Emphasis

- Encourage the children to think about heavy, slow, direct, or restricted movements.
- Encourage strong links in the train of elephants.
- The children should listen for the command to change directions and reorganise themselves as quickly as they can.

Variation   Give the command to change directions—the train has to reorganise itself with the last elephant now at the front.

CONCLUSION (10 MINUTES)

The Hunter Is Coming
Setup and Description

1. Allocate the children to groups of animals so that, for example, six children are monkeys, six children are crocodiles, six children are lions, and six children are snakes. The children move in different pathways and when the hunter signal is given, they have to find the other animals like them and move together in a huddle.
2. When all children are in groups and are resting together on the floor, ask each group of animals to line up at the door, ready to go back to the classroom.

Points of Emphasis

- Encourage the children to show versatility and variety in their actions.
- Encourage them to cooperate with others in their groups.
- Can they evaluate their own work via questions and answers with you?

Variations

- The animals could hide at different times—the biggest first, the smallest last.
- The children could decide to huddle together in different shapes.
- Ask the children to get in groups with one type of animal per group.

Lesson 13

Share Ideas and Roles
STANDARD 1, GOAL 1

OBJECTIVES
At the end of the lesson, children will be able to

- work safely and creatively in individual space,
- work in shared space with a partner,
- share ideas and roles creatively with a partner,
- comment on their own work and that of others,
- participate in activities without disturbing others,
- appreciate their own work and that of others, and
- work in groups.

EQUIPMENT
- Marching music (teacher's choice)
- Percussion instruments (cymbal recommended)
- 1 hoop per child
- Pictures of insects (caterpillar, bee, butterfly, ant, spider, and so on)
- 1 ball per six children
- 1 beanbag per child
- Hoops

EVALUATION
Ask the children to circle the face that describes how they worked in today's lesson.

1. I shared my ideas with a partner.
    a. ☺
    b. ☺
    c. ☹
2. I worked in a group.
    a. ☺
    b. ☺
    c. ☹
3. I have enjoyed seeing other children's work.
    a. ☺
    b. ☺
    c. ☹

INTRODUCTION: MARCHING BAND, WORKING ANTS, AND INCY WINCY SPIDER ACTIVITIES (12 MINUTES)

Marching Band (5 minutes)
Setup and Description
1. Ask the children to enter the space and stand to attention like toy soldiers on their magic spots.
2. Play some marching band–type music and ask the children to march on the spot, suggesting that they move like toy soldiers, marching ants, and so on.

3. Instruct the children that when the music stops, they should stand to attention again.

4. Ask the children to begin marching to the music again, this time marching away from their spot. If they are moving towards somebody else, ask them to march on the spot until the other child is safely past. The children can use lines on the floor to march along.

5. Use a percussion instrument (e.g., cymbal) to instruct the children to change direction.

Points of Emphasis

- Remind the children to show upright posture, swinging rhythmical arms and legs (alternating) in time to the music.
- When the music stops, say "Show me your best standing!"
- Emphasise changes in levels.

Working Ants (3 minutes)

Setup and Description

1. Group children into lines of six (one child behind the other).

2. Give the child at the front of the group an object (e.g., beanbag, ball, hoop).

3. When you say "Go", the ball is passed over the head of each child in the line. When the ball reaches the end of the line, the last child runs to the front of the line and passes overhead again.

4. In this way, the group works its way down the space to a predetermined finish line.

Points of Emphasis

- Stress cooperation and communication.
- Encourage the children to keep in line like very good ants!

Incy Wincy Spider (4 minutes)

Setup and Description

1. This activity is based on the "Incy Wincy Spider" poem. If this poem is not known in your country, use a story or nursery rhyme about a spider to encourage the children to move like spiders.

2. Ask the children to think about how a spider moves and encourage them to work in their own space to show you.

Points of Emphasis

- Encourage work at a low level and changes in level in accordance with the rhyme.
- How would the spider move when it is washed away (thus having to start again)?

MAIN LESSON: INSECTS AND METAMORPHOSIS ACTIVITIES (18 MINUTES)

Insects (10 minutes)

Setup and Description

1. Show the children various pictures of insects.

2. Discuss three insects (e.g., caterpillar, butterfly, bee).

3. Practise each one in turn, changing the insect on percussion beat. Then have the children choose their favourite.

Points of Emphasis

- Can the children move as though they were these insects?
- Use vocabulary such as *scuttling*, *scurrying*, *floating*, and *wriggling*.
- Encourage use of various speeds, levels, and directions.

> continued

Metamorphosis (8 minutes)

Setup and Description

1. Discuss how a caterpillar becomes a butterfly.
2. Ask the children to collect a hoop and place it on their magic spot. Play some music and ask the children to move around the space, in and out of all the hoops. Now ask them to move as though they were a caterpillar, low and wriggly.
3. As they move around the space, ask the children to collect food (beanbags), which is littered around the space (you can do this while you are explaining about metamorphosis).
4. On a signal (e.g., drum, cymbal), the children head for their cocoons (hoops). On the next signal, they emerge from the cocoons as beautiful butterflies.
5. Reduce the number of hoops so that children have to share their cocoons with others.

Points of Emphasis

- Ensure that the children work at different levels.
- Ensure that the children understand how they can move gracefully, with swooping and hovering actions.

CONCLUSION (5-10 MINUTES)

Spider's Web

Setup and Description

1. Ask the children to return to their individual magic spots.
2. Ask the children to move around the space freely like spiders. Give the command, "Here comes the rain." The children then have to scurry back to their webs (hoops placed throughout the space).
3. Reduce the number of hoops so that six children have to share each web.
4. Ask the six children inside the hoops to hold hands in a circle.
5. When sitting quietly holding hands, tell the children that they are ready to go back to the classroom.

Lesson 14

Share Ideas and Roles
STANDARD 1, GOAL 1

OBJECTIVES

At the end of the lesson, children will be able to

- participate in activities without disturbing others,
- participate in balancing activities,
- appreciate their work and that of others,
- work safely and creatively in individual space,
- work in shared space with a partner,
- share ideas and roles creatively with a partner, and
- comment on their own work and that of others.

EQUIPMENT

- Pictures of letters
- Pictures of children holding balance positions (you may have to make these using the children in your class)
- 1 mat, beanbag, and hoop per child
- Percussion instrument

EVALUATION

Ask the children to circle the face that describes how they worked in today's lesson.

1. I can work well in my own space.
   a. ☺
   b. ☺
   c. ☹

2. I have worked well with my partner.
   a. ☺
   b. ☺
   c. ☹

3. I can balance in a number of ways.
   a. ☺
   b. ☺
   c. ☹

4. I enjoy watching other children show their work.
   a. ☺
   b. ☺
   c. ☹

INTRODUCTION: STATUES AND ALPHABET SOUP ACTIVITIES (8 MINUTES)

Statues (3 minutes)

Setup and Description   Make sure that the space is clear of obstacles.

1. As soon as the children enter the space, ask them to become statues by making shapes with their bodies.
2. Can they be tall, short, wide, curled, or stretched statues? Position yourself to see all children working.

> continued

Points of Emphasis

- Ensure that the children are in good individual spaces.
- Remind the children to work carefully, accurately, neatly, and with increasing control.
- Ask the children to work quietly, stressing quality of movement.

Alphabet Soup (5 minutes)

Setup and Description

1. Show the children pictures or a poster of the letters of the alphabet.
2. Ask the children to make letters with their bodies. Start by suggesting which letters they make and then ask the children to choose their own letters.

Points of Emphasis

- Ensure that the children are in good individual spaces.
- Remind the children to work carefully, accurately, neatly, and with increasing control.
- Remind them to work quietly, stressing quality of movement.

Variations

- Can the children link with a partner to make letter shapes?
- The children make up their own simple words in a group or spell their own names with their bodies.

MAIN LESSON: HOLD AND MORE AND AIM AND FOLLOW ACTIVITIES (18 MINUTES)

Hold and More (10 minutes)

Setup and Description   Place mats at the edge of the space in more than one pile to allow for easy access by all children and to avoid queuing.

1. Ask the children to collect individual mats and to then sit on them. You may need to ask the children to work in pairs depending on the size and weight of the mats. Ask the children to place their mats so that they have lots of room around them.
2. Explain that the children are to make a balance position of their own choice on the mat and then move around their mat in a way of their choice. This linking of balance with travelling is repeated several times—how many ways can the children think of and show you? (For example, children could perform a wide balance and then hop around the mat or perform a narrow balance and then slide around the mat.)
3. Suggest some shapes that the children can make. This would be helped with picture cards showing children balancing.
4. Encourage the children to have a look at what others are doing and think of things they could do that are similar to or different from others. Ask the children to tell you what they like about others' work. What would they like to improve about their own work?

Points of Emphasis

- Emphasise safe lifting and carrying of mats: knees bent and back straight.
- Remind the children to balance and travel at various levels, with wide and narrow bases, and with different points of balance.
- Can the children travel in different directions, levels, and speeds?
- Can the children work close to and far away from their mats?

Variations

- Have the children work with a partner on the same mat to share the space.
- Have the children work in small groups around and on the same mat or groups of mats joined together.
- Have the children use a variety of equipment to mark a pathway (e.g., beanbags, hoops, cones).

Aim and Follow (8 minutes)

Setup and Description

1. Ask the children to collect a beanbag and return to their mat.
2. Ask the children to send the beanbag (by throwing, sliding, or another action) to a new mat.
3. When they arrive at the new mat, they should pick up the beanbag, perform a balance position, and then travel around the mat again. Ask the children to try this and check their understanding—a demonstration may be necessary!
4. Challenge the children to aim their beanbag to the middle of the mat.
5. Encourage them to spend a little time looking at others' work and giving feedback.

Points of Emphasis

- When sending beanbags, the children should look for free space and not throw at other children.
- Look for variety and contrast in sending and travelling skills.
- Emphasise accuracy of throw rather than distance.

Variations

- Work with a partner sharing the mats and beanbags.
- Take turns throwing the beanbag away and collecting it.
- Can one person work high while the other works low?
- Can one person work quickly while the other works slowly?
- How many balances and ways of travelling can the children think of?

CONCLUSION (10 MINUTES)

Busy Bees

Setup and Description

1. While the children are returning their mats to the piles, place a number of hoops around the space.
2. Ask the children to move like bees, buzzing around the whole space, which has been littered with enough hoops for one between two people.
3. Give a signal (such as a word or a percussion instrument) that means that the children have to move into a honey pot (hoop) and hold hands with a partner.
4. Ask the children to move again, but first remove some hoops. More children have to go to each honey pot as the game progresses, ending up with the whole class in one space holding hands.

Points of Emphasis

- Emphasise safe lifting and carrying, working well with another child to do this.
- Emphasise that the children must work cooperatively to share the honey pots, even if there are lots of bees!

Variation Ask the children to balance at various levels inside the hoops.

Lesson 15

Share Ideas and Roles
STANDARD 1, GOAL 1

OBJECTIVES
At the end of the lesson, children will be able to

- work safely and creatively in individual space,
- work in shared space with a partner,
- share ideas and roles creatively with a partner,
- comment on their own work and that of others,
- participate in balance activities,
- travel and balance by taking weight on the hands as well as the feet, and
- participate in activities without disturbing others.

EQUIPMENT

- Simple apparatuses or obstacles (e.g., benches, tables, skittles, cones)
- Dice (or spinner)
- Music and music player
- Pictures of animals (e.g., rabbit, kangaroo, frog, kitten)
- Chalk, skipping ropes, or beanbags to make lines on the floor

EVALUATION
Ask the children to circle the face that describes how they worked in today's lesson.

1. I can work well in my own space.
    a. ☺
    b. ☺
    c. ☹

2. I worked well with my partner.
    a. ☺
    b. ☺
    c. ☹

3. I can travel in a number of ways.
    a. ☺
    b. ☺
    c. ☹

4. I enjoy watching other children show their work.
    a. ☺
    b. ☺
    c. ☹

INTRODUCTION: STICKY TREACLE AND STICKY HANDS ACTIVITIES (8 MINUTES)

Sticky Treacle (3 minutes)

Setup and Description Before the lesson starts, place some obstacles such as benches, mats, gymnastic tables, hoops, and cones in the space to mark out a pathway. You can also improvise by placing canes between skittles to make low hurdles and so on.

1. Ask the children to enter the space and to sit in their own space next to (but not touching) an obstacle.

2. Ask the children to move in between and around the obstacles in a haphazard fashion, as though they were in sticky honey.

3. Play music while the children are moving. When you stop the music, ask the children to freeze and hold their shape until the music starts again.

3. Ask the children to make shapes when they freeze.

4. Ask the children to balance low, high, narrow, or wide.

Points of Emphasis

- Emphasise the space between and around the obstacles, also explaining the importance of not touching them.
- The children should start by moving slowly, exaggerating their actions and stretching their ankles and toes.

Sticky Hands (5 minutes)

Setup and Description   Make sure that you are in a position to see all the children moving and to check for safe use of the space.

1. Ask the children to continue moving in and around the obstacles, but when they are given a signal (e.g., percussion), they are asked to touch an obstacle with their hands and hold a balance position against that obstacle with weight on the hands.

2. Make the signal again to ask the children to carry on moving once more (at different speeds, levels, and directions).

2. Introduce the children to different signals (e.g., different number of drum beats, different types of percussion) to signify touching the apparatus with different body parts—hands, feet, back, side, and so on.

3. As the activity progresses, ask the children to work in pairs to hold balance positions around and on the obstacles.

Points of Emphasis

- Emphasise taking weight on different parts of the body. Make sure the children show increasing control.
- See if the children can hold the balance positions for 2 to 3 seconds.
- Make sure the children are showing variety and contrast in their work (different levels and speeds of travel).

MAIN LESSON: HOPPING MAD, CHASE THE RABBIT, AND PERFORMANCE AND EVALUATION OPPORTUNITY ACTIVITIES (22 MINUTES)

Hopping Mad (8 minutes)

Setup and Description

1. Ask the children to move in between, onto, off, and around the obstacles in response to visual cues in the form of animal cards: frog, rabbit, kangaroo, and kitten.

2. Give the children an open-ended instruction to move like any of these animals.

3. Then show a card for them to move like that animal. Explain that they are now expected to jump, hop, leap, and begin to take weight on both the hands and feet. This may require a demonstration!

Points of Emphasis

- Encourage the children to show variety and versatility in their movements and to apply jumping and weight on hands to different contexts.

> continued

- Encourage the children to consider safety in their surroundings and the sharing of obstacles.
- The children may slide, roll, stretch, hop, leap, skip, and so on. For each movement, give positive feedback to reinforce actions and skill development.

Chase the Rabbit (8 minutes)

Setup and Description

1. Ask the children to stop and stand in their own space.
2. While they are resting, ask the children to find a partner. Then ask them to decide who the old rabbit is and who the young rabbit is. The old rabbit will be the leader and the young rabbit will be the follower.
3. Instruct the children to work in their pairs around the space, leading and following, considering others and working safely. The children do not have to copy movements exactly; they work at their own ability levels.
4. The children should take it in turns to be the leader and the follower, changing roles several times.

Point of Emphasis   Emphasise control and careful actions—it is not a race or an obstacle course! Accuracy and neatness of movement should be stressed.

Performance and Evaluation Opportunity (6 minutes)

Setup and Description

1. Provide the children with opportunities to watch others working and to provide feedback.
2. Ask the children, "Who can tell me what they like about *X's* and *Y's* movements?

CONCLUSION (5 MINUTES)

Frogs in a Pond

Setup and Description   Make two lines on the floor (use chalk, rope, or beanbags) to signify two pond banks.

1. Ask the children to form groups of four and to stand in their groups along one side of the pond.
2. Ask the children to guess how many frog jumps they can use to cross the pond.
3. Encourage the children to attempt to cross the pond in this way. Can they beat their previous score?
4. Now place a number of small items (beanbags, discs, cones) in the pond. Ask the children to collect the equipment from the pond as they travel across. The equipment that you have placed will mark out a pathway for them.
5. Ask the children to work together to help each other and to find the best way to return all of the equipment.

Points of Emphasis

- Provide verbal instructions, especially when telling the children to cross the pond (e.g., "Can you think of a different route?").
- Emphasise skilful jumping and travelling in a variety of pathways.
- Encourage the children to help each other.

Lesson 16

Share Ideas and Roles
STANDARD 1, GOAL 1

OBJECTIVES

At the end of the lesson, children will be able to

- participate in activities without disturbing others,
- enjoy moving in a variety of ways,
- work with a partner to follow clues,
- move in response to visual and auditory stimuli, and
- share their ideas with the class.

EQUIPMENT

- Animal trail markers or chalk
- Laminated pictures of animals or toy animals
- Apparatuses and objects to hide pictures behind, under, and so on
- Recording sheets to answer questions and clues
- Bell or whistle

EVALUATION

Ask the children to circle the face that describes how they worked in today's lesson.

1. I can work well in my own space.
   a. ☺
   b. ☺
   c. ☹
2. I worked well with my partner.
   a. ☺
   b. ☺
   c. ☹
3. I enjoy moving in a variety of ways.
   a. ☺
   b. ☺
   c. ☹
4. I enjoy sharing my ideas with others.
   a. ☺
   b. ☺
   c. ☹

INTRODUCTION: LET'S GO ON AN ANIMAL HUNT AND ANIMAL TRACK ACTIVITIES (10 MINUTES)

Let's Go On an Animal Hunt (8 minutes)

Setup and Description   This lesson is based on movement and simple navigation in the form of an animal trail. It will ideally take place outdoors; otherwise a trail can be set up indoors.

At the centre of the space, place a selection of animal tracks going outwards in a variety of pathways for the children to see straightaway. (The size of the space is based on space and equipment available, availability of other staff, and so on.) Make enough tracks for the children to work in

> continued

pairs or groups of three. You can draw the tracks with chalk on the floor or make animal footprints from paper. Place a picture of the animal or a toy animal at the end of each trail (hidden from view under an object or behind an apparatus).

1. At the start of the lesson, show the children pictures of animals. The picture cards could also have footprints on the reverse side. Ask the children if they can see that different sizes and shapes of animals make different-shaped footprints.

2. The children work in pairs or groups of three to follow a different trail from the start. Once they have located the first animal (which can be a picture of the animal or a toy), they perform the task (written on the card or next to the toy). This task could be a question for them to respond to or a physical action to perform. You will need to plan these tasks according to the children's abilities.

4. You must also specify a loud signal (e.g., bell, whistle) to tell the children to report back to the start. It is advisable for you to remain in a position where you can see the whole class.

5. Once the children have performed the task, they return to the start and choose a different track to follow.

Points of Emphasis

- Careful explanation is required. This lesson may be worth delivering twice—the second time the children will fully understand what is required.

- It is worth spending longer on the explanation to save time later.

- Check understanding carefully before asking the children to go on the trail. Check understanding by asking questions such as, "Who can tell me what you have to do first? Who can tell me what you have to do when you have found an animal? Then what do you have to do?"

- Emphasise that the children have a responsibility to work with their partner or group and to help other pairs or groups who may be lost.

Animal Track (2 minutes)

Setup and Description

1. Ask the children to look at the tracks on the floor. What animals do they think made the tracks? Can they move as though they were those animals?

2. Tell the pairs or groups of children which track they are to follow.

3. Ask, "Is everyone ready? Let's go!"

4. The children move in the space to represent the tracks that are made by a selection of animals.

MAIN LESSON (25 MINUTES)

The Hunt

Setup and Description

1. Ask the children to follow the animal footprints, encouraging them to move like the animal that they expect to find in the hiding place.

2. When they find the animal, ask the children if they were right.

3. Support the children as they respond to the task that has been set.

4. Ask the children to return to the start and choose another track to follow.

Points of Emphasis

- Encourage the children to work quickly and carefully.

- They should move vigorously and skilfully when moving like the animal.

- Look for cooperation with partners and the whole class, as well as effective response to your signals.

Variations

- Use your imagination when choosing places to hide the pictures or soft toys and deciding what questions or tasks the animals hide.
- The questions and tasks can be made harder or easier depending on the ability of the children.
- The children could complete the course against the clock as a race.

CONCLUSION: BACK TO BASE AND SLEEPING LIONS ACTIVITIES (6 MINUTES)

Back to Base (3 minutes)

Setup and Description

1. Give the prearranged signal for all children to come back to the start. Check that everyone is back. Ask the children to count to see how many people they are waiting for.
2. Instruct the children to collect the animal cards and then sit with you to decide who got all the correct answers to the tasks. Did they find all the animals?
3. Engage the children in questions and answers to check understanding. This should also be a time for pairs to congratulate each other and to say how they helped each other. Don't worry if the children didn't get every answer correct.

Point of Emphasis   Emphasise that the children must respond as quickly as possible to the signal to return to the base.

Sleeping Lions (3 minutes)

Setup and Description   Children need to be relaxed and calmed down after so much fun. This activity requires the children to work in individual space.

1. To finish the lesson, ask the children to be lions at nighttime. They are to find some individual space and rest on the floor.
2. Have one final big stretch—up, out, and so on—and then settle down to sleep. Tell the children to concentrate on their breathing so that it slows down and they slowly drift off to sleep and dream about chasing other animals.

Point of Emphasis   Instruct the children to stretch slowly and take deep breaths. They close their eyes and imagine they are a sleepy lion.

Lesson 17

Appreciate Own Work and That of Others
STANDARD 1, GOAL 2

OBJECTIVES
At the end of the lesson, children will be able to
- coordinate within teams,
- show improved cooperation skills,
- show improved motor skills,
- appreciate their own contribution to a common aim, and
- recognise the contributions of the other members of the team.

EQUIPMENT
- 1 animal card per child
- 1 box
- 2 long ropes (4 m each), chalk, or tape
- 2 to 4 hula hoops
- 1 or 2 sheets of fabric (2 by 2 m)
- 2 or 3 small gymnastic or soft (foam) balls
- 1 plastic cube per child

EVALUATION
Give each child a sheet of paper that only contains the answers (e.g., 1. a, b, c; 2. a, b, c). After you slowly read each question and the possible answers, ask the children to circle the appropriate answer.

1. Everyone can participate and has something to offer to a team.
    a. yes
    b. no
    c. not sure
2. I can be a member of any team and contribute to its success.
    a. yes
    b. no
    c. not sure
3. Any of my classmates can contribute to a team and its success.
    a. yes
    b. no
    c. not sure

INTRODUCTION (7 MINUTES)
Setup and Description   Put the animal cards in a box. In a previous lesson you can ask the children to draw an animal that they like and then use the drawings to perform this activity.

1. Each child picks an animal card, shows it to the other children, and describes the way the animal moves (suggested animals: elephant, kangaroo, lion, rabbit, frog, mouse, bear, horse, duck).
2. The child prompts the other children to move like the animal.

Points of Emphasis

- Encourage the class to try moving according to one child's suggestion.
- Point out that they have to try the ideas of others, just as the others have to try their own ideas.

MAIN LESSON: FROG RACE, NAVIGATE THE SHIP, AND THE TOWER ACTIVITIES (20 MINUTES)

Frog Race (7 minutes)

Setup and Description   Use two long ropes and place them on the floor (4 m between them) to represent the starting and termination lines.

1. Divide children in groups of five. Each group begins from the starting line.
2. The first player has to make a long-distance jump (like a frog). At the landing point, place a hula hoop (around the child). The next member of the group continues from this point.
3. The procedure continues until the fifth child jumps. The goal of each team is to arrive at the termination line with five jumps (or as many jumps as there are children in each team). The distance between the two lines must be set up so that all groups can be successful.
4. Repeat the activity a few times.

Points of Emphasis

- Reward all the children personally for their performance.
- Ask the children in each group to encourage their teammates and cheer their performances.

Navigate the Ship (7 minutes)

Setup and Description

1. Divide the children into two groups. Each group stands around a big sheet of fabric (approximately 2 by 2 m, coloured blue if possible) and holds it at hip height. The sheet mustn't be completely strained.
2. At the centre of the sheet, place a ball that represents the ship. Each group must navigate the ship when the sea is calm, when the sea has small waves, and when the sea is rough.

Points of Emphasis

- Make it clear that the success of each team depends on the weather and on avoiding the rocks (i.e., preventing the ball from falling down).
- For each team to succeed, team members have to cooperate, control their movements, and do a coordinated performance for the common goal (e.g., coordinate hand movements, footsteps, pacing, and so on).
- Reward the children who make a real effort.

Variations

- Play the game with a bigger sheet of fabric and only one team.
- Two teams play the game separately rather than simultaneously (one by one).

The Tower (6 minutes)

Setup and Description

1. Divide children into three teams of six to eight and place them behind a starting point (line made from rope, chalk, or tape). Children of each team are one behind the other and the distance between the teams is approximately 1.5 metres.
2. On the other side of the class, put three hula hoops on the ground, one for each team, and outside each hula hoop put small, equal-sized cubes, the same number as there are children on each team.

> *continued*

3. The goal of each team is to make a tower with the cubes in a specific time. With the starting signal, one at a time each player must run to the hula hoop and place a cube inside the hoop, one upon the other, building a tower.

Points of Emphasis

- Point out that players must move as fast and carefully as they can.
- Encourage each child personally to run faster or to carefully place a cube on the tower.
- Create a warm climate using appropriate music, prompts, encouragement, and so on.

CONCLUSION (6 MINUTES)

The Watchmaker

Setup and Description

1. Divide the children into two teams. Each team forms a circle. The distance between the children in circles is approximately 1 metre, or as wide as throwing and receiving can be successfully achieved according to the children's abilities.

2. One child of each team holds a ball. You represent the watchmaker and the teams are the watches. Check to see if your watches are wound up well by giving the order to count 6 hours, 10 hours, 12 hours, and so on. One hour means one pass of the ball from one child to the other, starting clockwise. Each unsuccessful pass must be repeated.

Points of Emphasis

- Encourage the children to count together.
- Reward successful counting and trials.

Lesson 18

Appreciate Own Work and That of Others
STANDARD 1, GOAL 2

OBJECTIVES

At the end of the lesson, children will be able to

- coordinate within teams;
- show improved cooperation skills;
- show improved motor skills;
- appreciate their own contribution, achieving a common goal with ideas and actions;
- listen to and appreciate their teammate's ideas; and
- appraise others' trials and contributions.

EQUIPMENT

- Music player
- Music (Latin or rock and roll)
- 4 cones
- Cards with letters
- 4 hula hoops
- 8 balls
- 8 cubes
- 8 small plastic bags

EVALUATION

Give each child a sheet of paper that only contains the answers (e.g., 1. a, b, c; 2. a, b, c). After you slowly read each question and the possible answers, ask the children to circle the appropriate answer.

1. When I have some ideas that might benefit my team, I have to
    a. share them with my team
    b. keep them to myself
    c. be quiet
2. When I am a member of a team, it's good to listen and pay attention to the other teammates' ideas.
    a. true   ☺
    b. false   ☹
    c. don't know ☺
3. The most important thing to do when you are a member of a team is to appreciate someone's trials for success and not only the success.
    a. true   ☺
    b. false   ☹
    c. don't know ☺

INTRODUCTION (7 MINUTES)

Shapes

Setup and Description

1. Divide the class into two teams and place them on two sides of the space.
2. Put some music on (Latin or rock and roll) and ask the teams to dance freely in their space.

> continued

3. Each time the music stops, ask each team to form a shape (e.g., lake, orange, half-moon, square). Ask teammates to cooperate and give them enough time to decide how they will form the shape.

Points of Emphasis

- Help the children when they seem to have problem cooperating with each other or when they seem stuck.
- Point out that there is enough time for all to suggest their opinions and ideas.
- Reward the teams for creative performances and for cooperative performances.

MAIN LESSON: ROLLS, TRANSPORTATION, DIFFICULT BALANCES, AND SCULPTORS ACTIVITIES (27 MINUTES)

Rolls (7 minutes)

Setup and Description

1. Divide the class into two teams. Each team forms a line (one child behind the other) so that lines of teams are facing each other. The distance between the teams is approximately 8 metres.
2. In the middle of this space, put two cones close to each other to form a narrow passage of 40 to 50 centimetres. Give a ball to one team and let the activity begin.
3. Each child of each team takes turns trying to roll the ball through the narrow passage to the opposite team. The goal for each team is to pass the ball 10 times through the passage. The winner is the team that succeeds first.

Point of Emphasis Ask the teams to encourage their players while they try, regardless of the result.

Transportation (6 minutes)

Setup and Description

1. Divide the class into two teams. Each team forms a line (one child next to the other) so that lines of teams are facing each other.
2. Place a hula hoop on the floor in front of the first and last child of each team. Inside the hula hoop in front of the first child of one team, place some objects (e.g., four balls, four cubes, and four beanbags), and do the same for the other team.
3. The goal of each team is to transfer the objects hand to hand from the hula hoop in front of the first child to the hula hoop in front of the last child as fast as they can.

Point of Emphasis The goal of each team (common goal) can be achieved only if all team members
- try their best,
- pay attention to their team and their goal, and
- cooperate well with the other members of their team.

Variations

- Change the shape of the team's lines (e.g., circle, zigzag).
- Change the transported objects.
- Divide the children into more teams.
- Ask for more complicated transportation.

Difficult Balances (7 minutes)

Setup and Description

1. Divide the class into pairs.
2. Ask pairs to experiment to find many balance and support positions that each child alone wouldn't be able to achieve. This means that they should support each other.
3. After awhile, ask the children to change partners.

Points of Emphasis

- Encourage the children to create strange and difficult balance and support positions.
- Ask the children to use their hands, bodies, legs, and the floor and to change the level of their movements.
- Show and reward children's balance and support positions.

Variation Use some equipment (e.g., a wooden bench, chairs) that the children can use for support.

Sculptors (7 minutes)

Setup and Description

1. Divide the children into teams of four or five.
2. In each team, one child represents the potter's clay and the other children are the sculptors. Ask the sculptors to create many sculptures (e.g., police officer, woodchopper, hero, football player, dancer). Give enough time for them to experiment with their sculptures—how they will put the arms, legs, body, and head—to create a representative sculpture.

Points of Emphasis

- Reward the teams for their creations.
- Ask them to pay attention to details and the characteristics of the sculpture.
- Encourage them to find solutions to possible problems.

CONCLUSION (7 MINUTES)

Shape Letters

Setup and Description

1. Divide the children into groups of three.
2. Ask each team to form letters with their bodies. Show each letter on a board or a card. Give enough time for each team to think, cooperate, pose ideas, and try them.

Points of Emphasis

- Reward all groups for their ideas and for their final results.
- Encourage them to use all parts of their bodies.

Variation Ask the children to try their ideas in different levels.

Lesson 19

Appreciate Own Work and That of Others
STANDARD 1, GOAL 2

OBJECTIVES
At the end of the lesson, children will be able to

- coordinate within a team,
- show improved cooperation skills,
- show improved motor skills,
- comprehend their contribution to teamwork, and
- appreciate the contributions of other team members.

EQUIPMENT
- 4 to 8 ropes, tape, or chalk
- 4 hula hoops
- 4 bases or cubes for hoops or plastic bars or sticks
- 2 to 4 balls
- Coat, hat, scarf, gloves, umbrella, sunglasses, raincoat, sea towel, and other equipment and clothes that represent the four seasons (as much as you need)
- 4 pieces of cardboard (70 by 50 cm)
- Colourful markers (enough for all children)
- Colours for drawing on wood (enough for all children)

EVALUATION
Give each child a sheet of paper that only contains the answers (e.g., 1. a, b, c; 2. a, b, c). After you slowly read each question and the possible answers, ask the children to circle the appropriate answer or the face that they feel.

1. When you are a member of a team, you have to work together and cooperate in order to achieve the goals of the team.
    a. true   ☺
    b. false   ☹
    c. don't know ☺

2. When I cooperate with the members of a team for a common goal, I feel
    a. ☺
    b. ☺
    c. ☹

3. Everyone's contribution to the achievement of a common team goal is important.
    a. true   ☺
    b. false   ☹
    c. don't know ☺

INTRODUCTION (5 MINUTES)
Setup and Description
1. Divide children into pairs.
2. Ask them to try the following:
    - While they are holding their hands, seated, and facing each other, try to stand up simultaneously (stand up together).

- While they are holding each other by their elbows, seated, and back to back, try to stand up simultaneously (stand up together).

3. Ask the children to change partners.

Points of Emphasis
- Emphasise that the children have to work together in their pairs and cooperate in order to achieve their goals.
- Reward the children for their successful attempts.

Variation Divide the children into groups of three and try the same.

MAIN LESSON: CATERPILLAR, TRAVELLING BALL, GUESS THE CHANGE, AND PANTOMIME ACTIVITIES (32 MINUTES)

Caterpillar (8 minutes)

Setup and Description Form a path on the floor (with ropes, chalk, or tape) about 10 to 15 metres long. The path has curves and four tunnels (hula hoops, plastic bars, or sticks vertically on bases or cubes in order to form some short obstacles). You can also form different paths (e.g., zigzag, or a combination with curves, zigzags, and straight paths).

1. Divide the children into two teams.
2. Each team forms a caterpillar (children line up on hands and knees and link together by holding onto the ankles of the child in front of them). The goal for each team is to have a slithery excursion across the prescribed path as a caterpillar, cooperatively and without breaking the connection (without separating hands from ankles).

Points of Emphasis
- Point out that everyone contributes to the common goal and the success of the team.
- Reward the teamwork.

Variations
- Use other equipment to form the paths.
- Divide the children into smaller teams (three or four children per team).

Travelling Ball (5 minutes)

Setup and Description
1. Divide the children into two teams. Each team forms a line (one child behind the other and close together).
2. The first player of each team holds a ball. The ball must travel backwards above the heads of the children until it reaches the last child of the line. Then it returns forwards through the spread legs of the children until it reaches the first child.

Points of Emphasis
- Ask the children to pass the ball quickly but carefully.
- Encourage each one personally.
- Point out that they have to pay attention to their performance to achieve their team's goal.
- Reward the teams for their success.

Variations
- Form more teams.
- Have the children perform the activity within a certain time (e.g., 40 seconds), or have the teams compete against each other.
- Roll the ball or ask for different ways of passing.

> *continued*

Guess the Change (7 minutes)

Setup and Description

1. Divide the children into two teams and have them face each other.

2. Each team has a player in front who represents the statue. The statue of the first team takes a position.

3. After observing the other team's statue for a few seconds, the children of the second team turn away for 10 seconds and the statue of the first team changes positions (only one body part each time, such as an arm).

4. The second team faces the first team again and tries to guess the change that the statue made. Each team has three chances to find the change.

Points of Emphasis

- Encourage the teams to carefully observe the position of the opposite statue, and to announce their decision after consideration and cooperation.
- Reward the children for their cooperation.

Variations

- Each time have a different child be the statue.
- Ask two or three children to represent the statues simultaneously.

Pantomime (12 minutes)

Setup and Description

1. Divide the children into four teams. Each team goes to a corner of the class and secretly takes a phrase from you that represents one of the four seasons (e.g., "Someone wears coat, hat, scarf, and gloves, and plays in the snow", or "Someone holds an umbrella and plays in the puddles in the street", or "Someone places an umbrella in the sand for protection against the sun, lays out a towel, puts on tanning oil, and wears sunglasses.").

2. Each team takes a turn acting out the phrase, and the goal of each team is to make the other teams understand the season with representative movements, clothing, and props.

3. Children in each team change roles (represent different movements each time). Give enough time for teams to represent their subject.

Points of Emphasis

- Help children if they have difficulty with their pantomimes.
- Reward the teams for their representative pantomimes.

Variation   Have one child from each team represent the phrase, or assign separate roles for each team member.

CONCLUSION (7 MINUTES)

Art Activity

Setup and Description

1. Keep the children in the same teams of the previous activity. Each team has to represent a season on cardboard using colourful markers and other art materials.

2. After the artworks are finished, hang them on the walls of the classroom.

Points of Emphasis

- Encourage each child to draw or paint something that is relevant to the season assigned.
- Reward all teams for their teamwork.

Lesson 20

Appreciate Own Work and That of Others
STANDARD 1, GOAL 2

OBJECTIVES
At the end of the lesson, children will be able to

- coordinate within teams,
- show improved cooperation skills,
- show improved motor skills,
- suggest their ideas,
- accept and work with others' ideas, and
- work together and cooperate to achieve a common goal.

EQUIPMENT
- 4 to 6 balloons
- 1 piece of fabric (1 m by 1 m) for each team
- 2 to 4 hula hoops
- 3 elastic bands (each 2 m long)

EVALUATION
Give each child a sheet of paper that only contains the answers (e.g., 1. a, b, c; 2. a, b, c). After you slowly read each question and the possible answers, ask the children to circle the appropriate answer or the face that they feel.

1. I have opportunities to express my ideas to my teammates.
    a. true ☺
    b. false ☹
    c. don't know ☺

2. Sometimes, a teammate's ideas are better than mine.
    a. true ☺
    b. false ☹
    c. don't know ☺

3. When my teammates appreciate and accept my ideas, I feel
    a. true ☺
    b. false ☹
    c. don't know ☺

INTRODUCTION (7 MINUTES)
Setup and Description
1. Divide the children into two teams.
2. Ask each team to create a flower with their bodies. Hold a hula hoop, and when you start to raise the hoop, it means that the sun rises and the flowers have to bloom. When the sun goes down, the flowers have to fold.
3. Allow enough time for children to think of and create their flowers.

Points of Emphasis
- Help and reinforce the children when needed.
- Reward the teams for their good ideas and their creations.

Variation   Use other equipment (e.g., ribbons, ropes, scarves, fabric).

> continued

MAIN LESSON: BALLOONS ON THE AIR, THE TURTLE, FORM A SHAPE, AND JUGGLERS ACTIVITIES (26 MINUTES)

Balloons on the Air (8 minutes)

Setup and Description

1. Divide the children into teams of four and five.
2. Play music and give a balloon to each team.
3. At the beginning, have teams move one at a time through the space without dropping the balloon (continuously bouncing the balloon and trying to keep it in the air). Players can't hit the balloon twice in a row, and each player is allowed to hit the balloon one time. The winning team is the one that drops the balloon the least. After playing the game a few times and if there is enough space, have teams to play the game simultaneously.

Points of Emphasis

- Give appropriate instructions to help teams have effective hits and keep the balloon in the air (e.g., hit the balloon not too soft or strong, try to keep it in the centre of the team, and so on).
- Point out that all the players perform for their team and for a common goal—the victory of their team.

Variations

- Have the two teams simultaneously perform at their own marked places in the space.
- Each team has more than one balloon.

The Turtle (7 minutes)

Setup and Description

1. Divide children into groups of three.
2. Each trio represents a turtle and has to move like one. Cover each turtle with a piece of fabric and ask the turtles to move from the one side of the class to the other without losing their house (piece of fabric).
3. Let the children make any formation they want under the fabric (i.e., who is going to be the guide in front and who is going to be at the sides).

Points of Emphasis

- Emphasise that they have to move slowly, carefully, and in coordination so that they don't lose their house.
- Point out and reward the groups that perform well and finish successfully.

Variations

- Have more than one team move simultaneously.
- Use equipment to represent obstacles on the road.

Form a Shape (5 minutes)

Setup and Description

1. Divide the children into three teams.
2. Take 2-metre elastic bands and tie the ends together, forming a ring. Each team gets its own ring.
3. Have each team hold the ring stretched out. Play some music and let the children dance outside the ring while holding it.
4. When the music stops, ask the children to form a shape (e.g., square, triangle, circle). Give enough time for teams to form the shapes.

Points of Emphasis

- Help the teams if needed.
- Reward the teams for their creations and their successful performances.

Variations

- Shapes can be formed at high, medium, or low levels.
- Use ribbons instead of elastic bands.

Jugglers (6 minutes)

Setup and Description

1. Divide the children into teams of four or five.
2. One child from each team holds a hula hoop vertically at waist height, holding it away from her body.
3. Each time, the leader of the team (a different leader each time) passes through the hula hoop in any way he chooses. The rest of the teammates then try to pass through the hoop in the same way (e.g., hands first, legs first, backwards, sideways).

Points of Emphasis

- Reward the leader for finding different ways to pass through the hula hoop.
- Reward each child for passing through the hula hoop in the same way as the leader.

Variation Use other equipment (e.g., ropes, bench, table).

CONCLUSION (7 MINUTES)

Make Shapes With a Partner

Setup and Description

1. Play music and have the children dance freely throughout the space.
2. When the music stops, ask the children to find a partner and form a shape or object together (e.g., small boat, cross, bridge, roof, cave).

Point of Emphasis Point out and reward as many pairs or teams as you can.

Variations

- Ask the children to form an object or a shape in groups of three.
- Ask pairs to connect with other pairs to form a bigger shape or object.
- Have the children suggest an object or shape.

Lesson 21

Help Others
STANDARD 1, GOAL 3

OBJECTIVES
At the end of the lesson, children will be able to

- show improved motor abilities,
- have a sense of a cooperative help towards others,
- show team spirit,
- show improved cooperation,
- recognise the basic meaning of the expression "All for one", and
- cooperate to reach a common goal—to help one person.

EQUIPMENT
- 1 object for hiding (e.g., eraser)
- 1 percussion instrument per child
- 1 handkerchief or ribbon

EVALUATION
Give each child a sheet of paper that only contains the answers (e.g., 1. a, b, c; 2. a, b, c). After you slowly read each question and the possible answers, ask the children to circle the appropriate answer or the face that they feel.

1. When I participate in teamwork, I have to be
   a. independent
   b. selfish
   c. cooperative
2. When I take the responsibility to help a person, I have to be
   a. careless
   b. reliable
   c. inconsiderate
3. When I cooperate with other people to benefit another person, I feel
   a. ☺
   b. 😐
   c. ☹

INTRODUCTION (7 MINUTES)

Hidden Treasure
Setup and Description
1. Have the children sit on the floor.
2. Have one child leave the class. The other children have to decide where they will hide an object (e.g., eraser). The object must be hidden somewhere in the space where the child can easily find it (behind, under, or on another object).
3. The child comes back and searches for the hidden object. While the child searches, the other children clap their hands at different rates (tempos) to indicate how close the seeker is to the hidden treasure—the closer the child is to the treasure, the faster the other children clap. Children may use percussion instruments instead of clapping.

Points of Emphasis
- Advise the children to hide the object in unlikely places but to be honest and reliable while helping the seeker.

- Positive information will help the seeker discover the treasure more quickly. This fact reflects the common goal and the main objective of the class.

MAIN LESSON: SHIP AND LIGHTHOUSE, CAT AND MOUSE, AND PANTOMIME ACTIVITIES (30 MINUTES)

Ship and Lighthouse (10 minutes)

Setup and Description

1. Blindfold one child with the handkerchief or ribbon and have the child walk from one side of the class to the other. The child represents a ship trying to enter a foggy harbour and arrive safely (to the other side of the room).
2. The other children represent lighthouses. They are spread throughout the class and transmit a repeated sound at different volumes. Low volume means the lighthouse is far away from the harbour and high volume means the opposite. In this way the ship is being helped by the signals of the other lighthouses to safely arrive to the harbour.

Points of Emphasis

- Help the effectiveness of the game (if needed) by setting the pace of the lighthouses, especially the one that is closest to the harbour.
- Explain to the children that to effectively help the ship, they have to be very careful and reliable with the pace of the sound they make.

Variations

- Change the location of the harbour.
- Have different children play the role of the ship.
- Allow children to volunteer to play the role of the ship (some children don't like being blindfolded).

Cat and Mouse (10 minutes)

Setup and Description

1. Have the children form a nest by standing close to each other in a circle holding hands. One child inside the circle represents the mouse, and one child outside the circle represents the cat.
2. At your signal, the cat tries to catch the mouse, running inside, outside, and around the nest.
3. Children help the mouse by making openings in the circle, raising their arms and letting the mouse go under. They make it difficult for the cat to catch the mouse by lowering their arms to prevent the cat from going under. Have different children play the role of the mouse and cat. Define the duration of chasing, such as by playing a fast piece of music (1 minute per round).

Points of Emphasis

- Emphasise that the nest must continuously be surveyed to effectively help the mouse.
- Point out that the common goal and success is the rescue of the mouse, and that requires the cooperative help of the nest.

Pantomime (10 minutes)

Setup and Description

1. Divide the children into groups of five or six.
2. One person from each group leaves the class (each group decides the person who is going to leave).
3. Either you or the rest of the children define the theme for the pantomime. The chosen theme must be understandable to all children and also easy for imitation of the movements, such as everyday life scenes.

> continued

4. Teams have approximately 2 minutes to choose how they want to perform the pantomime so that their teammate guesses the theme as quickly as possible.

Points of Emphasis

- Motivate all children to participate. If necessary, help them perform their pantomimes.
- Point out that their movements must be simple and understandable to help their teammate guess the theme.

CONCLUSION (5 MINUTES)

Setup and Description

1. Have children sit on the floor in a circle.
2. Choose one child to go away for few minutes and have the other children think of an object or thing (e.g., an animal).
3. The child returns and asks questions about the object or thing that the rest of the group chose. The answers must be one word (e.g., yes or no). The other children have to answer the questions. Give some sample questions (e.g., Does this animal live on land? Does it have horns?).

Points of Emphasis

- Ask the children to be honest when they give instructions or answer the questions.
- Encourage the searcher to keep asking questions.

Lesson 22

Help Others
STANDARD 1, GOAL 3

OBJECTIVES

At the end of the lesson, children will be able to

- show improved motor abilities,
- accept and respect other children while exercising,
- understand the meaning of *offering* and *solidarity,* and
- recognise that they have to offer help to less capable people.

EQUIPMENT

- Enough handkerchiefs or ribbons for half the class
- 5 or 6 small pillows
- 5 or 6 chairs
- 5 or 6 schoolbags
- Slow music

EVALUATION

Give each child a sheet of paper that only contains the answers (e.g., 1. a, b, c; 2. a, b, c). After you slowly read each question and the possible answers, ask the children to circle the appropriate answer.

1. Everyone can face difficulties when performing a task.

    a. yes

    b. no

    c. not sure

2. I must help people who are less capable than me.

    a. yes

    b. no

    c. not sure

3. I can help a person who is less capable than me.

    a. yes

    b. no

    c. not sure

INTRODUCTION (5 MINUTES)

Blinds and Guides

Setup and Description

1. Separate the children into pairs. In each pair, one child represents a blind person (blind-folded) and the other represents the guide.
2. The guide must lead the blind person to as many locations inside the play area as possible. Create small obstacles throughout the area using chairs, small pillows, schoolbags, and so on to make the guide's mission more serious and realistic. Play some slow music with a stable rhythm to help the children concentrate and make the activity more pleasant.

Points of Emphasis

- Encourage blind children to trust their guides.
- Reward the guides for their responsibility, attention, and help.

> *continued*

MAIN LESSON: EAGLES AND SWALLOWS, PARAMEDICS, AND HEN AND CHICKS ACTIVITIES (30 MINUTES)

Eagles and Swallows (10 minutes)

Setup and Description

1. Separate the children into groups of five and ask them to form nests by holding hands in a circle.
2. One child is the eagle that watches the nests from a certain distance, and one child from each nest is the swallow. The swallows fly around the nests and enjoy the sun and the air. On your signal, the eagle tries to catch the swallows while they try to run and hide in their nests.
3. Change the children who represent the eagle and try to have as many children as possible play this role.

Points of Emphasis

- Emphasise the role of the nests. The nests must observe the movements of their swallows and help them escape from the eagle. (Nests raise their arms quickly when the swallows come closer and want to come in, and they lower their arms immediately to close the openings for eagle.)
- Emphasise that the nests have to try to rescue all the swallows.

Variation Flying can be accompanied by appropriate music, such as "Spring" from Vivaldi's *Four Seasons*. When the music stops, that means the eagle is coming.

Paramedics (10 minutes)

Setup and Description

1. Divide the children into groups of three and place them at one side of the room.
2. One child from each group represents an injured person and the other two children are the paramedics. The paramedics help transport the injured person to the hospital (the other side of the room). For example, the paramedics can link arms and support the injured person while walking.
3. Ask the children to change roles.

Points of Emphasis

- The paramedics have to pay attention to the transportation of the injured person.
- Reward the paramedics for their responsibility, effectiveness, and help. Also, reward the most creative methods of transportation.

Hen and Chicks (10 minutes)

Setup and Description

1. Divide the children into groups of five.
2. One child from each group is the hen, three are the chicks, and one is the fox. The chicks grab the waist of the child in front of them and form a line with the hen in the lead. The fox tries to catch the last chick, which is being protected by its hen and the other chicks with appropriate maneuvers.
3. Ask the children to change roles.

Points of Emphasis

- Explain that the role of chicks and hen is to cooperate to put themselves between the fox and the last chick and thus help the last chick escape from the fox.
- Emphasise the importance of cooperation and synchronisation to help the less capable person (last chick).
- Point out that the common goal of each team is to rescue the last chick.

CONCLUSION (5 MINUTES)

Setup and Description

1. Gather the children in the centre of the space and ask them to sit on the floor.
2. Discuss cases where it is necessary to intervene and help the less capable, either humans or animals. Refer to particular cases with specific examples of intervention and help.

Lesson 23

Help Others
STANDARD 1, GOAL 3

OBJECTIVES

At the end of the lesson, children will be able to

- show improved motor abilities,
- think in order to help others,
- volunteer to benefit others, and
- undertake risks to help others.

EQUIPMENT

- 1 long, wooden bench
- 1 long rope (10-15 m) or a few smaller ropes
- 5 or 6 hula hoops
- 5 or 6 chairs

EVALUATION

Give each child a sheet of paper that only contains the answers (e.g., 1. a, b, c; 2. a, b, c). After you slowly read each question and the possible answers, ask the children to circle the appropriate answer or the face that they feel.

1. When my team and I want to achieve a common goal, we have to
    a. help each other
    b. compete with each other
    c. work each one by ourselves

2. Sometimes I have to undertake risks to help other people.
    a. true   ☺
    b. false   ☹
    c. don't know   ☺

3. When I undertake risks to help other people, I feel
    a. ☺
    b. ☺
    c. ☹

INTRODUCTION (6 MINUTES)

Setup and Description

1. Have six children stand inside a formed circle (approximately 2 m in diameter). These children represent prisoners.
2. Outside the circle, two children are the guards and have to continuously move around the circle to prevent the rest of the class, who are the liberators, from freeing the prisoners.
3. Ask the prisoners to place themselves close to the edges of the circle with extended arms, waiting for the liberators to touch them in order to free them. If liberators are tagged by the guards, then they become prisoners. After each round, count the prisoners that the guards kept in the prison.
3. Ask the children to change roles after awhile.

Points of Emphasis

- Encourage the children to undertake risks.
- Help the children find strategies to solve problems and find ways to liberate their friends.

Variation Give each liberator a ball. Each liberator tosses a light ball or beanbag to the prisoners. If a prisoner catches it without the ball bouncing or falling to the floor, the prisoner is freed.

MAIN LESSON: LIFE BELT, MOUNTAINEERS, AND FREEDOM ACTIVITIES (30 MINUTES)

Life Belt (10 minutes)

Setup and Description

1. Divide the children into pairs and place them in a circle. Pairs have to be a little apart from each other. Children in each pair are close to each other and are linked together using their elbows (bent arms), while their free hand holds their own waist.

2. Two children outside the circle represent the hunter and the runner. The hunter tries to catch the runner. Whenever the runner is in danger or getting tired, he or she can link to the free arm of a child standing in one of the pairs (life belt). The link between the original pair is now broken, creating a new runner.

3. Each child has to play the role of hunter and runner. If an arrest doesn't take place after a minute, change the hunter.

Points of Emphasis

- At the beginning, have a discussion with the children about how they should offer their help to the child on the run.
- Encourage the pairs to call to the child on the run and offer their life belt.

Mountaineers (10 minutes)

Setup and Description Use a long rope (10-15 m) or a few smaller ropes to make a spiral or curved trail. Put small obstacles such as chairs, hula hoops, and so on along the trail to represent rocks, bridges, and caves that the children must pass.

1. Ask the children to form teams of five, holding hands in lines. Tell them that they have to help each other in order to travel the path and pass the obstacles without letting go of their hands.

2. When a team arrives at the destination, the next team begins. If a team unfastens hands, then it has to begin again from the start.

Points of Emphasis

- Point out the meaning of cooperation and mutual help so that the teams might succeed in their goals.
- Repeat that each team must cooperate in every moment.

Variation Create a harder or easier trail depending on the abilities of the children.

Freedom (10 minutes)

Setup and Description Clear the area of obstacles so that the children can run safely without danger.

1. One child is the hunter and chases the other children.

2. Children who are caught by the hunter have to stop immediately and sit still, curling their bodies into a ball. The other children can try to free the child by shouting "Freedom!" and passing a leg over the child. The aim of the hunter is to catch as many children as possible.

3. After 1 to 2 minutes, a different child becomes the hunter.

Points of Emphasis

- Encourage and reward the children who undertake risks to free a child who is caught.
- Help the children find strategies to solve problems and find ways to free their friends.
- Point out the enjoyment of offering help.

CONCLUSION (5 MINUTES)

Setup and Description Have the children sit in a circle and discuss the meaning of offering help. Refer to cases where someone has to pay attention in order to help the person who needs it (e.g., car accidents, mountaineering).

Lesson 24

Help Others
STANDARD 1, GOAL 3

OBJECTIVES
At the end of the lesson, children will be able to
- show improved motor abilities,
- offer specialised help,
- show team spirit and cooperation,
- take the responsibility to provide specialised help, and
- cooperate and help, working together for the success of the team.

EQUIPMENT
- 1 long, wooden bench
- Cubes for supports
- 4 to 6 gymnastic mats

EVALUATION
Give each child a sheet of paper that only contains the answers (e.g., 1. a, b, c; 2. a, b, c). After you slowly read each question and the possible answers, ask the children to circle the appropriate answer or the face that they feel.

1. If I know something better than the others and I feel sure, I have to
   a. keep it to myself
   b. offer my help
   c. make them feel stupid
2. When I offer my help to the others, I have to make them feel
   a. secure
   b. insecure
   c. unstable
3. When I cooperate with my team to achieve a common goal, I feel
   a. ☺
   b. ☺
   c. ☹

INTRODUCTION (7 MINUTES)

Setup and Description   Place a long, wooden bench about 2 metres long and 15 to 20 centimetres wide in the room.

1. Divide the children into pairs.
2. One child from each pair represents the acrobat and tries to walk on the bench. The other child from each pair is the assistant and helps by gently holding the acrobat's hand and supporting the acrobat whenever necessary (e.g., when losing balance).

Points of Emphasis
- Point out that the assistant has to be there to give a sense of security.
- Let children walk on the bench without help whenever they feel secure.

Variations
- Change the dimensions of the bench depending on the abilities of the class.
- Use more than one bench so that more children can practise at the same time.

MAIN LESSON: ROCKING AND STANDING, CANDLE, AND SOMERSAULT ACTIVITIES (32 MINUTES)

Rocking and Standing (10 minutes)

Setup and Description

1. Divide the children into groups of three.

2. One child from each team is the trainee and is sitting down, curled up into a ball (with legs bent and knees close to his jaw, hands embracing his legs). The other two children of each team stand on opposite sides of the trainee.

3. The trainee rolls backwards onto the back of his neck (like a barrel) and then forwards again, using the momentum to try to stand up. The moment his feet touch the ground, he extends his hands out to the sides so the assistants can support him as he stands up.

4. When the trainee stands up, he must stay still for few seconds with arms extended out to the sides.

5. Before the performance, the children try to roll in different ways (movements like a barrel) in order to familiarise themselves with the movement.

6. Ask the children to change roles.

Points of Emphasis

- Point out that the assistants must intervene at the appropriate moment to help their trainee.
- Reward groups for their cooperation and synchronization when they result in a perfect performance.

Variation When children are familiar enough with the movement, have many groups do the exercise simultaneously.

Candle (12 minutes)

Setup and Description

1. Divide the children into groups of three.

2. One child from each team represents the trainee and is sitting down curled up into a ball (with legs bent and knees close to her jaw, hands embracing her legs). The other two children of each team stand on opposite sides of the trainee.

3. The trainee rolls backwards onto the back of her neck (like a barrel). When she is supported on her neck, she tries to lift her legs vertically while supporting her waist with her hands from behind. The assistants help the trainee by holding her legs and bringing them as vertical as they can in the candle position. The back of the trainee's neck must touch the gymnastic mat and her hands must support her waist. The torso must be straight in a vertical position.

4. Before the performance, all children try to do the exercise by themselves.

5. Ask the children to change roles.

Points of Emphasis

- Advise the assistants to hold the trainee for few seconds in the candle position (e.g., count to 5) and then easily lower the legs.
- Reward the assistants for their careful and responsible performance.
- Reward the groups that had an effective performance (correct candle position).

Variation When the children are familiar enough with the movement, have many groups do the exercise simultaneously.

Somersault (10 minutes)

Setup and Description Set up the gymnastic mats with a small incline of 30°, with the highest point at the beginning.

> continued

1. Divide the children into groups of three.
2. The general instructions for the trainee and the assistants are the same as the previous exercises. The trainee puts his hands in front of him flat on the mat and his head between his hands and then gently pushes his feet to do the somersault. The assistants kneel and help the trainee put his head inside his hands and also support him so that he does not fall to the right or left.
3. Stay close to the performing group and help out and give the appropriate instructions.
4. Ask the children to change roles.

Points of Emphasis

- Emphasise the difficulty of this exercise. Point out to the assistants that they must be very careful and responsible.
- Reward the assistants who provide appropriate help to the trainee, who will perform the exercise with security.

CONCLUSION (5 MINUTES)

Setup and Description   Have the children sit on the floor in a circle and discuss the following topics:

- What is security?
- When should security and help be provided?
- When we can provide them?
- If you don't know how to do something, is right to ask for help?
- Are there some cases where we have to know how to give specialised help (we have to know exactly what to do)?
- When is it easier to learn something difficult—alone or with others' help?
- What does it mean to feel secure?

Points of Emphasis

- Emphasise the meaning of specialised help (knowing something well and knowing how to help).
- Point out the value of teamwork (working together and helping each other in order to achieve something).

Chapter 7

Healthy Behaviour Lesson Plans

Reprinted in part from E. Zachopoulou, N. Tsangaridou, J. Liukkonen, I. Pickup, P. Innila, E. Konstantinidou, A.M. Pontinen, A. Saarikangas, E. Trevlas and P. Valkama, 2007, Early Steps Physical Education Curriculum (ESPEC) — Lesson plans. In *Early Steps: Promoting healthy lifestyle and social interaction through physical education activities during preschool years* (Thessaloniki, Greece: Xristodoulidi Publications), 47-143. Early Steps project funded by a grant from the European Commission Socrates Programme, Comenius 2.1 Action, Project number: 118192-CP-1-GR-COMENIUS-C21.

Lesson 25

Travel in Many Ways Showing Variations in Direction, Level, and Speed
STANDARD 2, GOAL 1

OBJECTIVES
At the end of the lesson, children will be able to
- regulate movement speed,
- develop reaction skills, and
- adapt their movement according to the space and other children.

EQUIPMENT
- Plastic cones for each student
- Hula hoops for each student
- Parachute or a piece of fabric
- Music player and music
- Chalk
- Marking tape
- 1 hat representing a hawk, made by the teacher

EVALUATION
Tell the children to circle the face according to the way they feel. Then ask the following: Which way of moving is easiest to get into the nest?

1. Changing direction
   a. ☺
   b. ☹
   c. ☹

2. Running fast
   a. ☺
   b. ☹
   c. ☹

3. Viewing which nest is empty before starting to move
   a. ☺
   b. ☹
   c. ☹

INTRODUCTION (10 MINUTES)

Setup and Description   Place the parachute on the floor before the lesson starts. Teach the children how to use the parachute.

1. Have the children grip the sides of the parachute and start moving it up and down.
2. Name two children to change places by moving under the parachute.

Point of Emphasis   Make sure the children don't take their hands off the parachute without your permission.

MAIN LESSON: BIRDS AND HAWK AND CATCHING ACTIVITIES (30 MINUTES)

Birds and Hawk (20 minutes)

Setup and Description   All the children must have their own nests. All nests are spread around the space. If outdoors, draw the nests in the sand or on asphalt with chalk. If indoors, mark the nests with cones or hoops fixed on the floor with tape.

1. At the beginning, ask children to stand inside the nests (one per child). Tell them to pretend they are birds.
2. Name one child to be the hawk, who has to stand in the middle of the room.
3. The hawk calls the birds by shouting, "All birds come here!" Every bird has to move with a predetermined movement style (e.g., jumping) to find a new nest. Returning to their old nest is not allowed.
4. The hawk also starts to find a free nest. The person who is left without a new nest becomes the hawk.

Points of Emphasis
- Observe the action and help if needed.
- If the way of moving between the nests is jumping, make sure that the children perform the movement correctly.
- Encourage everyone, especially the shy ones, to participate.

Variations
- The activity can be made more difficult by changing the movement style so that one style is used several times until it is changed to another movement style and so on.
- Players can suggest their own movement styles, in which case one player will be chosen to demonstrate.
- The nests can be made of ribbons hanging from trees (or from the ceiling). The children get in the nests after they have jumped up and touched the hanging ribbons.

Catching (10 minutes)

Setup and Description   The room should have two large nests (safety areas) marked with tape, plastic cones, and so on. Place one nest at each end of the room.

1. Tell the children to stand in one of the safety areas. One of the children should stand outside of the safety areas and is the hawk inside the play area.
2. When the hawk gives a sign, all birds (children) start to fly to the nest at the other end of the room.
3. The hawk tries to catch as many birds as possible.
4. The birds that have been caught change roles and start to chase other birds together with the hawk.
5. The play goes on until there is only one bird left.

Point of Emphasis   Make sure the children catch each other in a safe way without harming each other.

CONCLUSION (5 MINUTES)

Discuss different ways of escaping the hawk and catching the birds. Ask their opinion about which ways of moving are most effective. Discuss what a hare does when escaping a fox.

Lesson 26

Travel in Many Ways Showing Variations in Direction, Level, and Speed
STANDARD 2, GOAL 1

OBJECTIVES
At the end of the lesson, children will be able to
- show improved control movements, and
- show variation in movement skills.

EQUIPMENT
- Music player
- Space music, such as Gustav Holst's *The Planets*
- Armbands for teams (two colours)
- Several triangles, squares, and circles in four colours, made of paper or cardboard big enough for children to step inside them
- 4 pictures of different planets
- 3 to 5 silver ribbons per child
- Musical instrument that sounds like a firecracker or sparkler, such as a wood block, tambourine, or maracas

EVALUATION
Tell the children to circle the face according to how they feel. Then ask the following: Which movement styles were easy or difficult for you?

1. Zigzagging
   a. ☺
   b. ☻
   c. ☹
2. Round-movement running
   a. ☺
   b. ☻
   c. ☹
3. Tiptoeing
   a. ☺
   b. ☻
   c. ☹
4. Squatting
   a. ☺
   b. ☻
   c. ☹

INTRODUCTION (10 MINUTES)

Space Travel

Setup and Description   Have the armbands, silver ribbons, and music ready before the lesson begins.

1. Discuss outer space with the children, and ask them how they think it is possible to move up there (e.g., softly, horizontally and vertically, and in different levels). Ask some of the children to show how they can move in space, giving instructions when necessary. Give all children silver ribbons. Show the children how to move in round movements and with zigzag movements.

2. The adventure starts when the children go inside their own spaceships. They build the ships around themselves with silver ribbons using their imaginations.

3. The children go to space in their imaginary spaceships when the music starts playing. On your signal, each spaceship lands on the moon.

4. Two kinds of people come out from the ships. Give the children coloured armbands: Half of the group gets red bands and the other half gets green ones. The reds move in round movements and the greens with zigzag movements. Each group moves independently. When the zigzag movers are moving, the others go to the sides of the room and squat or kneel, and vice versa.

Points of Emphasis

- Point out that they all must use their imaginations.
- Point out cooperation so that the children notice when their group has to move or wait.

MAIN LESSON (30 MINUTES)

On the Moon

Setup and Description   Place shapes on the walls, such as three triangles, three squares, and four circles. Place the shapes on opposite walls and at different places. You must have a musical instrument that sounds like a sparkler (star rain).

1. Talk with the children about space and how they can move there with, for example, smooth, round movements; with zigzag movements; and on different levels. Ask the children to demonstrate these ways to move and give them advice.

2. Ask the children to come to the middle of the room and tell them about the coming adventure. There is a danger of star rain (sparklers) in the space, and when that happens, everybody has to move towards a more secure planet or a star on the opposite wall. At this point it's time to rehearse colours and forms with children.

3. Journeying to another planet happens by running. Changing places in the room happens first according to shape, repeating this several times. After that, places can be changed according to shape and colour (e.g., yellow triangle).

4. At the end, the children can travel to any planet they want.

Points of Emphasis

- Help the children identify open spaces and pay attention to the shapes.
- Emphasise the need for concentration, especially when moving according to a given sign.

Variations

- When the star rain (sparkler) begins, the children change place by running, walking silently, jumping, leaping, and so on.
- The children can suggest and show different ways to move.
- Have the children move from one planet to another by running, walking silently, leaping, jumping, crawling, rolling, and so on. They should use their imaginations.
- If forms are still unclear to the children, concentrate on one form at a time that comes in different colours.

CONCLUSION (5 MINUTES)

- Discuss different ways of moving.
- Ask their opinion about how easy or difficult it was to react to the takeoff signs of movement.
- Give small pieces of paper to the children to evaluate the learning outcome of the lesson (see evaluation).

Lesson 27

Travel in Many Ways Showing Variations in Direction, Level, and Speed
STANDARD 2, GOAL 1

OBJECTIVES

At the end of the lesson, children will be able to

- move in different spaces in various ways,
- show improved balance skills, and
- show improved body control.

EQUIPMENT

- Several stars made of cardboard
- 1 rope per child that is strong enough for the children's weight
- 3 to 5 pinecones (or other natural items for throwing) per child
- 3 to 5 sticks (from a tree) of varying thickness per child
- Painted treasure stones or other small items
- Flags in four colours representing directions (e.g., north = blue, south = red, east = yellow, west = green)

EVALUATION

Tell the children to circle the face according to the way they feel. Then ask the following: Which way is easy when travelling along a narrow bench?

1. Walking
    a. ☺
    b. ☺
    c. ☹
2. Running
    a. ☺
    b. ☺
    c. ☹
3. Jumping
    a. ☺
    b. ☺
    c. ☹
4. Jumping with one leg
    a. ☺
    b. ☺
    c. ☹

INTRODUCTION (10 MINUTES)

Magician

Setup and Description

1. One of the children is chosen as the tagger, or magician. The magician captures children and solidifies them into different positions, such as a pineapple.
2. A fellow child can save the captured child in various ways:
    - Banana: Child goes into a bridge position. Saving her is possible by creeping under the bridge.

- Apple: Child makes a tight kink of his body on the floor. Saving him is possible by running around him.
- Pear: Child makes a crab position. Saving her is possible by creeping under him.
- Pineapple: Child makes a *T* position. Saving him is possible by running under one of his hands.

Point of Emphasis   Point out that the children must take others into account and learn to follow common rules.

Variation   Two taggers are chosen and one or two solidifying positions are given at the start.

MAIN LESSON (30 MINUTES)

Setup and Description   Organise the room before the beginning of the lesson. Fasten several stars to a tree trunk at various heights. There can be several accuracy throwing trees. Hang several stars on tree branches at various heights. Set a stick on a tree stump or a stone. Place several throwing sticks in a basket near the throwing place (throwing distance is about 1 m). The obstacles can be a pile of twigs on the ground, a small ditch, and so on. Create an obstacle that the children go under. It can be made of twigs or strings, or it can be a tunnel made from a bedsheet or other piece of fabric. In the end the children search for star treasures (painted stones) in a marked area.

1. Divide the children in pairs. Tell them to make imaginary spaceships that will start the space adventure towards the moon after your signal.
2. Lead each pair to a specific activity point and instruct the pairs as follows:
   - The children draw themselves up to the star using the rope and bench in a diagonal position.
   - Balance over the craters on the star surface (e.g., stones, tree trunks, benches).
   - Practise accuracy by throwing pinecones at the stars. The trip continues only after four successful throws.
   - Do springing jumps to the stars. The trip can continue only when at least one of the pair has succeeded in touching small stars hanging high up.
   - Knock over a stick by using another stick. The star obstacles have to be cleared, so, for example, a stick crossing another stick on the ground has to be moved with the throwing stick. Before the trip goes on, the pairs have to put the obstacle sticks back for the next space travellers.
   - Jump over a ditch or another obstacle, jumping over a row of star canyons.
   - Go under the obstacle and search for treasure stones.
3. The children go back in pairs to the spaceship. Following your sign, the spaceships travel back to earth.
4. The children climb up from the ship and come to you in a circle. Discuss the trip experiences and atmosphere.

Points of Emphasis
- Encourage the children to move together as pairs according to their mental images of varying open terrain.
- Encourage the children to take responsibility for the success of their pair's trips.
- Encourage them to work on their own initiative.
- Emphasise that partners should pay attention to each other in pair work.

CONCLUSION (5 MINUTES)
- Discuss different ways of moving.
- Ask the children's opinion about how easy or difficult the movements were.
- Give small pieces of paper to the children to evaluate the learning outcome of the lesson (see evaluation).

Lesson 28

Travel in Many Ways Showing Variations in Direction, Level, and Speed
STANDARD 2, GOAL 1

OBJECTIVES
At the end of the lesson, children will be able to
- show improved balance skills, and
- show improved body control.

EQUIPMENT
- Small flag for each student
- 4 large pictures of fruit (pineapple, pear, apple, and banana)
- 2 gymnastics benches
- Music player
- Tranquil music

EVALUATION
Tell the children to circle the face according to the way they feel. Then ask the following: Which way is easy when travelling along a narrow bench?

1. Tiptoeing
   a. ☺
   b. ☺
   c. ☹
2. Running
   a. ☺
   b. ☺
   c. ☹
3. Jumping down from the bench
   a. ☺
   b. ☺
   c. ☹
4. Hopping with one leg
   a. ☺
   b. ☺
   c. ☹
5. Creeping
   a. ☺
   b. ☺
   c. ☹

INTRODUCTION (10 MINUTES)

Setup and Description Mark a big circle on the ground and set out small flags indicating the four directions (north, south, east, and west).

1. Before the start of the game, explain the meaning of the colours and directions to the children (e.g., yellow = north). Tell the children to go inside the big direction circle. Give each one a direction flag.

2. The leader (first the teacher, then one of the children) is standing outside the circle and shouts out one direction, showing at the same time the flag indicating that direction (e.g., north). All those who have that colour of flag run to the direction mentioned and stay there.

3. The play continues until all have found their direction.

4. The leader can be changed a few times. Flags can be left away as the play becomes familiar to the children.

Points of Emphasis   Help the children understand the four directions.

Variation   The leader gives commands to the participants (e.g., everyone has to take one step or horizontal jump towards the direction mentioned).

MAIN LESSON: FRUIT PLAY AND FRUIT SALAD ACTIVITIES (30 MINUTES)

Fruit Play (20 minutes)

Setup and Description   Place pictures of the fruits (banana, apple, pear, and pineapple) on the walls of the room. Put two gymnastic benches near the picture of the pear.

1. The children stand on the bench and start the game after teacher's sign.

2. The leader gives a direction. (In the beginning, the teacher is the leader.)
   - Run to the pineapple.
   - Creep to the banana.
   - Travel to the apple on tiptoe.
   - Move with jumps to the banana.
   - Hop on one leg to the pineapple.
   - Leap to the pear and stand up on the bench.
   - Jump down from the bench and gallop to the banana.
   - Jump to the apple.
   - Leap to the pear.
   - Stand on the bench and jump down.

3. Ask the children to come up with a way to move. One by one the children take the role of leader by choosing the way of moving and the fruit.

Point of Emphasis   Ask the children to follow movement directions and control their movements.

Fruit Salad (10 minutes)

Setup and Description   The fruit pictures are still on the wall. Have some tranquil music ready to listen to at the end of the game.

1. Divide the children into four groups, one near each fruit picture.

2. Shout out the names of two fruits, and the groups have to change places with each other.

3. The play goes on until you shout "Fruit salad!" Then the children lie on the floor in a comfortable position and relax. Play tranquil music.

Point of Emphasis   Ask the children to listen to their bodies and thus learn to relax their muscles after physical activity.

CONCLUSION (5 MINUTES)

- Discuss different ways of moving.
- Ask the children's opinion about how easy or difficult the movements were.
- Give small pieces of paper to the children to evaluate the learning outcome of the lesson (see evaluation).

Lesson 29

Participate in Balancing Activities
STANDARD 2, GOAL 1

OBJECTIVES
At the end of the lesson, children will be able to

- balance better,
- control their bodies better, and
- jump and leap horizontally.

EQUIPMENT

- Red and white ribbons or hare and fox hats
- Rhythm instruments (e.g., tambours, tambour sticks, maracas)
- Music player and instrumental music
- Chairs and benches
- Big fabric sheets to cover the benches
- 3 to 5 beanbags per child
- Hula hoop
- Bear hat

EVALUATION
Tell the children to circle the face according to the way they feel. Then ask the following: If you want to develop your balance, which of the following are good for that purpose?

1. Walking
   a. ☺
   b. ☺
   c. ☹
2. Sitting
   a. ☺
   b. ☺
   c. ☹
3. Tiptoeing
   a. ☺
   b. ☺
   c. ☹
4. Jumping on one leg
   a. ☺
   b. ☺
   c. ☹
5. Leaping
   a. ☺
   b. ☺
   c. ☹
6. Walking with a beanbag on your head
   a. ☺
   b. ☺
   c. ☹

INTRODUCTION (10 MINUTES)

Fox and Hare

Setup and Description

1. Divide the children into two groups, foxes and hares. Give red ribbons to foxes and white ribbons to hares. (Alternatively, animal hats can be used.) Hares go to one end of the room and foxes to the other.

2. Give a sign for the animals to start to move in the way they are advised. They move in the space in slow tempo. Hares move with horizontal jumping, foxes with long leaps. Animals may move forwards, sideways, or backwards.

3. Foxes touch hares with one hand when they manage to come near enough. Then the hares stop and stay still.

4. When all hares have been caught, the children change roles and exchange identification marks: Hares will become foxes and vice versa.

Points of Emphasis

- Help the children move slowly in order to stay balanced after a long jump or leap.
- Help children to control their movement in the direction where they should proceed to catch a hare or to avoid getting caught by the fox.

Variations

- The hares may save each other. When the fox has been able to touch the hare, another hare may touch the frozen hare.
- Choose only three or four foxes. The foxes may have ribbons or hats as identification marks.

MAIN LESSON: ANIMAL GYMNASTICS, TUNNEL, AND BEAR IS SLEEPING ACTIVITIES (30 MINUTES)

Animal Gymnastics (10 minutes)

Setup and Description

1. Show the children pictures of animals. With the children, name the animals and decide their way of moving. By combining a rhythm instrument and the animal, children move in the predetermined way.
   - Maracas = squirrel
   - Rhythm sticks = hare
   - Tambour (slide part) = bear
   - Tambour (edge part) = fox

2. One child shows the way an animal moves and the others follow that example. For example, the hare leaps; the squirrel runs, quickly changing directions; the bear stamps its feet; and the fox walks around cunningly on tiptoe. Play instrumental music while the children are moving.

Tunnel (10 minutes)

Setup and Description   Make a tunnel using chairs and covers. Place beanbags all around the room: on rungs, on windowsills, and so on.

1. A rhythm instrument (e.g., slide part of the tambour) tells which animal travels through the tunnel (e.g., bear). The children travel in the tunnel on all fours in line as long as the instrument is played.

2. When the maracas are playing, the children find out that the squirrel does not have a track of its own. In the middle of the room there is a common nest of squirrels, where they gather one by one. Beanbags are transported on the head, back, or shoulder or between the knees. Ask the children to discover different ways of transporting the beanbags.

> continued

Point of Emphasis   Help the children combine the auditory signal with the correct animal and its way of moving.

Variation   Have the squirrels find their own place in the nest. The children transport beanbags one at a time from the common nest to their own place using various methods of transportation. In the end, count the beanbags that have been gathered in the nest.

Bear Is Sleeping (10 minutes)

Setup and Description

1. Tell the children to form one big circle. One child is a bear and wears a bear hat. This child goes to sleep in the middle of the circle

2. Children sing or rhyme the following: Bear is sleeping, bear is sleeping in its winter lair. There's no danger at all, this is how we play. Bear is sleeping, bear is sleeping—no, it doesn't sleep!

3. Children move in a circle hand in hand around the sleeping bear. When they say, "No, it doesn't sleep", the bear wakes up and starts to catch the escaping children.

4. When the bear catches someone, that child becomes the next bear.

Variation   Have the children move in various ways, such as creeping, creeping on tiptoe, running on tiptoe with dainty steps, and stamping.

CONCLUSION (5 MINUTES)

- Discuss which ways of moving the children discovered and which ways they liked most.
- Give small pieces of paper to the children to evaluate the learning outcome of the lesson (see evaluation).

Lesson 30

Participate in Balancing Activities
STANDARD 2, GOAL 1

OBJECTIVES
At the end of the lesson, children will be able to
- balance better, and
- control their bodies better.

EQUIPMENT
- 1 hula hoop per child
- Music player
- Relaxing, tranquil music
- Brisk, cheery music

EVALUATION
Tell the children to circle the face according to the way they feel
1. It was difficult to get into the hula hoop when several children tried to do that at the same time.
   a. ☺
   b. ☻
   c. ☹
2. Which ways of travelling through the hula-hoop track were easy?
   a. hopping
      - ☺
      - ☻
      - ☹
   b. leaping
      - ☺
      - ☻
      - ☹
   c. hopping on one leg
      - ☺
      - ☻
      - ☹

INTRODUCTION (10 MINUTES)

Capturing a Hula Hoop

Setup and Description   Set out as many hula hoops as the number of children minus one. Have music ready for this activity.
1. When the music is on, the children move around the space as you instruct them: walking, running, tripping, leaping, jumping, jumping on one foot, inverted walking, and walking in a squat position.
2. After awhile, stop the music. The children have to move inside a hoop as quickly as possible. One of the hula hoops has been removed, which means that two children will have to go inside one of the hula hoops.

> continued

3. As the play proceeds, remove more hula hoops one by one so that two, three, and more players will have to go inside one hoop. At the end of the game, there is only one hoop left that the children try to get in. Those who have been left out can touch the area inside the hoop with a toe or fingertip.

Point of Emphasis Ask the children to pay attention to each other.

Variation Newspapers can be used instead of hula hoops. In the end, the last newspaper can be folded in quarters and the players touch the paper with a toe or a fingertip.

MAIN LESSON: HULA-HOOP TRACK, HULA-HOOP SLIPPING TRACK, JUMP ROPE, AND RELAXATION ACTIVITIES (28 MINUTES)

Hula-Hoop Track (7 minutes)

Setup and Description Make a track from hula hoops. Also, the children can plan their own tracks to travel through.

1. The children hop from one hula hoop to another.
2. Place the hula hoops in a line or some other kind of track. The children show different ways of travelling through the track (e.g., hopping on one leg, leaping).
3. Travel through the hula-hoop track in time with a rhyme or song (for example, "Hickory Dickory Dock").

Point of Emphasis Check that the hula hoops are not too far from each other.

Hula-Hoop Slipping Track (7 minutes)

Setup and Description

1. On your signal, the children slip their hula hoops from the waist over the upper body and head and lay it down on the floor in front of them.
2. After putting the hula hoop on the floor, the children jump inside. Slipping starts again and continues until a certain distance has been travelled or until a certain amount of time has passed.

Jump Rope (8 minutes)

Setup and Description

1. Give each child a hula hoop. The children use the hula hoop as a jumping rope and jump along to a rhythm drummed by you.
2. Once the drumming stops, each child moves to another person and slips the hoop over the pair. Now there are two children together in the hoops.
3. In the next phase there will be four children together and so on. The game proceeds until as many children as possible have managed to get inside their shared hula hoops.

Relaxation (6 minutes)

Setup and Description

1. Play peaceful music as the children lie on their backs with hula hoops around their waists.
2. Visit each player and slip the hoop from waist to ankles and then back.

Point of Emphasis Advise the children to listen to their bodies to learn how to relax their muscles after physical activity.

CONCLUSION (5 MINUTES)

- Discuss various ways of travelling through the hula-hoop track.
- Ask their opinion about how easy or difficult the movements were.
- Give small pieces of paper to the children to evaluate the learning outcome of the lesson (see evaluation).

Lesson 31

Participate in Balancing Activities
STANDARD 2, GOAL 1

OBJECTIVES
At the end of the lesson, children will be able to

- balance better, and
- use stabilising movement skills.

EQUIPMENT
- Tambourine and mallet (tambourine stick)
- Benches and strings
- Kangaroo (big) ball
- Activity instructions at both ends of the balance tracks
- 1 small beanbag per child
- Music player
- Relaxing classical music

EVALUATION
Tell the children to circle the face according to the way they feel.

1. It was easy to get into the hula hoop when several children tried to do that at the same time.
    a. ☺
    b. ☺
    c. ☹

2. Which ways of travelling through the hula-hoop track were easy?
    a. hopping
        - ☺
        - ☺
        - ☹
    b. leaping
        - ☺
        - ☺
        - ☹
    c. on one leg
        - ☺
        - ☺
        - ☹

INTRODUCTION (15 MINUTES)

Crane and Frog

Setup and Description

1. Drum a tambourine and have the children hop like frogs freely in the space. Once the drumming stops, the players freeze on the spot.
2. A crane starts to travel among the frogs (teacher starts the play by being the first crane) and touches one of the frogs with the mallet (tambourine stick). The frog that has been touched hops to the side of the room and sits on the floor.
3. The last frog becomes the new crane.

> continued

Point of Emphasis   Make sure the children stop moving once they hear the signal (tambourine stops).

Variation   At the end of the lesson, give each player a beanbag. The children move like frogs in a way they like while listening to peaceful music. In the end they all lie down, putting the beanbags on their stomachs. The beanbags will thus rise and fall along with the rhythm of breathing. Collect the beanbags from children's bellies.

MAIN LESSON (25 MINUTES)

Track

Setup and Description   Set up 10 apparatus tracks starting in the middle of the room. At the end of each track place a picture that clearly shows the children what they have to do. The whole track will be travelled through three to five times. Give a sign when the children are expected to move from one track to another.

- Track 1: Walk or hop in a squatting position to stall bars, take a few steps along the stall bars upward and hanging awhile, and return along the track while moving in the same way as before.

- Track 2: Do a horizontal jump from side to side over and along a short bench, and jump with a kangaroo ball at the end of the bench.

- Track 3: Walk along a bridge or balance track, and balance for a few seconds at the end of the track on one foot and then on the other.

- Track 4: Walk along certain marks or small bricks on the floor, and X-jump (hands and legs spread at the same time) at the end of the track

- Track 5: Crab-walk with a small beanbag on the stomach, and stand up and perform tricks with the beanbag at the end of the track (i.e., travelling the bag around the body and under the feet, throwing it from one hand to another).

- Track 6: Walk below and jump over strings and benches, and squat six times at the end of the track.

- Track 7: Jump on one foot along a zigzag track made of cones, and lie prone and lift the upper body at the end of the track.

- Track 8: Balance-walk along a long rope while moving pea-bags from one side to the other side of the rope, and stretch up and to the side while holding a pea-bag at the end of the track.

- Track 9: Jump vertically with legs together from one to the other side of a long rope; reach hands towards the toes at the end of the track.

- Track 10: Lie prone on a bench and pull body along the bench using arms. Reach the floor with upper body and touch the floor with nose (hands may touch the floor) at the end of the bench.

Points of Emphasis

- Help the children act according to pictorial instructions.
- Help the children vary their jumping techniques and balancing activities according to what they are asked to do at different points of the apparatus track.

Variations

- Put different-coloured or different-shaped tags (e.g., alphabets, numbers) at the end of each track. After passing a track, the child will bring the tag to a specified place. A certain number of tags can be set as the task to be collected by each child and in this way the number of performing tracks can be controlled.

- The children travel through the tracks without performing the tasks at the ends of the tracks.

- A lesson task can be executed in pairs (five tracks per task): The children go in pairs so that one of the pair waits at the end of the track for the other, who performs the track first.

CONCLUSION (5 MINUTES)

- Discuss the various ways of moving in the tracks.
- Ask the children which movements they liked and which were easiest or most difficult.
- Give small pieces of paper to the children to evaluate the learning outcome of the lesson (see evaluation).

Lesson 32

Participate in Balancing Activities
STANDARD 2, GOAL 1

OBJECTIVES

At the end of the lesson, children will be able to

- balance better, and
- move in various ways.

EQUIPMENT

- Cone poles or other marking poles
- 2 to 5 skipping ropes
- Sticks made of newspaper
- Empty juice and milk cartons
- Pictures of various travelling styles
- Marks (e.g., tags, ribbons, or pieces of material) to be fitted or stuck on the children's left legs

EVALUATION

Show the (unmarked) right leg and ask the children to make a jump trial to rehearse the motion. Repeat the procedure with marked (left) leg. Then tell the children to circle the face according to the way they feel.

1. It is easy to jump with the unmarked (right) leg.

    a. ☺

    b. ☺

    c. ☹

2. It is easy to jump with the marked (left) leg.

    a. ☺

    b. ☺

    c. ☹

INTRODUCTION (10 MINUTES)

Wonder Person

Setup and Description   Mark the play area with lines or tapes that the players have to cross when the Wonder Person shouts. Determine the ways in which the children have to move across the space, such as jumping with both legs, leaping, jumping with one leg, or something the players come up with themselves.

1. One of the children stays in the middle of the room, pretending to be the catcher (Wonder Person) and the others stand in a row behind a line at the other end of the room.
2. When the Wonder Person shouts "Who's afraid of Wonder Person?", the players try to reach the line at the opposite end of the room without being tagged by the Wonder Person. If the children get caught, they become assistants of the Wonder Person.
3. The game ends when there is only one child left to catch. This child becomes the new Wonder Person.

Point of Emphasis   When the children are jumping, instruct them to focus on pushing against the floor with force for taking off (beginning part of jump) and touching down carefully and softly while they bend their knees (when they land).

Variations

- Designate more than one Wonder Person in the beginning.
- Ask the children to suggest ways of travelling.

MAIN LESSON: JUMPING TRACK AND MOUSE TAIL ACTIVITIES (30 MINUTES)

Jumping Track (25 minutes)

Setup and Description   Build the track indoors or outdoors. You can make the equipment in imaginative ways. For example, fill juice or milk cartons with water or sand. Make sticks of rolled newspapers, and put up hurdles by installing the sticks on top of two posts (filled cartons). The best posts are bailed juice cans (cans with a handle). Post pictures of the ways of travelling near the checkpoints to direct movement to the next checkpoint. Repeat the jumping track at least twice.

1. From checkpoint 1 to 2: X-jumping
2. From checkpoint 2 to 3: Jumping with both legs together (long jump without speeding)
3. From checkpoint 3 to 4: Moving forwards by vertical jumping
4. From checkpoint 4 to 5: Galloping
5. From checkpoint 5 to 6: Hurdle race (five hurdles)
6. From checkpoint 6 to 7: Jumping with marked (left) leg
7. From checkpoint 7 to 8: Jumping with unmarked (right) leg
8. From checkpoint 8 to 9: Squat jumping
9. From checkpoint 9 to 10: Own style

Points of Emphasis

- Put marks on the children's left legs.
- Make sure the children travel using the correct style.

Mouse Tail (5 minutes)

Setup and Description

1. Depending on the number of children, divide them into two or more groups, with four to six children in each group.
2. Have a child in each group turn a mouse tail (rope) along the surface of the floor in a circle like the hand of a clock (the child turns many times on the same spot while holding the rope). The other children stand in a circle and try to avoid touching the rope by jumping over it.
3. The first person to hit the rope so that the rope stops is the next to turn the mouse tail.

Point of Emphasis   Ask the children to position themselves so that each of them will be close enough to the end of the rope that they will need to jump at least once.

CONCLUSION (5 MINUTES)

- Discuss the various ways of moving at the checkpoints.
- Ask the children which movements they liked and which were easiest or most difficult.
- Give small pieces of paper to the children to evaluate the learning outcome of the lesson (see evaluation).

Lesson 33

Send and Receive a Variety of Objects in Many Ways
STANDARD 2, GOAL 1

OBJECTIVES
At the end of the lesson, children will be able to
- send and receive a ball in various ways, and
- travel in various ways with a ball.

EQUIPMENT
- Soft balls and big gymnastic balls of different colours (1 per child)
- 1 shield per pair (made of expanded plastic or cardboard)
- 1 hula hoop per pair
- Music player and music
- Treasure box
- 1 giant gymnastic ball per child

EVALUATION
Tell the children to circle the face according to the way they feel.
1. It is easy to receive the ball with one hand.
   a. ☺
   b. ☺
   c. ☹
2. It is easy to receive the ball with two hands.
   a. ☺
   b. ☺
   c. ☹
3. It is easy to bounce the ball through a hula hoop to my partner.
   a. ☺
   b. ☺
   c. ☹

INTRODUCTION (10 MINUTES)
Setup and Description Take care that all equipment and music are at hand when needed.
1. Have the children form a circle in the middle of the room and tell the children the rules of the game (they are not allowed to bump each other, hit or kick the balls, the speed can't be too fast, they can carry the balls only when the music is on, and when the music stops, they should touch or stop the balls with their feet).
2. Ask a few children to show some ways of carrying, rolling, and handling a ball.
3. Give each child a big gymnastic ball and put the music on to start the activity. Ask children to travel freely with the ball throughout the space when the music is on. Repeat the same activity with a soft ball.

Point of Emphasis Instruct the children to change movement speed if needed so that moving while carrying a ball is possible. It is important for them to handle the ball whatever the speed and style of moving.

MAIN LESSON: FIND A PARTNER, BOUNCING THROUGH HULA HOOPS, SHIELD AND BALL, CARRYING BALLS WITH BODY PARTS, AND RELAXATION ACTIVITIES (30 MINUTES)

Find a Partner (5 minutes)

Setup and Description   Bring different kinds of balls.

1. Explain the rules and discuss them carefully with children. Pairs will match up only by using eye contact (speaking is not allowed). Ask two children to demonstrate.
2. Have the pairs carry or roll their ball to each other when the music is on.
3. When the music stops, the children stop their balls (using their feet) and exchange their balls with another player.

Point of Emphasis   Your role as facilitator is important so that the play proceeds regularly. Ask children to perform the activity according to the rules and not to rush.

Bouncing Through Hula Hoops (5 minutes)

Setup and Description   Bring different kinds of balls and hoops.

1. Explain the rules and discuss them carefully with the children. Ask a child to demonstrate.
2. The children form pairs and place a hoop on the floor between them. They stand on opposite sides of the hula hoop and bounce the ball to each other through the hoop. Bouncing continues until it is fluid.

Point of Emphasis   Ask children to pay attention to cooperation with partners and as members of the group.

Variation   In pairs, one child throws the ball in the air while the other holds a hoop and tries to get the ball go through it.

Shield and Ball (5 minutes)

Setup and Description   Bring shields and various balls and hoops

1. Explain the rules and discuss them carefully with the children. Ask a pair to demonstrate.
2. Each pair takes a shield and a soft ball. One partner throws a ball towards the other, who blocks the ball using the shield.
3. Change roles after awhile. Instruct the children actively if needed.

Variation   The defender stays inside the hula hoop, and the thrower stays at a distance (e.g., 3 m).

Carrying Balls With Body Parts (5 minutes)

Setup and Description   Bring different kinds of balls.

1. Explain the rules and discuss them carefully with the children. Ask a pair to demonstrate.
2. Each child takes a ball and moves with it by carrying it with a part of the body.
3. Each child has a chance to show a carrying style and others try to copy it.

Relaxation (10 minutes)

Setup and Description

1. Children choose a relaxation ball from the treasure box.
2. They lie on the floor and place the ball so that it touches a certain part of the body (for example, on the shoulder, belly, or chest). They stay still with the ball in one place, listening to beautiful music.

Point of Emphasis   Create a peaceful and relaxing atmosphere and try to create a feeling of well-being.

Variation   Relax in pairs using giant balls.

CONCLUSION (5 MINUTES)

- Discuss which ball-handling methods were easy and which were difficult.
- Ask the children's opinion about which methods they liked most.
- Give small pieces of paper to the children to evaluate the learning outcome of the lesson (see evaluation).

Lesson 34

Send and Receive a Variety of Objects in Many Ways
STANDARD 2, GOAL 1

OBJECTIVES

At the end of the lesson, children will be able to

- send and receive a ball in various ways, and
- travel in various ways with a ball.

EQUIPMENT

- 1 ball per child
- Music player and music
- Targets to rest against the wall (for example, 3 hula hoops)
- Boxes of different sizes for accuracy throwing (yellow, red, blue, and green)
- Triangles, bells, or rhythmic wooden sticks
- 1 piece of coloured paper per child (for handmade paper ball)
- A piece of fabric about 2 by 2 metres
- Armbands or other marks for the left arm or hand of each child to help them distinguish between the left and right sides

EVALUATION

Tell the children to circle the face according to the way they feel.

1. It was easy to hit targets on the wall with the ball using my marked (left) hand.

   a. ☺

   b. ☺

   c. ☹

2. It was easy to hit targets on the wall with the ball using my unmarked (right) hand.

   a. ☺

   b. ☺

   c. ☹

3. It was easy to throw balls into the boxes with my marked (left) hand.

   a. ☺

   b. ☺

   c. ☹

4. It was easy to throw balls into the boxes with my unmarked (right) hand.

   a. ☺

   b. ☺

   c. ☹

INTRODUCTION (10 MINUTES)

Setup and Description   Make sure you have coloured paper, a music player, and stimulating music nearby.

1. Have the children sit down around a piece of fabric about 2 by 2 metres. Give each child a piece of coloured paper to wrinkle into a ball.
2. Play stimulating music while the children throw their balls into the middle of the fabric.
3. When all balls are in the fabric, the children grab the fabric with both hands. Give a sign and ask the children to stand up while lifting the fabric and wave it so that the balls fly all over.
4. The children lay the fabric down together and collect the balls. Play the game several times.

Points of Emphasis
- At the beginning it's important to work together as a unit.
- Remind the children that they are not allowed to step on the fabric.
- Everybody should work in favour of the team and avoid individual competition.

Variations
The game becomes more difficult when children have to identify their own teams and colours.

1. Divide the children into four animal families, such as squirrels, bears, deer, and birds. Each family has a winter storage box of a different colour.
2. Each family has to collect as many pinecones (paper balls) as possible for the winter.
3. After throwing the paper balls in the air with the fabric, the children should collect the balls into the boxes of their colour.
4. At the end, the families count their pinecones.

MAIN LESSON: BALL SCHOOL AND RELAXATION ACTIVITIES (30 MINUTES)

Ball School (20 minutes)

Setup and Description
1. Have the children sit down in a circle.
2. At ball school, there are different stations with activities. Have two children show the others, according to your advice, what they have to do in each station. Some of the activities at the stations are carried out in pairs.
3. Divide the children into groups of four or five and show them where each group starts.
4. The stations are as follows:
   - Accuracy throwing into three hula hoops on the wall. They can be of different sizes. Ask children to aim at the centre of the hoops while throwing their balls.
   - Accuracy throwing to four boxes of different colours and sizes
   - Ask two children to hold a hoop vertically while touching the floor. The other two children of this team try to roll or push the balls through the hula hoops. After a few times, pairs in this team change roles.
   - Bouncing the balls through an obstacle track (the obstacles should be small and short for safety reasons)
   - Throwing the balls to the wall from different distances
   - Lifting the balls between their ankles when lying on their backs

Points of Emphasis
- Help children tighten the armband or put the mark on their left arms.
- Ask the children to use both hands.

Variations
- A child stands behind the boxes and announces scores by playing a triangle, bells, or wooden sticks.
- In station 3, children roll or push their balls under their partner's legs. The partner tries to stop the ball with their legs.
- In station 4, make a double line from 10 hula hoops, 5 hoops in each line, with a distance of 2 to 5 metres between the lines. Ask children to throw and catch the ball in pairs while slowly walking inside the hoops.

Relaxation (10 minutes)

Setup and Description
1. Have the children lie on their backs in a circle, with their hands next to their bodies and their eyes closed.

> continued

2. While relaxing music is playing, go around silently and rub everybody's arms and legs with a soft ball or massage ball.

Variations Half of the children form a circle lying on the floor and their partners pretend they are masseurs. In this case, the ball can be smaller, such as tennis ball or massage ball. The masseur rubs the arms and legs of someone lying on the floor while relaxing music plays. After a couple of minutes the children change roles.

CONCLUSION (5 MINUTES)

- Discuss which ball-manipulating methods were easy and which were difficult.
- Ask the children's opinion about which methods they liked most.
- Give small pieces of paper to the children to evaluate the learning outcome of the lesson (see evaluation).

Lesson 35

Send and Receive a Variety of Objects in Many Ways
STANDARD 2, GOAL 1

OBJECTIVES
At the end of the lesson, children will be able to

- move in many ways,
- adjust their movements in relation to other children, and
- use a wider variety of movement skills.

EQUIPMENT
- 5 big, soft balls
- Tape (indoors) or chalk (outdoors)
- Cones for marking
- Music player and music

EVALUATION
Ask the children to circle the face according to the way they feel.

1. It was easy to avoid getting hit by the ball without bumping into others when I was inside the circle.

    a. ☺

    b. ☺

    c. ☹

2. It was easy to roll the ball and hit other children inside the circle.

    a. ☺

    b. ☺

    c. ☹

3. It was easy to bounce the ball and hit other children inside the circle.

    a. ☺

    b. ☺

    c. ☹

4. It was easy to throw the ball and hit other children inside the circle.

    a. ☺

    b. ☺

    c. ☹

INTRODUCTION (15 MINUTES)

Setup and Description

1. Separate the children into 2 or 3 teams (4 or 5 children in each team). Ask children on each team to stand in a line, one behind the other, with their legs open to form a tunnel.
2. The first child of each line rolls the ball backward through the tunnel.
3. The last child of each line tries to catch the rolling ball and runs to the beginning of the line.
4. Children in each line should roll the ball through the tunnel at least 3 times.

Points of Emphasis

- Point out that the children should be very careful when they roll the ball in order to send it straight backward.
- Help children fix their lines when needed.
- The children should pay attention to the rolling ball.

> continued

MAIN LESSON (25 MINUTES)

Burning Ball

Setup and Description   Make a big circle on the ground using chalk or tape.

1. Explain to the children that they should not throw the ball above the height of their waists; wrong throws won't be accepted. Ask the children to show the accepted maximum height of ball throws.

2. There are three burning balls. One child holds a burning ball outside the circle and the other children inside the circle will try to escape being burned by the ball. Start the game by asking the child with the burning ball to throw, bounce, or roll the ball towards the other children. The child who is the thrower can use all three burning balls.

3. After being hit, children step outside the circle to join the first thrower and become throwers themselves, taking another burning ball (the number of throwers increases until the end of the game).

4. The play goes on with the three burning balls until one child is left inside the circle. That child becomes the first thrower in the next game.

Points of Emphasis

- Encourage children outside the circle to cooperate with each other while throwing the three burning balls at the children inside the circle.
- Enhance self-esteem by giving positive feedback to everybody.
- Ask children to pay attention and be very careful when moving all together.

Variations

- Modify the size of the circle and the ball.
- Children crawl on the floor on all fours, protecting themselves from the burning ball with their feet. Burning balls are rolled instead of thrown. Children become rollers once they are struck by a burning ball on any part of their body other than their feet.
- Inside the circle, the children stand on one leg and defend themselves from the rolling ball with the free leg.

CONCLUSION (5 MINUTES)

- Discuss which of the ball-handling methods (throwing, rolling, and bouncing) were most effective in hitting the children inside the circle and which were the least effective.
- Ask the children which kinds of skills they liked most.
- Give small pieces of paper to the children to evaluate the learning outcome of the lesson (see evaluation).

Lesson 36

Send and Receive a Variety of Objects in Many Ways
STANDARD 2, GOAL 1

OBJECTIVES

At the end of the lesson, children will be able to

- balance better, and
- demonstrate improvement when using various moving skills.

EQUIPMENT

- 2 pieces of paper (1 yellow on one side and red on the other and 1 blue on one side and green on the other)
- Wooden stick or soft object
- 1 small ball per child (made of newspaper or old socks inside a plastic bag)

EVALUATION

Ask the children to circle the face according to the way they feel. Then ask the following: Is it easy to travel along a narrow bench while

1. Squatting
   a. ☺
   b. ☺
   c. ☹
2. Tiptoeing
   a. ☺
   b. ☺
   c. ☹
3. Leaping
   a. ☺
   b. ☺
   c. ☹
4. Jumping on one leg
   a. ☺
   b. ☺
   c. ☹

INTRODUCTION (15 MINUTES)

Traffic Police

Setup and Description

1. Show two coloured pieces of paper (one yellow and red, the other green and blue) to the children. Each colour represents a different action.
   - Yellow—leaping
   - Red—one-foot jumping
   - Blue—walking on tiptoes
   - Green—walking in squatting position

   Other options: running, hopping, knee-lift walking, creeping, sliding, skipping, and so on
2. When you hold up a colour, the children have to respond with the corresponding movement.

Point of Emphasis Make sure the children pay attention to your signals, responding properly by changing their movement styles.

> continued

Variations

- Use three colours as traffic lights:
  - Red—Stop.
  - Yellow—Wait and listen to instructions for the next movement skill.
  - Green—Go.
- Change the movement skills: jumping on one foot, walking on tiptoes, crawling on all fours, jumping with open arms and legs, and so on.
- Children can perform in pairs. One child can be a leader who moves in the front and decides the movement skill while the other child follows the leader.
- Three children make up a leader team. They decide the movement skill that they want to use and show a connection style (e.g., arms around each others' waists). The other children imitate the leader team.

MAIN LESSON: TAR POT, TAIL BALL, AND SHAKING ACTIVITIES (30 MINUTES)

Tar Pot (15 minutes)

Setup and Description   Draw a big circle on the ground (diameter at least 5 m) surrounded by smaller circles for all children except one, who will be the first stick carrier. You may choose to use a soft object for safety with younger children.

1. The children stand in the smaller circles, facing the centre of the big circle. One child moves outside all circles, carrying a stick or soft object and drops it at random in another player's circle.
2. After dropping the stick, the stick carrier starts running around the circle. The child who received the stick grabs it and starts running in the opposite direction around the circle. The child who first arrives at the small empty circle stays inside the circle while the one who has been left outside continues the activity.

Point of Emphasis   Point out that once the stick or soft object has been dropped, the children should run in opposite directions.

Variations

- A handshake takes place when the two children meet each other while running.
- Play the same activity in pairs.

Ball Tail (10 minutes)

Setup and Description   Draw a long, straight line in the middle of the room. Set an equal number of balls on both sides of the line.

1. Divide the children into two teams and give each child a ball made of newspaper. The teams stand on both sides of the line.
2. The children try to throw to the other side all balls that have come to their side.
3. When the time is out, count the balls. The winner is the team with the fewest balls.

Shaking (5 minutes)

Setup and Description

1. The children gallop around the circle clockwise, changing directions at your signal.
2. They shake their left and right legs in turn. Then they bend their bodies forward, and their hands touch the ground. Finally they rise up shaking their entire bodies.
3. At the end they shake hands with each other.

CONCLUSION (5 MINUTES)

- Discuss different ways of moving.
- Ask the children how easy or difficult the movements were.
- Give small pieces of paper to the children to evaluate the learning outcome of the lesson (see evaluation).

Lesson 37

Identify Changes in Heart Rate
STANDARD 2, GOAL 2

OBJECTIVES
At the end of the lesson, children will be able to
- understand the effect of physical activity on the development of a healthy heart,
- understand the relation of physical activity and a healthy heart, and
- understand the cardiovascular system.

EQUIPMENT
- 4 to 8 ropes
- 7 to 10 pairs of ankle weights or beanbags (enough for half the class)
- 1 or 2 pictures of the cardiovascular system
- 1 or 2 stethoscopes
- 4 to 6 hula hoops
- 4 to 6 big cardboard boxes
- 2 or 3 light balls
- 2 or 3 foam couch cushions

EVALUATION
Give each child a sheet of paper that only contains the answers (e.g., 1. a, b, c; 2. a, b, c). After you slowly read each question and the possible answers, ask the children to circle the answer that they believe is correct.
1. The more exercise I get, the healthier my heart will be.
    a. true ☺
    b. false ☹
    c. don't know ☺
2. My heart rate (HR) increases when I do high-impact exercises.
    a. true ☺
    b. false ☹
    c. don't know ☺
3. When I'm motionless, my HR is
    a. high
    b. low
    c. medium

INTRODUCTION (6 MINUTES)
Setup and Description
1. Explain the cardiovascular system to the children and show them a picture. Try to describe the basic functions with simple words (the heart sends blood to the brain, muscles, and all parts of the body through veins so that the body can work properly).
2. Explain how and where they can feel their heartbeat (heart, wrist, and carotid). Ask the children to put their hands on their hearts and feel their heartbeats.

Points of Emphasis
- Explain that the heartbeat is a basic function of the human body.
- Emphasise the importance of developing and keeping a healthy, strong heart.
- Tell the children that physical activities help them keep a healthy heart.

> continued

MAIN LESSON: LISTEN TO YOUR HEART, RABBITS AND KANGAROOS, RABBITS AND TURTLES, AND TRAINING IN STATIONS ACTIVITIES (26 MINUTES)

Listen to Your Heart (6 minutes)

Setup and Description

1. Use a stethoscope to show the children how their heart beats and how they can hear it. (It's better if you have more than one stethoscope.) Ask the children to pay attention to the tempo of their heart rate (HR).

2. Help the children count their HR for 10 seconds and multiply this rate by six to get their HR per minute. Explain that this is their HR when they are calm.

3. Ask the children to run and move for a few minutes and then repeat the HR measurement. Explain that this is their HR after exercising.

4. Repeat the activity. Ask the children if they notice any difference in HR.

Point of Emphasis Emphasise that when exercising, HR increases and simultaneously the heart gains benefits.

Rabbits and Kangaroos (6 minutes)

Setup and Description

1. Divide the children into two teams (rabbits and kangaroos).

2. Ask the rabbits to jump for few minutes in a shaped alley (use ropes or tape to make the alley), while kangaroos, who are spread through the area, put on the ankle weights or hold beanbags and jump.

3. After moving, the children feel and count their HR. Ask them if they notice that kangaroos have faster HRs than rabbits.

4. Ask the teams to change roles.

Points of Emphasis

- Diversify the intensity of the activities—make sure you use activities of two intensities (i.e., low- or medium-impact exercises and high-impact exercises).

- Emphasise that extra weight causes more weariness.

- Explain why people with extra weight get tired more easily and how being overweight affects the human body.

Rabbits and Turtles (6 minutes)

Setup and Description

1. First, the children take their initial HR.

2. Separate the children into two teams (rabbits and turtles). Rabbits spread through the area bouncing, leaping, and jumping while turtles crawl slowly on the ground.

3. After moving for a few minutes, ask them to count their HR and see which team has the faster HR.

4. After finishing, ask the teams to change roles.

Point of Emphasis Emphasise the relation of exercise intensity to HR.

Variation Find other kinds of animals whose movements have noticeable differences in HR.

Training in Stations (8 minutes)

Setup and Description Divide the space into four to six stations with activities that are in sequential order from medium to high impact. Here are some possible stations: jumping inside small lakes (hula hoops), passing through cardboard boxes, jumping onto foam couches, and throwing and catching light balls.

1. Divide the children into four to six teams and have them take their HR.
2. Assign each group to a station and begin the activity clockwise.
3. Ask the children to move for 20 to 30 seconds at each station.
4. Signal them to stop and count their HR.
5. Ask them to rest for 20 to 30 seconds.
6. Repeat the same for each station. Ask them to notice the difference in their HR at each station.

Point of Emphasis Explain that the heart circulates blood through the veins according to the intensity of movement.

Variations

- Each team passes through each station.
- Change the activities of the stations.

CONCLUSION (9 MINUTES)

Setup and Description

1. Have the children sit on the floor at the centre of the room. Ask the children to think of and present everyday activities that have differences in HR.
2. Have the children count their HR with you. Ask the children if they have the same HR as you and as at the beginning of the lesson.

Point of Emphasis Emphasise that improved function of the heart is due to the combination of exercise and healthy nutrition.

Lesson 38

Identify Changes in Heart Rate
STANDARD 2, GOAL 2

OBJECTIVES
At the end of the lesson, children will be able to

- count their HR,
- identify differences between physical activities that increase or don't increase HR,
- explain physical activities that help keep their heart healthy,
- understand the importance of exercise for health and a strong heart,
- increase HR with different movements,
- stabilise low HR with different movements, and
- be creative in moving in a variety of ways.

EQUIPMENT
- 4 boxes
- Pictures of physical activities or games that don't change HR (as many pictures as children or more; these can be made by you and the children, perhaps in another class)
- Music player
- Music with fast, cheerful tempo and slow, calming tempo
- Chalkboard or other kind of board
- 10 to 12 gymnastic balls
- 10 to 12 tennis balls
- 10 to 12 foam balls

EVALUATION
Give each child a sheet of paper that only contains the answers (e.g., 1. a, b, c; 2. a, b, c). After you slowly read each question and the possible answers, ask the children to circle the answer that they believe is correct.

1. I can count my HR if I put my left thumb to
   a. the left side of my neck
   b. the left side of my knee
   c. the left side of my belly
2. A race makes your heart beat
   a. slow
   b. medium
   c. fast
3. Balancing makes your heart beat
   a. slow
   b. medium
   c. fast
4. Which of the following activities help keep my heart healthy?
   a. running
   b. sitting
   c. moving in a variety of ways
   d. watching TV

INTRODUCTION (10 MINUTES)

Setup and Description

1. Remind the children of the previous lesson about changes in HR. Emphasise the importance of being active in order to have a healthy, strong heart. Tell them that doctors recommend people exercise at least three times per week for at least 20 minutes each time.

2. Have the children brainstorm activities that increase HR and activities that don't increase HR.

3. Divide the class into two teams and place them in parallel lines on one side of the room. In each line, the children stand one behind the other. Lines have approximately 3 metres between them. Each team faces a box filled with pictures of activities that either increase or don't increase HR. On the other side of the room, place two empty boxes, one for activities that increase HR and one for activities that don't increase HR.

4. One by one the children take a picture from the box that they face, run to the opposite appropriate box, and throw it in the correct box.

Points of Emphasis

- Emphasise the importance of a healthy, strong heart and its connection with movement activities.
- Ask the children appropriate questions: Have you ever felt changes in your HR? Why do you think your HR changes? Can you name physical activities or games that increase HR?

Variation Have the children move in a variety of ways from the full boxes to the empty boxes (e.g., run, jump, turn, and crawl).

MAIN LESSON: NOTICE THE DIFFERENCE BETWEEN FAST AND MOTIONLESS; NOTICE THE DIFFERENCE AMONG FAST, MEDIUM, AND MOTIONLESS; AND BALL ACTIVITIES IN THREE PARTS ACTIVITIES (27 MINUTES)

Notice the Difference Between Fast and Motionless (7 minutes)

Setup and Description Choose a fast piece of music. Create two columns on the chalkboard, one for HRs from energetic activities and one for HRs from passive activities.

1. Separate the children into two groups (one energetic and one passive) and ask them to spread throughout the room.

2. Have the energetic group dance for a few minutes with the cheerful music while the passive group stands still while balancing.

3. After finishing the activity, write the HRs of the children in the appropriate column.

4. Repeat the activity, changing roles. After writing down all HRs, have the children find the lowest and the fastest HR for each column. Ask them to notice the differences.

Points of Emphasis

- Ask each team to play its role appropriately (fast or motionless).
- Ask the children to dance with the whole body, making vivid and fast movements and moving both legs and arms.

Variation Ask the children to dance or balance in different ways (e.g., change directions, levels of movement).

Notice the Difference Among Fast, Medium, and Motionless (7 minutes)

Setup and Description Choose two pieces of music, one fast and one slow. Make another column on the chalkboard for medium HR.

1. Ask the children to spread throughout the room and dance to fast music.

2. After they dance for a few minutes, stop the music and have them check their HRs and write them on the board in the energetic column.

> continued

3. Tell the children to dance again to the slow music.

4. After they dance for a few minutes, stop the music and have them check their HRs and write them down on the chalkboard in the medium column.

5. At the end, ask the children to find the lowest and fastest HR for each column. Ask them to notice the differences.

Points of Emphasis

- Ask the children to dance using the whole body, making vivid and fast movements or slow and soft movements.

- Ask them to suddenly and sharply change levels and directions while they are dancing fast or to do so gently and softly while they are dancing slowly.

- Tell them to pretend they are dancing in a speed dance contest or in a slow dance contest.

- Use appropriate questions: Can you move your hands while dancing? Can you change levels while dancing? Show me that you can dance using your whole body.

Variation Ask the children to dance or balance in different ways (e.g., change directions, levels of movement).

Ball Activities in Three Parts (13 minutes)

Setup and Description Draw with chalk or mark with tape a starting point on one side of the room and a finishing point on the other side.

1. Leave the three columns on the chalkboard (fast, medium, and low HR). Ask the children to name various games, sports, or physical activities that use a ball and write them in the appropriate HR column. For example, rolling the ball in pairs while sitting causes a low HR, volleyball or throwing the ball while standing in a circle causes a medium HR, and basketball causes a fast HR.

2. Discuss their opinions and solve possible questions or confusions.

3. Divide the children into two teams. Each team is half on one side of the room and half on the other. All children are one behind the other, standing behind the marked lines.

4. Organise a funny contest with a ball. Beginning with the first child of each team on one side of the room, ask them to find a funny way to carry one or more balls while they move to the opposite child of their team (other side of the room).

5. After the contest, tell them to check their pulses and ask them in which column they think this activity belongs.

6. Divide the children into pairs with approximately 2 metres between each pair.

7. Give a ball to each pair and ask the pairs to invent their own way of rolling the ball. Give some examples of rolling at the beginning. Leave them for a few minutes to roll the balls.

8. Tell them to check their HRs and ask them in which column they think this activity belongs.

Points of Emphasis

- Use appropriate questions for part 2: Can you imagine a different way to carry the ball? Show me how many balls you can carry while running. Can any other part of your body help you to carry the ball?

- Use appropriate questions for part 3: In which other ways can you roll the ball? Show me another way to roll the ball without hands. Can any other part of your body help you roll the ball?

Variations

- Ask the children to use different locomotive movements (e.g., running, jumping, or changing the level of the movement, such as on all fours or crawling).

- Use two or three balls together or a variety of balls (e.g., tennis ball, basketball, foam ball).

- Ask for a bigger space between each pair.

- Separate the children into groups of three and ask them to roll the ball to each other.

CONCLUSION (6 MINUTES)

- Have the children sit on the floor. Repeat the importance of exercising for a healthy, strong heart.
- Explain the differences in HR among different movement activities.
- Give small pieces of paper to the children to evaluate the learning outcome of the particular lesson.

Points of Emphasis

- Repeat the importance of a healthy, strong heart and its connection with movement activities.
- One last time, show the children the chalkboard with the activities and their HRs.

Lesson 39

Identify Changes in Breathing
STANDARD 2, GOAL 2

OBJECTIVES
At the end of the lesson, children will be able to

- recognise the function of breathing,
- identify changes of pace in their breathing, and
- recognise activities that affect the pace of breathing.

EQUIPMENT
- 1 sheet of paper per child
- 1 balloon per child
- Tape or chalk
- Music player and music (fast and slow)
- 2 long, thin ropes
- Painting and artistry materials for half the class

EVALUATION
Give each child a sheet of paper that only contains the answers (e.g., 1. a, b, c; 2. a, b, c). After you slowly read each question and the possible answers, ask the children to circle the answer that they believe is correct.

1. When I am motionless, my breathing is
   a. slow
   b. medium
   c. fast
2. When I start running, my breathing
   a. gets faster
   b. gets slower
   c. stays the same
3. Which of the following activities affects my breathing?
   a. running
   b. sitting
   c. moving in a variety of ways
   d. watching TV

INTRODUCTION (6 MINUTES)
Setup and Description

1. Ask the children how they blow out the candles of a birthday cake. Discuss the two functions of breathing: inhaling and exhaling.
2. Ask the children to lie down, spread throughout the room, and give them each a piece of paper. Have them place the papers on their chests and observe the papers while they breathe. Ask them what they notice and also to observe other children's papers.

Point of Emphasis Emphasise that when the children are calm, their pace of breathing is slow.

MAIN LESSON: FIVE ACTIVITIES (32 MINUTES)

Activity 1: Blow Up the Balloon (2 minutes)
Setup and Description Each child blows up a balloon and throws it as high as possible.

Activity 2: Direct Your Balloon (6 minutes)

Setup and Description   Make two circles on the floor with tape or chalk. In the centre of each circle, place a balloon.

1. Separate the children into two teams, one for each circle. Place each team outside and around the perimeter of their circle.

2. One at a time, the children enter the circle and try to move the balloon out of the circle with their breathing.

Variations

- Make more than two circles if you have plenty of space.
- Divide the children into pairs and have them pass the balloon back and forth with breathing.

Activity 3: Feel Your Breathing (8 minutes)

Setup and Description

1. Divide the children into two teams, 6 to 10 children per team.

2. One team participates in art activities (e.g., painting, collage) for a few minutes. The other team participates in high-impact activities.

3. After the children finish the activities, ask them to put their hands on their chests or in front of their mouths to feel their breathing, specifically the slow pace of breathing of the art team and the fast pace of breathing of the training team. Teams switch activities.

Point of Emphasis   Explain the difference between breathing during calm activities and high-impact activities.

Variations

- The duration of the activity depends on the intensity.
- Ask the moving team to run, jump, and dance with the whole body.

Activity 4: Breathing Facts on Paper (8 minutes)

Setup and Description   Choose two musical pieces, one slow and one fast. Tie one or two long ropes from one side of the area to the other and hang pieces of paper, one per child.

1. Play slow music for a few minutes and ask the children to move and dance slowly with the rhythm.

2. After finishing the activity, ask the children to stand in front of a piece of paper and observe the movement of paper as they breathe (slow movement).

3. Repeat the activity with the fast music. Ask the children what they observe about the paper (fast, sharp movement).

Point of Emphasis   Emphasise the relation of low- or medium-impact exercise to regular breathing and the relation of high-impact exercise to heavy, strong breathing.

Activity 5: Breathing Questions Game (8 minutes)

Setup and Description

1. Place the children in two lines facing each other. Create a line with tape or chalk on the floor between them. Each line of children must have a 3-metre distance from the centre line.

2. Ask each line a question relevant to the lesson (about breathing). If the team answers correctly, the team members take a step forwards, but if the answer is wrong, they take a step backwards. The winner is the team that first touches the centre line. Be careful, because the first team laps the other team. You must make the same number of questions for both teams.

> *continued*

Point of Emphasis

Ask the children appropriate questions about breathing: Does riding a bicycle affect breathing? How is your breathing when you watch TV? How is your breathing when you swim?

Variation

Separate the children into four teams and place one team in each corner of the class. Put an object in the centre of the class to represent the winning point.

CONCLUSION (4 MINUTES)

Explain why the pace of breathing changes when exercising (need for more oxygen and so on).

Lesson 40

Identify Changes in Breathing
STANDARD 2, GOAL 2

OBJECTIVES
At the end of the lesson, children will be able to

- recognise the function of breathing in relation with exercise,
- identify changes in HR and in breathing,
- recognise which activities affect the pace of breathing and HR, and
- understand the function of HR in relation to breathing when exercising.

EQUIPMENT
- 1 small, light ball per child
- 1 balloon per child
- Tambourine
- Long mirror
- Music player
- Music with fast, medium, and slow tempos

EVALUATION
Give each child a sheet of paper that only contains the answers (e.g., 1. a, b, c; 2. a, b, c). After you slowly read each question and the possible answers, ask the children to circle the answer that they believe is correct.

1. When I start running, the need for oxygen is
   a. more
   b. less
   c. the same
2. In which of the following activities is more oxygen needed?
   a. walking
   b. running
   c. painting
3. When your HR is fast, how is your breathing?
   a. fast
   b. slow
   c. medium

INTRODUCTION (6 MINUTES)

Setup and Description
1. Ask the children how they blow up a balloon or how they blow on their food to cool it. Discuss the two functions of breathing: inhaling and exhaling.
2. Ask the children to lie down throughout the space. Give each child a ball. Tell the children to place the balls on their chests. Ask them what they notice and also to observe the other children's balls.

Point of Emphasis Emphasise that when the children are calm, the pace of breathing is slow.

> continued

MAIN LESSON: FIVE ACTIVITIES (33 MINUTES)

Activity 1: Understanding Breathing Functions (6 minutes)

Setup and Description

1. Have the children lie on their backs throughout the space.
2. Ask them to count slowly to five while they inhale. Do the same while they exhale.
3. Repeat a few times.

Variation   Try to count to six or seven or as long as the children can inhale or exhale.

Activity 2: Blow Up the Balloon (5 minutes)

Setup and Description   The children blow up their balloons and try to blow them as high as they can. They must keep the balloons in the air with their breathing.

Activity 3: Two Feet Join Together (6 minutes)

Setup and Description

1. Divide the children into pairs and have them lie on their backs throughout the space.
2. Put a balloon between the legs of each child and have them hold it in this way while they raise and lower their legs. When they raise their legs, they inhale, and when they lower their legs, they exhale.

Activity 4: Feel Your Breathing (8 minutes)

Setup and Description

1. Divide the children into two teams.
2. With the accompaniment of a tambourine, one team runs, jumps, and dances while the other team does sit-ups on the floor. Let children exercise for a few minutes.
3. After the children finish the activities, have them hold their mouths in front of a mirror or put their hands on their chests and tell them to count their HR.
4. Ask the teams to change roles.

Point of Emphasis   Emphasise the relation of low- or medium-impact exercise to regular breathing and the relation of high-impact exercise to heavy, strong breathing.

Variations

- Separate the children into three teams that do three activities: one low impact, one medium impact, and one high impact.
- Change the elements of movements (e.g., directions, levels, movements).

Activity 5: Compare Your Breathing Paces (8 minutes)

Setup and Description

1. Divide the children into two teams.
2. Play fast music and ask one team to hop on one foot while the other balances on one foot.
3. Compare the pace of breathing and the HR of both teams.

Points of Emphasis

- Emphasise the relation of low- or medium-impact exercise to regular breathing and the relation of high-impact exercise to heavy, strong breathing.
- Ask the children appropriate questions: When your HR is fast, how is your breathing? When you are calm, how are your breathing and your HR?

Variation   Separate the children into three teams: one motionless, one doing low-impact exercise, and one doing high-impact exercise. Ask them to observe the differences in breathing and HR.

CONCLUSION (3 MINUTES)

Explain why the pace of breathing and HR change when exercising (need for more oxygen and so on). Remind the children of the relation of breathing and HR to the intensity of activities.

Lesson 41

Identify Changes in Body Temperature
STANDARD 2, GOAL 2

OBJECTIVES

At the end of the lesson, children will be able to

- understand the function of perspiration,
- understand the need to consume an adequate quantity of water,
- identify changes in body temperature when they exercise, and
- recognise which activities affect body temperature changes.

EQUIPMENT

- 1 bottle with cold water per child
- Extra clothes (a few for each child), such as coats, raincoats, sweaters, blouses, pants, and jackets
- Painting and artistry materials for half of the class
- Tambourine
- Music player
- Music with fast tempo
- Parachute or a big piece of fabric

EVALUATION

Give each child a sheet of paper that only contains the answers (e.g., 1. a, b, c; 2. a, b, c). After you slowly read each question and the possible answers, ask the children to circle the answer that they believe is correct.

1. During summer, I sweat
    a. more than in winter
    b. less than in winter
    c. the same as in winter
2. When I exercise, my body releases
    a. heat
    b. cold
    c. viruses
3. When do you sweat more?
    a. while painting
    b. while dancing
    c. while watching TV

INTRODUCTION (6 MINUTES)

Setup and Description On the previous day, ask the children to bring a bottle of water with them. The day of the lesson, put the bottles in a fridge so they are cold for the lesson. Have some extra bottles in case some kids forget to bring theirs.

1. Discuss with the children why they sweat. Ask them when they feel it and what they observe about their body temperature.
2. Give the children their chilled bottles and ask them to observe that the bottles sweat and there are drops of water on the bottles. Ask the children to observe their own bottles as well as the others' bottles.
3. Explain why this happens and how the human body functions in this way. (Bodies release heat when people exercise, and that's why they sweat.)

Point of Emphasis   Emphasise the perspiration effect in relation to the environmental temperature (i.e., during the summer, people sweat more because of the heat, so the warmer the environment, the sweatier we become).

MAIN LESSON: DRESS AND UNDRESS, WHO SWEATS MORE?, PARACHUTE 1, PARACHUTE 2, AND DANCE ACTIVITIES (36 MINUTES)

Dress and Undress (6 minutes)

Setup and Description

1. Have the children spread throughout the area and put on as many clothes as they can.

2. The children then stand or walk with the accompaniment of a tambourine. After a few minutes they notice that they are sweaty because of the heat that they produce and feel.

3. Ask them to slowly take off the extra clothes and realise how the body gradually returns to its initial temperature before the exercise. Tell them that each body has its own pace for when and how it sweats.

Point of Emphasis   Ask the children appropriate questions: Why do you think you start to sweat? When do you sweat more?

Variation   Change the movements (e.g., run, jump, dance with the whole body).

Who Sweats More? (6 minutes)

Setup and Description

1. Separate the children into two teams. One team participates in art activities (e.g., painting, collage) for a few minutes while the other team participates in high-impact activities with the accompaniment of a tambourine or music.

2. After finishing the activity, ask the children which team is sweating more and why. Also ask them why exercise changes body temperature and how. Explain that the muscles become warmer and the blood circulates faster, and that produces heat. Teams should switch roles.

Point of Emphasis

- Emphasise the relation of sedentary activities to slow breathing and no perspiration and the relation of high-impact activities to fast breathing and perspiration.

- Ask the children appropriate questions: When do you sweat more, when drawing or when exercising?

Variation   Exercise can be indoors or outdoors, with or without extra equipment (e.g., balls, hula hoops).

Parachute (16 minutes)

Setup and Description

1. The children form a circle at close intervals holding a parachute with their hands (not from the handles for safety reasons).

2. Challenge the children to lift the parachute when you count slowly to four and lower it in the same way. They have to inhale when they lift it and exhale when they lower it. Start this activity with a very slow tempo and gradually accelerate it. Ask them to observe when they start to sweat or when they start to get tired.

Points of Emphasis

- Emphasise that when people move, their body temperature increases and they start to sweat.

- Explain the difference in perspiration from low- or medium-impact exercise and high-impact exercise.

- Ask appropriate questions: Why do you think you start to sweat? When did you sweat more—with slow or fast movements?

Variations

- Exercise can be indoors or outdoors.
- Change the way the children move (e.g., walking or running in a circle).

Dance (8 minutes)

Setup and Description

1. Separate the children into two teams.
2. Play music with a fast tempo. One team must be motionless, like statues, while the other team dances for a few minutes.
3. After the children finish, ask them what they notice. Which team sweat the most?
4. Ask teams to change roles.

Point of Emphasis Emphasise the relation of low-impact activities to slow breathing and no or little perspiration and the relation of high-impact activities to fast breathing and perspiration.

Variation Exercise can be indoors or outdoors.

CONCLUSION (3 MINUTES)

1. Explain changes in body temperature, including what happens when they exercise and why they sweat (e.g., body heat, need for oxygen).
2. After the discussion, have the children drink some water.

Understand the Function of Perspiration
STANDARD 2, GOAL 2

OBJECTIVES

At the end of the lesson, children will be able to

- understand the usefulness of perspiration,
- understand the need to consume an adequate quantity of water,
- identify changes in body temperature when they exercise, and
- recognise which activities affect body temperature.

EQUIPMENT

- 6 to 10 balls (enough for half of the class)
- 1 long rope or 2 or 3 smaller ropes
- 2 music players
- Music with slow, medium, and fast tempos
- 6 to 10 blank cards (each card 30 by 30 cm)
- 6 to 10 cards that each list one sedentary activity, such as watching TV or playing computer games (each card 30 by 30 cm)
- 6 to 10 cards that each list one physical or athletic activity, such as running or dancing (each card 30 by 30 cm)
- 10 to 20 cards that each list a result of sedentary and physical activities, such as athletic body, overweight child, sweaty athletic child, increase in HR or temperature, or same HR or temperature (each card 30 by 30 cm)

*All the aforementioned cards could be made by the instructor and the children, perhaps in another class.

EVALUATION

Give each child a sheet of paper that only contains the answers (e.g., 1. a, b, c; 2. a, b, c). After you slowly read each question and the possible answers, ask the children to circle the answer that they believe is correct.

1. When I exercise, my body loses water and expels toxins.
   a. true   ☺
   b. false   ☹
   c. don't know   ☺

2. When I start exercising, my body temperature
   a. increases
   b. decreases
   c. doesn't change

3. Which of the following causes the biggest changes in body temperature?
   a. from painting to walking
   b. from painting to running
   c. from painting to watching TV

INTRODUCTION (4 MINUTES)

Setup and Description Remind the children when they sweat and why. Ask them why they sweat when they exercise and what other changes happen during physical activity in relation to perspiration (e.g., body loses water and expels toxins; explain using simple words).

Points of Emphasis

- Emphasise the relation of perspiration to loss of water and the need to drink water.
- Explain what toxins are and why the body must expel them (this happens with perspiration when they exercise).

MAIN LESSON: FOUR ACTIVITIES (31 MINUTES)

Activity 1: Different Action, Different Function 1 (7 minutes)

Setup and Description

1. Separate the children into two teams and have them spread through the area.
2. Play some music with slow and fast tempos. One team must dance slowly while the other team dances fast for a few minutes.
3. After the children finish, ask them to count their HRs and feel if they are sweaty. What did they notice? Which team sweat the most?
4. After finishing, ask teams to change roles.

Points of Emphasis

- Explain the difference in perspiration from low- or medium-impact exercise and high-impact exercise.
- Ask appropriate questions: Why do you think you start to sweat? When did you sweat more—with slow or with fast movements?
- Emphasise the relation of low-impact activities to slow breathing and no or little perspiration and the relation of high-impact activities to fast breathing and perspiration.

Variations

- Give the children athletic or other equipment (e.g., ropes, ribbons, scarves, soft balls).
- Ask the children to change the level of their movement as they dance.

Activity 2: Different Action, Different Function 2 (8 minutes)

Setup and Description

1. Divide the children into three teams and have children pair up within teams. Give a ball to each pair of one team and give one rope to the second team. Have the teams go to different corners of the room.
2. Ask the children on the first team to find many ways to roll their balls in pairs. The members of the second team jump over the low-level rope in many ways, and the members of the third team move and jump fast in many ways from one side of the room to another.
3. After the children have exercised for some minutes, ask them to count their HRs and feel if they are sweaty. Also ask them what they noticed. Which team sweat the most and why?
4. Ask teams to change roles.

Point of Emphasis Remind each team to concentrate on its role (low-impact activity, medium-impact activity, and high-impact activity).

Variations

- Give the children athletic or other equipment (e.g., ropes, ribbons, scarves, soft balls).
- Ask the children to change the level of their movement as they move.

Activity 3: Rhymes for Body Functions (8 minutes)

Setup and Description

1. Have the children form a circle, seated on the floor. Inside the circle, spread out 10 to 20 cards with sedentary and physical activities so that the activities are facedown.

> continued

2. Each child picks a card and shows it to the others. If the card has a physical activity that changes body temperature (perspiration), the child runs outside the circle and the other children sing rhythmically, "If you move and dance and run, you are healthy and it's fun." If the card has a sedentary activity, the child returns to his spot in the circle and the other children sing rhythmically, "It's no good not to move." You can create the rhymes with the children in a previous lesson and use them in this activity.

Point of Emphasis Remind the children to pay attention to the cards and help them to sing rhythmically.

Variation Change the way the children move (e.g., running, jumping, hopping, galloping, crawling).

Activity 4: Match and Remember (8 minutes)

Setup and Description Place in a line 6 to 10 cards that each list a physical activity. Mix up 6 to 10 blank cards and 6 to 10 cards that each list a result of physical activities, and place the cards on the floor away from each other.

1. Separate the children into three or four teams.

2. After the children observe the cards (blank and results) for 1 minute, turn the cards face-down.

3. A child from each team must take and show a card with a physical activity from the first line of cards and the other children on the team have to remember where a result is from the mixed-up cards (blank and results).

4. After the game finishes for one team, mix up the cards again and show them to the children of the next team. Repeat the same procedure for every team. The team that remembers and finds the most pairs of cards (physical activity with a result) wins.

Points of Emphasis

- Remind the children to observe the cards and remember where the cards with results are.
- Point out the meaning and the importance of perspiration.

Variation Play with more or fewer cards according to the age and cognitive level of children.

CONCLUSION (5 MINUTES)

1. Explain changes in body temperature. What happens when they exercise and why they sweat (e.g., increases body heat, need for more oxygen)?

2. Remind the children that when they sweat, they have to drink water because the body loses a considerable amount of water. Also, with perspiration they expel toxins that are bad for the body.

3. After the discussion, have the children drink water.

Lesson 43

Enjoy Moving in a Variety of Ways
STANDARD 2, GOAL 3

OBJECTIVES
At the end of the lesson, children will be able to

- enjoy participation in physical activities, and
- express their joy in many ways.

EQUIPMENT
- Music player
- Music with medium or fast tempo
- 1 hat per child
- 10 to 20 small bricks with animal pictures on them
- 10 to 12 hula hoops

EVALUATION
Give each child a sheet of paper that only contains the answers (e.g., 1. a, b, c; 2. a, b, c). After you slowly read each question and the possible answers, ask the children to circle the appropriate answer or the face that they feel.

1. When I exercise I feel
   a. ☺
   b. ☺
   c. ☹
2. Exercising is
   a. good for our health
   b. bad for our health
   c. neither good nor bad for our health
3. When I exercise and play games with others, I feel
   a. ☺
   b. ☺
   c. ☹

INTRODUCTION (5 MINUTES)
Setup and Description   Ask the children to narrate their morning awakening and act out all their movements and actions from that time until they come to the school. Remind them of the importance of exercising for their health.

Points of Emphasis

- Ask the children to pantomime their usual activities.
- Ask appropriate questions: Can you show me how you brush your teeth? Can you show me how you eat breakfast?

Variation   Have the children narrate and act out other everyday activities or favourite physical activities.

MAIN LESSON: FOUR ACTIVITIES (30 MINUTES)

Activity 1: Statues and Dancers (6 minutes)
Setup and Description

1. Divide the children into two teams.

> continued

2. The children of one team represent the statues and they are spread through the class. While music plays, the statues form a position and the children of the other team move and dance between the statues.

3. When the music stops, ask the active children to find a statue that they like and imitate it. Each child should imitate a different statue.

4. Ask teams to change roles.

Points of Emphasis

- Guide the children to move and dance in many ways.

- Ask the statues to stand motionless.

Variations

- Give the children athletic or other equipment (e.g., ropes, ribbons, scarves, soft balls).

- Ask the children to change the level of their movement as they dance.

Activity 2: Musical Hats (8 minutes)

Setup and Description

1. Divide the children into two circles. Each child wears a hat.

2. Play some music and have the children change their hats (one child takes the hat of another child).

Point of Emphasis   Guide the children to change hats in many ways: Can you pass your hat only with your right hand? Can you pass your hat with both hands? Show me that you can pass your hat with your left hand and take your partner's hat with your right hand. Can you pass your hat between your legs?

Variations

- Change the level at which the children stand.

- Ask the children to move or walk when they exchange hats.

Activity 3: Build an Animal Tower (8 minutes)

Setup and Description   Throughout the area, spread small, colourful bricks with animal pictures on them. It's best to have bricks of three or four animals (e.g., dog, cat, bird, mouse) in three or four colours for each animal (e.g., red brick with dog, blue brick with dog, yellow brick with dog, green brick with dog).

1. Divide the children into two teams. Create or name a special place for each team to make its tower. (It's better if the special places are in opposite corners of the room.)

2. Ask the children to find a certain brick, such as a red brick with a dog or a green brick with a mouse. After children find the brick, they put it in their team's place and make a tower of bricks. The tallest tower wins (team that finds the most bricks).

Points of Emphasis

- Repeat your instructions loudly at least twice (e.g., "Red brick with dog, red brick with dog.").

- Ask the children to observe and remember the place of each brick in order to find them quickly.

Variations

- Create more teams.

- Instead of bricks, use cardboard.

- Instead of animals, play with sports, flowers, letters, and so on.

Activity 4: Spiders (8 minutes)

Setup and Description   Within a marked area, place hula hoops on the ground.

1. A child stands inside each hula hoop. These children are the spiders. Make sure there are enough children (10-12).

2. The other children run from one side of the class to the other. The spiders try to catch the children who run, but they can't leave their webs (hula hoops). If a spider catches a child, they change roles.

Points of Emphasis

- Explain to the children that they must move fast and cleverly so that the spiders don't catch them.
- Give opportunities to all children to try both roles.

Variations

- Ask the children to change the level of their movement (e.g., on all fours, crawling).
- Change the way the children move (e.g., running, jumping, hopping, galloping, crawling).

CONCLUSION (6 MINUTES)

Ask the children to narrate a fun story that involves a game or a physical activity.

Lesson 44

Enjoy Moving in a Variety of Ways
STANDARD 2, GOAL 3

OBJECTIVES
At the end of the lesson, children will be able to

- enjoy participation in physical activities,
- express their joy in many ways when exercising, and
- enjoy their creative expression.

EQUIPMENT

- 1 chair per child or 2 to 4 long wooden benches
- Music or tambourine
- 6 to 8 ropes or masking tape or chalk
- 2 or 3 small tables
- 10 to 15 tall milk cartons hanging from strings (5 per table) or 10 to 15 tenpins or clubs
- 6 to 9 balls (2-4 per team)

EVALUATION
Give each child a sheet of paper that only contains the answers (e.g., 1. a, b, c; 2. a, b, c). After you slowly read each question and the possible answers, ask the children to circle the appropriate answer.

1. Exercising is
   a. exciting
   b. boring
   c. nothing special
2. I can exercise
   a. in many ways
   b. only with prescheduled activities
   c. only with the activities my teacher says
3. My teacher often helps me express my ideas through movement.
   a. true   ☺
   b. false   ☹
   c. don't know ☺

INTRODUCTION (5 MINUTES)
Setup and Description

1. Have the children spread out in one area of the room and sit on the floor.
2. Ask the children how many ways they can exercise. Discuss movements, dance, and sports and ask what their favourites are. Ask the children if they were athletic statues, what could their positions be?
3. Remind the children of the importance of exercising for their health.

MAIN LESSON: ROBOTS, BOWLING, TRAP ROOM, AND STATUE BALANCES ACTIVITIES (32 MINUTES)

Robots (8 minutes)

Setup and Description   Put as many chairs as children or a few long, wooden benches in two lines against a wall. In front of them, place ropes or tape to represent the aisles of a toy store.

1. The children are robots or dolls on the shelf of a toy store. When the night comes and the store is closed, they come alive. Play music that gradually fades out and becomes slow or use a tambourine in the same manner while the children dance as if they were robots or dolls, moving inside the store, on the shelves, and on the ground.

2. After a few minutes, tell them that their batteries don't last forever, so they gradually lose their power. With their remaining energy, they have to reach their positions on the shelves so that the shopkeeper doesn't know what they've been doing.

Points of Emphasis

- Emphasise the changes in tempo and intensity of movements.
- Tell the children that they can pretend to be whatever toy they like (e.g., robot, doll, ballerina, soldier, animals).
- Challenge them with questions (e.g., What will happen if you are a hard robot made of steel and you fall down?).

Variation   Make use of athletic or other equipment.

Bowling (8 minutes)

Setup and Description   Under two or three small tables, hang five large milk cartons side by side using tape and five strings of equal length. The space between the cartons should be about 5 to 10 centimetres, and the distance from the bottom of the milk cartons to the floor should be approximately 5 centimetres.

1. Explain the game of bowling. Place the children on one side of the room and divide them into two or three teams, depending on the number of tables. Have each team stand in lines, one behind the other.

2. Place a table 2 to 3 metres in front of each team.

3. One at a time, the children roll the ball in whatever way they want in order to hit the milk cartons.

Point of Emphasis

- When you have two or three teams, you can organise a simple competitive game: See which team can hit the most milk cartons. Count how many milk cartons each child hits and total the score for each team. The team that strikes the most milk cartons wins.
- Encourage and reward the children. Tell them to turn their attention to the target (milk cartons) before they roll the ball. Encourage them to roll the ball in various ways (e.g., with two hands, with one hand, between their legs).

Variation   Play on the floor with a ball and five tenpins or clubs.

Trap Room (8 minutes)

Setup and Description

1. Explain to the children that they are heroes in a computer game. To find the treasure or to save their friends, they must pass through all the trap rooms of a huge magical tower. Each room of this tower hides many traps and difficulties.

2. Place the children on one side of the room, one next to the other with small spaces between them. Give them instructions to keep the same amount of space between them while they move through the trap rooms.

3. Give the signal to go or the signal to break (stop moving) with a tambourine. Give the children enough time to think of their own imaginative movement based on the trap of the room.

4. After each time, change the conditions of the trap room to help the children imagine different ways of moving in the general space. Some ideas for trap rooms include a room full of water with waves, sharks, and so on; a room with oil on the floor; a very short room for elves; a room with lions; a room filled with jelly; a room with big holes in the floor; and a room with glue on the floor.

> continued

Points of Emphasis

- Explain to the children that they have to imagine and imitate a hero who could think of and perform many movements.

- Tell them that it's OK if their movements are different, because every hero has different ways to perform movements.

- Point out that it doesn't matter how much time it takes to pass through the trap room; the important thing is to move in the best way they can think of.

- Repeat the same trap room, asking for a different way to move (e.g., "Show me another way you can pass through the very low room for elves.").

- Encourage the children and choose one of the most original movements. Have that child show it to the others.

Variation Each child can determine boundaries for personal space in the general space (e.g., a hula hoop for each child on the floor). When an external danger comes into the trap room, such as a dragon or wizard, the children must run to their personal space for safety or to become invisible. If children fall into someone else, they are excluded from the next trap room and must stay and think of a movement within their personal space.

Statue Balances (8 minutes)

Setup and Description

1. Have the children spread throughout the space.

2. Play some music. Have children move and dance as they like. Every time the music stops, the children have to pose as statues. Challenge them to balance in a different way (e.g., "Put two palms and one foot on the floor", "Only two body parts can touch the floor.").

Point of Emphasis Ask the children appropriate questions: Can you show me how to balance using one hand and two feet? Can you show me that you can use your head when you balance?

Variations

- Give the children athletic or other equipment (e.g., ropes, ribbons, scarves, soft balls).

- Ask the children to change the level of their movement as they dance and as they balance.

CONCLUSION (6 MINUTES)

Ask the children which activity they prefer best and what are the benefits of exercise (e.g., strong heart, lungs, bones, and muscles; better blood circulation). Remind them of the joy of movement creation and participation.

Lesson 45

Identify Healthy Foods
STANDARD 2, GOAL 3

OBJECTIVES
At the end of the lesson, children will be able to
- understand the value of healthy foods,
- comprehend the need for healthy foods in their diets,
- discriminate healthy from unhealthy foods, and
- show improved observation skills.

EQUIPMENT
- 1 box
- 10 to 12 cards (size A4, 21 × 29 cm), each with an image of a healthy food (e.g., broccoli, carrots, fruit salad)
- 10 to 12 cards (size A4, 21 × 29 cm), each with an image of an unhealthy food (e.g., potato chips, fast food)
- 8 cards (size A3, 42 × 29 cm), each with three images of one healthy and two unhealthy foods (e.g., salad with fresh vegetables, pizza, and a hamburger)
- Music player
- Music

*All the aforementioned cards could be made by the instructor and the children, perhaps in another class.

EVALUATION
Give each child a sheet of paper that only contains the answers (e.g., 1. a, b, c; 2. a, b, c). After you slowly read each question and the possible answers, ask the children to circle the answer that they believe is correct.

1. Which of the following sweets builds a healthier body?
   a. chocolates
   b. cookies
   c. yoghurt with fruit and honey
2. If I prefer eating healthy rather than unhealthy foods, the possibility of building a stronger body is
   a. greater
   b. less
   c. the same
3. Which of the following foods has the least fat?
   a. salad
   b. chocolate
   c. potato chips

INTRODUCTION (7 MINUTES)
Setup and Description
1. Ask the children what foods they think are healthy or unhealthy and why. Ask them which ones they like. Point out the importance of eating healthy food or how a group of foods builds their body (e.g., dairy products build strong bones).

> continued

2. Have the children form a circle and sit on the floor. In the middle of the circle, place a box containing cards with many foods.

3. Each child picks a card and shows it to the others. Everyone discusses whether this food is healthy and why (e.g., pizza has a lot of fat).

Point of Emphasis   Emphasise the importance of healthy eating and give examples of the consequences of unhealthy foods and a sedentary life, such as obesity, heart disease, and so on.

Variation   Discuss the children's breakfast, lunch, or dinner.

MAIN LESSON: FIVE ACTIVITIES (30 MINUTES)

Activity 1: Find the Healthy Foods (8 minutes)

Setup and Description   On the floor, place eight cards in two lines (four and four). Each card has one healthy and two unhealthy foods on it. Lines have approximately 50 centimetres between them.

1. Separate the children into pairs.

2. After the children observe the cards for a minute, turn the cards facedown. Each pair must turn over the cards one by one and decide which of the three foods is healthy. If they find all eight healthy foods, they will have total of 8 points. The pair with the most points wins.

Point of Emphasis   Tell the children to observe the cards and remember the healthy foods.

Variations

- Have the same number of cards as children.

- Have more than one healthy or more than two unhealthy foods on one card.

- Separate the children into bigger teams (three to five children).

Activity 2: Steps for Health (6 minutes)

Setup and Description

1. Divide the children into three to five teams. Each team has a leader. The other children on each team form a line, one next to the other, 4 to 5 metres from their leader.

2. The leader shows the team a card that has a picture of a healthy or an unhealthy food. If the food is healthy, the children take a step forwards, and if it's unhealthy they take a step backwards.

3. After finishing the cards, ask the children to change roles (change leaders sequentially).

Variation   Change the way the children move in response to healthy or unhealthy food (e.g., jumping with both legs together, turning, crawling).

Activity 3: Rhymes for Foods (8 minutes)

Setup and Description

1. Have the children sit in a circle on the floor. Inside the circle, spread out cards with healthy or unhealthy foods so that the images are facedown.

2. One at a time, each child picks a card and shows it to the others. If the card has a healthy food, the child runs around the outer perimeter of the circle while the other children sing rhythmically, for example, "An orange is healthy" or "Oranges have vitamins." If the card has an unhealthy food, the child returns to the circle and the other children sing rhythmically, for example, "Eating chocolate all the time is so unhealthy" or "Lollipops, sweets, and chocolates, so much fat your body hates."

Point of Emphasis   Point out the meaning and the importance of healthy foods.

Variation   Change the way the children move (e.g., running, jumping, hopping, galloping, crawling).

Activity 4: Match With Your Opposites (4 minutes)

Setup and Description

1. Each child holds a card that shows a healthy or an unhealthy food.

2. While music plays, the children move and dance. When the music stops, the children must form pairs of healthy or unhealthy foods.

Point of Emphasis Every child must find a different healthy or unhealthy food partner each time the music stops.

Variation Create smart cards that form healthy or unhealthy combinations. For example, the broccoli card goes with the lemon card, the yoghurt card goes with the fruits card, the fast-food card goes with the potato chips card, and so on.

Activity 5: Get Energy (4 minutes)

Setup and Description

1. Have the children spread throughout the area.
2. When you call a healthy food, the children begin running, but when you call an unhealthy food, the children move sluggishly.

Variations

- Change the way the children move (e.g., jumping, hopping, galloping, crawling).
- Ask the children to be the leader.

CONCLUSION (8 MINUTES)

Setup and Description

1. Remind the children of healthy foods while showing them the healthy food cards.
2. Ask the children about the origin of each food. They divide the cards with healthy foods in two groups: foods that come from plants and foods that come from animals.

Point of Emphasis Remind the children about the importance of healthy eating and give examples of the consequences of unhealthy foods and a sedentary life, such as obesity, heart disease, and so on.

Variation The children can divide the foods into two boxes, or they can make two paper collages, one for foods that come from plants and one for foods that come from animals.

Lesson 46

Identify Healthy Foods
STANDARD 2, GOAL 3

OBJECTIVES
At the end of the lesson, children will be able to
- understand the value of healthy foods,
- comprehend the need for healthy foods in their diets,
- discriminate healthy from unhealthy foods and their consequences, and
- develop their observation skills.

EQUIPMENT
- A large card box
- Empty cans and boxes of foods (as many as the children)
- 6 to 10 cards, each showing one healthy food
- 6 to 10 cards, each showing a result of healthy eating (e.g., strong bones, strong muscles, a fit body, an *X* in front of the word *fat*)
- 20 to 45 cards, each showing a category of foods (4 or 5 of the same cards for each category, such as dairy products like milk, yoghurt, cheese, ice cream, or butter)
- Cards illustrating a maze, 1 per child
- Cards illustrating a park with hidden vegetables and fruits, 1 per child
- Crayons for colouring the park cards
- 1 magnetic fishing rod per child
- Magnetic cards with healthy and unhealthy foods

EVALUATION
Give each child a sheet of paper that only contains the answers (e.g., 1. a, b, c; 2. a, b, c). After you slowly read each question and the possible answers, ask the children to circle the answer that they believe is correct.

1. Obesity and heart disease are two major problems that may be caused by eating
   a. healthy foods
   b. unhealthy foods
   c. many vegetables
2. Which of the following foods helps you build stronger bones?
   a. dairy products
   b. fat
   c. potatoes
3. Vegetables and fruits have a lot of
   a. vitamins
   b. fat
   c. calories

INTRODUCTION (8 MINUTES)
Setup and Description
1. Ask the children which foods they think are healthy or unhealthy and why. Ask them which ones they like. Point out the importance of eating healthy food or how a group of foods builds their body (e.g., dairy products build strong bones).

2. Play Supermarket Basket: The children sit in a circle. Inside the circle, place a box that has empty cans and boxes of foods. The children each pick an empty box or can of food that they like as if they were shopping at the supermarket. Discuss whether this food is healthy or unhealthy and why.

Point of Emphasis   Remind the children about the importance of healthy eating and give examples of the consequences of unhealthy foods and a sedentary life, such as obesity, heart disease, and so on.

Variation   Discuss the children's breakfast, lunch, or dinner.

MAIN LESSON: MATCH AND REMEMBER, I EAT AND EXERCISE, MAZE GAME, AND HIDDEN VEGETABLES AND FRUITS ACTIVITIES (32 MINUTES)

Match and Remember (8 minutes)

Setup and Description   You will need 6 to 10 cards that each show one healthy food, as well as 6 to 10 cards that each show a result of healthy eating (e.g., fish helps make good vision, meat helps build strong muscles, milk helps build strong bones). Place the cards on the floor in two lines (equal number of cards in each line), with 50 centimetres between the two lines.

1. Separate the children into pairs. Have the children observe the cards for a minute and explain the type of healthy eating and its results.

2. After the minute is up, turn the cards facedown. A child of each pair must turn over one card with a healthy food and the other child has to remember where its result is. The winners are the partners who find the most correct pairs of cards.

Point of Emphasis   Emphasise that the children must observe the cards and remember where the results of healthy eating are.

Variations

- Have the same number of cards as children.
- Separate the children into bigger teams (three to five children).

I Eat and Exercise (8 minutes)

Setup and Description

1. Separate the children in three to six teams. Each team has a leader. The other children on each team form a line, one next to the other, 4 to 5 metres from their leader.

2. The leader shows the rest of the team a card that illustrates a category of food. Each category corresponds to a kind of movement (e.g., cereal and running, dairy and jumping, vegetables and turning). Ask the children to repeat each movement a few times.

3. Ask the children to change team leaders (the leader changes sequentially).

Point of Emphasis   Point out the meaning and the importance of healthy foods.

Variation   Change the way the children move (e.g., running, jumping, hopping, galloping, crawling).

Maze Game (8 minutes)

Setup and Description

1. Have the children stand on one side of the room.

2. Give each child a small card that shows a maze. At its dead ends, there are unhealthy foods, whereas at the exit there is a healthy food. Children try to find the exit on their cards.

3. When they finish, they run and put the cards in a box on the other side of the room.

Variation

- Change the way the children move (e.g., running, jumping, hopping, galloping, crawling).
- Put a time limit on this game. Have many cards with mazes. Each child tries to solve as many mazes as they can and puts them in the box.

> continued

Hidden Vegetables and Fruits (8 minutes)

Setup and Description

1. Each child has a card that shows a park with hidden vegetables and fruits. The children must find the hidden vegetables and fruits and colour them.

2. When they finish colouring, they run and put the cards in a box on the other side of the room.

Point of Emphasis

- Change the way the children move (e.g., running, jumping, hopping, galloping, crawling).

- Put a time limit on the activity. Give children many cards with hidden vegetables or fruits. Children colour in as many vegetables and fruits as they can find before the time is up.

CONCLUSION (8 MINUTES)

Setup and Description

1. Remind the children about healthy foods while showing them healthy foods cards.

2. Place magnetic cards inside a lake (circle). (Each magnetic card must show a healthy or an unhealthy food.) Ask the children to fish for the food with their magnetic rods. When they catch a healthy food, they take 2 points, and when they catch an unhealthy food, they take 1 point. (The children can construct magnetic rods and magnetic cards during a previous lesson.)

Point of Emphasis Remind the children about the importance of healthy eating and give examples of the consequences of unhealthy foods and a sedentary life, such as obesity, heart disease, and so on.

Lesson 47

Understand the Need for Rest
STANDARD 2, GOAL 3

OBJECTIVES
At the end of the lesson, children will be able to
- understand and experience tension and relaxation,
- understand and feel the contrast between motionlessness and movement,
- understand and feel the changes in body function between exercising and relaxing, and
- express themselves with their bodies and move creatively.

EQUIPMENT
- Pack of spaghetti and some already cooked spaghetti
- Pot or casserole dish
- Music player
- Music with fast and slow tempos
- 3 benches

EVALUATION
Give each child a sheet of paper that only contains the answers (e.g., 1. a, b, c; 2. a, b, c). After you slowly read each question and the possible answers, ask the children to circle the answer that they believe is correct.

1. Why do you think it's important to relax after exercising?
   a. because we need to recover and recapture energy
   b. because we need to drink water
   c. because we need more exercise afterwards
2. When I relax, my muscles have to be
   a. tight
   b. loose
   c. neither tight nor loose
3. Breathing, HR, and perspiration are three body functions that change between exercising and relaxing.
   a. true   ☺
   b. false   ☹
   c. don't know ☺

INTRODUCTION (4 MINUTES)

Setup and Description
1. Discuss with the children why they sleep at the end of the day. Ask them what the purpose of napping is and what the body does during the nap (relax, recover, and recapture energy and strength). Explain the need for rest after exercising. Ask them what body functions change during exercise and relaxation (e.g., breathing, HR, perspiration).
2. Ask the children to spread throughout the room and have them walk, run, and jump with the accompaniment of a tambourine.
3. After the children move for few minutes, have them inhale and exhale deeply and slowly to relax. Explain the need for more oxygen in order to relax.

> continued

Points of Emphasis

- Ask the children to inhale deeply and slowly exhale. When they exhale, tell them to do so until they don't have any more air in their lungs.
- Help them when they inhale and exhale by counting slowly (1, 2, 3, 4, 5, 6 . . .).

Variations

- Use fast music for the movement and easy listening for the relaxation.
- Give the children athletic or other equipment (e.g., ropes, ribbons, scarves, soft balls).
- Ask the children to change the level of their movement as they dance and move.

MAIN LESSON: SPAGHETTI DANCE, HAIL MELTS, AND DANCE AND BREATHE ACTIVITIES (30 MINUTES)

Activity 1: Spaghetti Dance (15 minutes)

Setup and Description

1. Separate the children into three lines around a big circle (pot).
2. Narrate a story of the spaghetti dance. Make use of a pack of spaghetti, a pot, and some already cooked spaghetti when storytelling. Then challenge the children to act it out. Ask them to pretend to be spaghetti, walking and jumping to enter the pot. At the beginning they are straight and inflexible like uncooked pasta and they jump and dance in this way through the pot. After a while they start to melt and become very flexible. The chef is in love and talking on the phone with his fiancée and forgets the spaghetti on the fire. After awhile the bubbles of the boiling water get bigger and bigger, pushing the spaghetti outside the pot. The children have to jump in many ways with flexibility, and they stick to the walls, forming many shapes. After awhile they start to slide slowly from the wall to the ground until finally they stand still on the floor.

Points of Emphasis

- Ask the children appropriate questions when they move: Can you show me that you can walk in another straight shape? Can you show me many ways that you can jump inflexibly through the pot? Can you show me many shapes of cooked and flexible spaghetti on the wall? Can you show me how you melt in the pot? Can you use all of your body?
- Make appropriate suggestions when they relax or melt: Breathe as slowly as you can, take a big breath and exhale slowly, and feel the relaxation of your body.

Variations

- Separate the children into more teams (lines) to jump through the pot.
- Form more than one circle (pot).
- Create and narrate a story (e.g., making cookies).

Hail Melts (8 minutes)

Setup and Description

1. Tell the children that they are hail in the sky and when the storm starts they land on the ground. Have them jump strongly and sharply for a few minutes with the accompaniment of a tambourine. They can clap their hands on the floor if they want.
2. After the storm passes, the hail starts to melt. Ask the children to imagine that they are melting and becoming liquid (water).
3. To become rain, hail, or snow again, they must evaporate in the sky, so they must be very light. Have them breathe deeply and slowly to relax and become lighter.
4. Repeat one more time.

Points of Emphasis

- Emphasise the contrast between motionlessness or slow movement and energetic movement.

- Ask the children to pretend that they are heavy, strong, and sharp when they are hail and that they are light, soft, and slippery when they are liquid.

Dance and Breathe (7 minutes)

Setup and Description
1. Play some music. You have to find music that changes a few times between a slow and fast tempo.
2. During the fast music, ask the children to imitate you and dance, showing happiness and vividness.
3. During the slow music, ask them to move their arms slowly up and down and breathe deeply with you (inhale and exhale slowly).
4. At the end of the activity, ask them to lie on the floor and take slow breaths when you count.

Point of Emphasis Emphasise the importance of small breaks with slow breathing and movements between the fast parts of the dance in order to relax and regain strength.

Variations
- Have the children make different formations or spread throughout the class.
- Change the way the children move (e.g., running, jumping, hopping, galloping, crawling).
- Ask the children to change the level of their movement as they dance and move.
- Ask the children to dance as they want, imitating you only in breathing.
- Have a child play your role as the dance leader.

CONCLUSION (7 MINUTES)

Setup and Description.
1. To promote deep breathing, ask the children to expand (by inhaling) and contract (by exhaling) like balloons, slowly inflating and deflating. Help them by demonstrating with a balloon.
2. Ask them if they notice the changes between motionlessness and movement (breathing, HR, perspiration). Ask them also what they noticed and felt when they were moving and when they were relaxing.

Points of Emphasis
- Explain the need for rest between or after exercising.
- Remind the children of the changes in body function during exercise and relaxation.

Lesson 48

Understand the Need for Rest
STANDARD 2, GOAL 3

OBJECTIVES
At the end of the lesson, children will be able to

- understand and experience tension and relaxation,
- understand and feel the contrast between motionlessness and movement,
- understand and feel the changes in body function between exercising and relaxing, and
- express themselves with their bodies and move creatively.

EQUIPMENT
- Music player and music
- 1 thick plastic bag or gunny sack per child (to put over the feet)
- 10 to 12 hula hoops
- Percussion instruments (tambourine, maracas, and bells)

EVALUATION
Give each child a sheet of paper that only contains the answers (e.g., 1. a, b, c; 2. a, b, c). After you slowly read each question and the possible answers, ask the children to circle the answer that they believe is correct.

1. After exercising, in order to relax, I have to inhale and exhale
   a. slow and deep
   b. fast and shallow
   c. the same as when exercising
2. It's important to have small breaks during exercise, because I need
   a. to regain strength
   b. to drink water
   c. to talk with my teacher
3. When I have small breaks during exercise, I feel
   a. ☺
   b. ☺
   c. ☹

INTRODUCTION (9 MINUTES)
Setup and Description
1. Have the children spread throughout the space or in a circle. Explain the need for rest during and after exercising. Ask them what body functions change during exercise and relaxation (e.g., breathing, HR, perspiration).
2. Have the children dance to medium-fast music.
3. After children move for few minutes, have them inhale and exhale deeply and slowly to relax. Explain to them the need for more oxygen in order to relax.

Points of Emphasis
- Remind the children of the changes in body functions during exercise and relaxation.
- Ask them to inhale deeply and slowly exhale.
- When they exhale, tell them to do so until they don't have any more air in their lungs.
- Help them when they inhale and exhale, counting slowly (1, 2, 3, 4, 5, 6 . . .).

Variations

- Give the children athletic or other equipment (e.g., ropes, ribbons, scarves, soft balls).
- Change the way the children move (e.g., running, jumping, hopping, galloping, crawling).
- Ask the children to change the level of their movement as they dance and move.

MAIN LESSON: FOUR ACTIVITIES (27 MINUTES)

Activity 1: Hopping Race With Bags (8 minutes)

Setup and Description

1. Divide the children into two teams, forming two lines on one side of the room. Give each child a bag and ask the children to wear the bags on their feet and hold them with their hands.
2. Ask the children to jump from one side of the room (start) to the other (end). One team must jump continuously to the end of the room and back, while the other team must jump to the end of the room and return to the start by walking.
3. Repeat a couple of times. After children finish the activity, ask them to find their HR and what they notice. Which team has the lowest HR (the jumping or walking team), and why?
4. Repeat the exercise, changing roles.

Variation   Change the way the children move (e.g., running, jumping, hopping, galloping, crawling).

Activity 2: Dance and Breathe (8 minutes)

Setup and Description

1. Play some music. You have to find music that changes a few times between a slow and fast tempo.
2. During the fast music, ask the children to imitate you and dance, showing vivid happiness.
3. During the slow music, ask them to move their arms slowly up and down and breathe deeply with you (inhale and exhale slowly).
4. At the end of the activity, ask them to lie on the floor and take slow breaths when you count. Ask them if the slow music helped them relax during the activity.

Point of Emphasis   Emphasise the importance of small breaks with slow breathing and movements between the fast parts of exercise in order to relax and regain strength.

Variations

- Have the children make different formations or spread throughout the room.
- Change the way the children move (e.g., running, jumping, hopping, galloping, crawling).
- Ask the children to change the level of their movement as they dance and move.
- Ask the children to dance as they want, imitating you only in breathing.
- Have a child play your role as the dance leader.

Activity 3: Summer Relaxation (3-4 minutes)

Setup and Description

1. Ask the children to lie on the floor.
2. Paint a picture in their minds. Ask them to imagine that it is spring and they are in the woods, lying next to a river. You can also play nature sounds in the background. Tell them that they start to feel a cool breeze on their bodies that refreshes and relaxes them. Also, they have to try to listen to the sound of the water as it runs down the river and to the birds that sing softly in the trees.

Point of Emphasis   Enhance children's ability to imagine, using appropriate verbs such as *feel, sense, listen,* and *hear.*

> *continued*

Variations

- Have the children make different formations or spread throughout the room.
- Make use of another imaginative scene, such as sunbathing on the beach in summer.

Activity 4: Observe the Difference (7 minutes)

Setup and Description   Spread hula hoops throughout the room.

1. Divide the children into two teams. The children of one team are inside the hula hoops (one child in each hula hoop) and the children of the other team are spread throughout the room, outside the hula hoops.

2. Show them a tambourine, maracas, and bells. Each instrument represents a level (tambourine for high level, maracas for medium level, bells for low level). When you hit an instrument, the children must react correctly and appropriately at the right level. The children inside the hula hoops must pose and balance at the appropriate level, while the children outside the hula hoops must move (run, jump, or hop) at the appropriate level.

3. After the children finish the activity, tell them to check their HR. Ask them which team sweat the most and which had the faster HR.

4. Ask teams to change roles.

Points of Emphasis

- Remind the children of the changes in body functions during exercise and while motionless.
- Emphasise that during exercise, they should have resting times or changes in the intensity of movement.

Variations

- Change the way the children move (e.g., running, jumping, hopping, galloping, crawling).
- Play some music.

CONCLUSION (7 MINUTES)

Setup and Description

1. Ask the children to pretend that they are ice cream cones. They are very cold and hard at the beginning, but as time passes, they start to melt.

2. Ask them if they notice the changes between motionlessness and movement in breathing, HR, and perspiration. Ask them also what they noticed when they were moving and what they noticed when they were relaxing.

Points of Emphasis

- Explain the need for rest during and after exercise.
- Remind children of the changes in body function during exercise and relaxation.

Variation   Make use of another imaginative scene or example of melting, such as ice or snowmen.

Chapter 8

Evaluation Methods

Vasilis Grammatikopoulos, PhD

University of Thessaly, Greece

KEY POINTS

- Evaluation in education is essential to improve policies, practice, and decisions in education.
- Evaluation in the early childhood setting gathers information that leads to appropriate decisions about children's psychoeducational development.
- The evaluation object is whatever is being evaluated. Goals are the reason why the evaluation is carried out, and they determine the evaluation criteria that will be selected.
- Programme evaluation applies evaluation processes to assess and improve programmes.
- Systems approach evaluation is characterised by its concern to the system under review, the subsystems, and the higher-order system.

This chapter provides information about evaluation theory and how it can formulate a solid foundation that every evaluation procedure can rely upon. It might seem that evaluation does not have much to offer in the everyday praxis of early childhood education. Yet, knowledge about evaluation procedures can lead to better understanding and communication between teachers and evaluators. It might also help educators overcome the counteractive attitude that is often detected among teachers. Moreover, mastering basic evaluation skills could help teachers in independence, decentralisation, and adoption of internal evaluation procedures.

Evaluation in Education

As defined by the American Evaluation Association, evaluation comprises procedures that estimate the strengths and weaknesses of programmes, policies, people, products, and organisations to improve their effectiveness. These procedures incorporate systematic collection and data analysis needed to make decisions. Scriven (1991) argued that evaluation is important in pragmatic terms (bad educational services cost society by lowering quality of life and wasting resources), ethical terms (evaluation is a tool in the service of justice), social terms (evaluation directs efforts where it is more needed), intellectual terms (evaluation refines the tools of thought), and personal terms (evaluation provides the basis for self-esteem).

Several definitions of the term *evaluation* can be found in literature. Fitzpatrick, Sanders, and Worthen (2004) offered a broadly accepted definition of evaluation as "the identification, clarification, and application of defensible criteria to determine an evaluation object's value (worth or merit) in relation to those criteria" (p. 5).

Educational evaluation is the process of appraising aspects in the educational setting. It is essential in any effective educational system, and it must be an integral part of any educational effort. The importance of educational evaluation has led some evaluators to consider evaluation as a panacea for all the ills of education. However, evaluation alone cannot solve all the problems in education (Fitzpatrick et al., 2004). One of the most common mistakes evaluators make is promising something that cannot be attained. Many problems can occur during any evaluation procedure. Arguments could arise about

the appropriate definition and objectivity of the criteria, or the report of correct assumptions, or even the interpretation of the results. Evaluation primarily exposes problems. It plays an important role in elucidating many aspects of education and providing useful tools for problem solving, but it is only one of many factors that influence policies, practice, and decisions in education.

Evaluation in Early Childhood Education

The main goal of evaluation in the early childhood setting is to gather information that can lead to appropriate decisions about children's psychoeducational development (Nagle, 2000). To better understand the role of the evaluation in early childhood education, it is helpful to group its purposes in specific areas. Nagle (2000) identifies four major purposes in early childhood evaluation: screening, diagnosis, individual programme planning and monitoring, and programme evaluation. Screening entails evaluation of many children to identify those who may need further assessment. Diagnosis is served by the follow-up evaluation procedures that are implemented for the children identified as needing further consideration. Individual programme planning and monitoring uses information from the evaluation. Finally, programme evaluation is every evaluation that deals with programme quality.

In each of these purpose groups, a different evaluation procedure is required because the information needed could serve different purposes. Thus, the procedure choice depends on evaluation purpose and should vary according to the information that has to be collected. Every evaluation procedure has to take into consideration general principles that apply to all evaluations. More specifically, every evaluation has to benefit children, and its design and use must serve a specific purpose. It has to be acknowledged that the validity and reliability increase with children's age, the content and methods should be age appropriate, and the parents and family are valuable sources of information for every evaluation.

Another point that should be stressed is that solely focusing on skills and competencies during this time of transition in a child's life may be the wrong way to collect information. Perhaps implementation curriculum is the key issue and not curriculum per se. As Pianta (2004) reported,

Evaluation must consider the age of the students.

"Policies that result in provision of direct and thorough feedback to teachers regarding high quality implementation may result in better outcomes for children than policies that focus on one or another curricular approach" (p. 6).

Evaluation Objects, Goals, and Criteria

The description of an evaluation procedure is one of the major concerns of evaluators. This description is essential in order to accurately depict the content and the procedures that were adopted. Moreover, to better understand the larger picture, all people interested in the evaluation procedure need a comprehensive and thorough description of it. Such a presentation would be ineffective if the evaluation objects, goals, and criteria were not indicated (Dimitropoulos, 1998; Grammatikopoulos, 2006). Following is a brief explanation of evaluation objects, goals, and criteria.

The evaluation object is whatever is being evaluated. For example, an evaluation object can be a book, a curriculum, an educational programme, or an educator. Evaluation literature has developed its own terminology, and the word *evaluand* is sometimes used to refer to the evaluation object, unless it is a person, who is then an *evaluee* (Fitzpatrick et al., 2004). Yet, the latter definitions are not usually adopted because most researchers prefer to refer to both as objects of the evaluation. In several areas, concern about how to evaluate broad categories of objects has led to the development of subareas within the field of evaluation, such as personnel evaluation, programme evaluation, and so on.

The goal of an evaluation is the reason why the evaluation is carried out. For example, common goals in evaluation are to reform an educational programme or to change a curriculum. Criteria are the foundation on which the conclusions of an evaluation stand. For instance, when a firm hires whoever succeeded in a math test, then the criterion is the math performance of the candidates.

The goals of any evaluation procedure help determine the criteria that will be selected. If the goal of an evaluation is to hire teachers, the criteria could be their experience, educational qualifications, recommendations, and so on. But, if the goal of an evaluation is to estimate teachers' abilities, then the criteria could be their efficacy, level of knowledge, acquired educational strategies, and so on. In this example, we have two evaluations with the same object (teachers), but different criteria due to different goals. Different criteria need to be determined to fulfil different causes.

Evaluation is the identification, clarification, and application of defensible criteria to determine the value of an evaluation object. Thus, a major concern is how these criteria are identified and clarified in order to be defensible. Valid and reliable ways to meet these requirements include relying on appropriate reference and prior research, past experience, experts' notions, evaluators' personal opinions, and the procedure itself (e.g., cause, objects).

Programme Evaluation in Education

For many years, educational evaluation was synonymous with children's performance assessment, yet in the last decades many evaluation efforts have been applied to other aspects of education. These efforts indicate alternative uses of educational evaluation, such as programme evaluation. Although *programme* and *programme evaluation* are common terms and are used widely in literature, their definition is essential in order to identify them precisely.

Programme appears to have several names in literature, such as treatment programme or action programme or even intervention programme. Nevertheless, programmes are all "organised efforts to enhance human well-being, whether by preventing disease, reducing poverty, or teaching skills" (Chen, 2005, p. 3). Programme evaluation is "the application of evaluation approaches, techniques, and knowledge to systematically assess and improve the planning, implementation, and effectiveness of programs" (Chen, 2005, p. 3). Similar is the definition of programme evaluation provided by Patton (1997), who stated that "program evaluation is the systematic collection of information about the activities, characteristics, and outcomes of programs to make judgments about the program, improve program effectiveness, and/or inform decisions about future programming" (p. 23).

Programme theory explains how a programme will achieve its desired goals. Theory-based evaluations consider not only the end result of a programme but also the programme theory itself: the intermediate steps to reach that end result. In the Early Steps case, the choice of evaluation procedure aspired to serve the purpose of the theory-based evaluations, and thus a dynamic approach was selected, as will be described in the appendix.

Systems Approach Evaluation

A system consists of a group of interdependent interacting parts that themselves are subsystems that belong to a higher-order system in which the subsystem is embedded. Any systems approach procedure is characterised by its concern to the system under review, the subsystems, and the higher-order system (Bawden, 2005, 2007). In our case, the system under review is the Early Steps project, the subsystems are all the parts of the project (e.g., design, training, curriculum), and the higher-order system is early childhood education.

Any system has five components: input, transformation, output, environment, and feedback (Chen, 2005). Its function is determined by interdependence, interaction, and self-control and self-correction. Self-control and self-correction are ensured by feedback, which is the basic idea in cybernetics (Midgley, 2007). An example of such a feedback mechanism is the thermostat that controls the heating system of a house. When the temperature reaches the desired level, the thermostat receives feedback from its thermometer and turns the heating off.

The systems approach to evaluation developed as a means to overcome the setting of narrowly defined goals, and it is characterised by a holistic view of the procedure under evaluation. These approaches are generally complex and could be confusing to practitioners. However, evaluations that utilise the theoretical concepts of the systems approach look promising (Harris, 2004).

The previously mentioned arguments about the systems approach were the foundation on which our choice of evaluation procedure was based. The general idea is that for complex problems,

One factor that programme evaluation considers is the outcome of the programme itself.

such as an educational project, there are no simple solutions. Systems approaches are not content specific and thus can be used to evaluate any programme. They provide a holistic view of the procedure under evaluation and are based on a strong theoretical background. On the other hand, evaluations based on the systems approach are not the only solution to the problem. They are situational procedures, and generalisation of their results is somehow problematic. Moreover, they are formative rather than summative and are suitable to evaluate programmes rather than people or products.

Practical Applications and Forms

The first two instruments used for the evaluation of the Early Steps project were developed and used for the evaluation of the training provided. The Early Steps Training Evaluation Questionnaire for Early Childhood Educators (form 1 on page 203) was an adaptation of the Professional Development Evaluation Form (PDEF), a newly designed tool for seminar evaluation (Grammatikopoulos, Zachopoulou, Tsangaridou, Liukkonen, & Pickup, 2008). The Follow-Up Seminar Evaluation Questionnaire for Early Childhood Educators (form 2 on page 204) was designed to evaluate the training after implementation of the project activities, a time thought to be ideal for judging every training procedure (Guskey, 2000).

Next, the Social Behaviour List (forms 3 and 4 on pages 205 and 206) and Healthy Lifestyle List (forms 7 and 8 on pages 209 and 210) were developed to gather direct evidence from the children participating in the project. Usually, observation from teachers or interviews from parents are the most common means to get information from children aged 4 and 5, but the current project aspired to provide direct evidence by developing valid and reliable instruments (Grammatikopoulos, Konstantinidou, et al., 2008).

Moreover, the Social Behaviour List for Early Childhood Educators (form 5 on page 207) and for Parents (form 6 on page 208) and the Healthy

Lifestyle List for Early Childhood Educators (form 9 on page 213) and for Parents (form 10 on page 215) search to define the attributes of a child's behaviour that should be adopted before and after implementation of the programme. Preliminary results for the instruments have already been published (Grammatikopoulos, Trevlas, & Zachopoulou, 2007).

Finally, the Programme Evaluation Questionnaire for Early Childhood Educators (form 11 on page 216) and the Supervision Sheet for Programme Implementation Evaluation (form 12 on page 217) were used for the internal and external evaluation of the programme implementation. The questionnaire was adjusted to the current project requirements from the Evaluation Scale of the Educational Programme Implementation (Grammatikopoulos, Tsigilis, Koustelios, & Theodorakis, 2005; Grammatikopoulos, Tsigilis, & Koustelios, 2007). The supervision sheet was used by the external evaluators of the lesson plans as a tool assisting their systematic observation.

REFERENCES

Bawden, R.J. (2005). Systemic perspectives on community development: Participation, learning and the essence of wholeness. *Perspectives on Community Development in Ireland, 1,* 45-62.

Bawden, R.J. (2007). A systematic evaluation of an agricultural development: A focus on the worldview challenge. In B. Williams & I. Imam (Eds.), *Systems concepts in evaluation: An expert anthology* (pp. 35-46). Point Reyes, CA: EdgePress.

Chen, H-T. (2005). *Practical program evaluation: Assessing and improving planning, implementation and effectiveness.* Thousand Oaks, CA: Sage.

Dimitropoulos, E. (1998). *Educational evaluation.* Athens: Grigori [in Greek].

Fitzpatrick, J.L., Sanders, J.R., & Worthen, B.R. (2004). *Program evaluation: Alternative approaches and practical guidelines.* Boston: Allyn & Bacon.

Grammatikopoulos, V., Tsigilis, N., Koustelios, A., & Theodorakis, Y. (2005). Evaluating the implementation of an Olympic education program in Greece. *International Review of Education, 51,* 427-438.

Grammatikopoulos, V. (2006). Educational evaluation: Evaluation models for educational programs. *Inquires in Sport & Physical Education, 4*(2), 237-246 [in Greek].

Grammatikopoulos, V., Trevlas, E., & Zachopoulou, E. (2007). Early Steps physical education curriculum evaluation: Preliminary results for the Social Behavior Instrument. 12th European Congress of Sport Psychology, September 2007, Halkidiki, Greece.

Grammatikopoulos, V., Tsigilis, N., & Koustelios, A. (2007). Influential factors of an educational program implementation evaluation: A cross validation approach. *Evaluation and Research in Education, 20*(2), 100-113.

Grammatikopoulos, V., Konstantinidou, E., Tsigilis, N., Zachopoulou, E., Tsangaridou, N., & Liukkonen, J. (2008). Evaluating preschool children knowledge about healthy lifestyle: Preliminary evaluation of the healthy lifestyle evaluation instrument. *Educational Research and Review, 3*(11), 351-352.

Grammatikopoulos, V., Zachopoulou, E., Tsangaridou, N., Liukkonen, J., & Pickup, I. (2008). Applying a mixed method design to evaluate training seminars within an early childhood education project. *Evaluation and Research in Education, 21*(1), 4-17.

Guskey, T.R. (2000). *Evaluating professional development.* Thousand Oaks, CA: Corwin Press.

Harris, B.M. (2004). A systems approach to formative evaluation of instructional programmes. *International Journal of Leadership in Education, 7*(1), 71-81.

Midgley, G. (2007). Systems thinking for evaluation. In B. Williams & I. Imam (Eds.), *Systems concepts in evaluation: An expert anthology* (pp. 11-34). Point Reyes, CA: EdgePress.

Nagle, R.J. (2000). Issues in preschool assessment. In B.A. Bracken (Ed.), *The Psycho-Educational Assessment of Preschool Children* (pp. 19-32). Neidham Heights, MA: Allyn & Bacon.

Patton, M.Q. (1997). *Utilization-focused evaluation: The new century text.* Thousand Oaks, CA: Sage.

Pianta, R.C. (2004). Transitioning to school: Policy, practice, and reality. *Evaluation Exchange, X*(2), 5-6.

Scriven, M.S. (1991). *Evaluation thesaurus* (4th ed.). Thousand Oaks, CA: Sage.

Description of the Early Steps Project

Evridiki Zachopoulou
Alexander Technological Educational Institute of Thessaloniki, Greece

The education of young children must cover their specific needs to feel confident and safe; to learn, think, and solve problems; to create; to develop their abilities; and to share their experiences with other children and adults. An effective way of meeting these needs is participation in a physical education programme that provides children with opportunities to practise their skills, express their capabilities, and develop their abilities. Preschoolers use movement in many ways. They move, for example, to explore the world around them, to learn concepts, to communicate with others, or to express their feelings and their thoughts.

Werner and Burton (1979) offered six reasons why physical activity is an effective learning medium.

1. Children more readily attend to the learning task. When children are physically active, they tend to be totally involved in the learning experience. This assists them in focusing on the relevant attributes of the learning task and prevents their attention from being distracted by extraneous factors.

2. The children are dealing with reality. The facts are tangible. An action-oriented learning task provides direct rather than vicarious experience. The children actually manipulate objects or situations, and this enables them to see the facts applied and the principles in operation. They do not just read about the content; they experience it.

3. It is a process approach in which development of the affective domain is a primary concern. Affective development is enhanced because the children must closely attend to the stimulus message and actively respond to it. The movement response is both natural and pleasurable and, therefore, acts as a positive reward. This promotes development of positive attitudes towards the learning process and the particular content being learned.

4. Action-centred learning compensates for some of the sensory deficiencies inherent in sedentary activities that only employ cognitive operations. When children are physically active, they receive sensory input from their tactual and kinesthetic senses. This makes learning a multisensory experience in which they are feeling as well as observing.

5. Physical activity is results oriented. Each learning activity culminates in achieving an observable goal. Thus, children experience immediate rather than delayed gratification.

6. It provides an incentive for self-directed learning. The learning process is exciting and satisfying, which promotes participation in self-initiated learning activities.

Adapted from *Learning through movement*, P. Werner and E. Burton. Copyright 1979, with permission from P. Werner.

For many years, physical education programmes were primarily focused on things to do, promoting participation and fun for all at the expense of developing movement and physical activity knowledge (Logsdon, Allenan, Straits, Belka, & Clark, 1997). More recent trends call for physical education programmes that emphasise quality alongside healthy lifestyle benefits and outcomes (McKenzie, 2003; Siedentop, 1996).

The main mechanism for health maintenance is participation in physical activities (Corbin & Pangrazi, 1999). This principle is well known, but the modern lifestyle leads to totally different results. Inactive everyday life, lack of participation in physical activities, systematic watching of TV, and unhealthy nutrition threaten children's health. The majority of prevailing health problems is thought to stem from sedentary lifestyles and habits that are acquired during preschool and school. An indicator of these problems is the continually increasing number of children who are classified as obese. The World Health Organization (2000) suggests that a sedentary lifestyle is one of 10 leading causes of death and disability in the world. In developed countries, it is estimated that more than half of adults are insufficiently active.

Young children seem to have a natural exuberance for movement and boundless energy. Despite this, it appears that some children are experiencing uncharacteristically inactive lifestyles. Guidance has shifted somewhat as a better understanding of appropriate activity for children has emerged. Evidence suggests that regular, moderate physical activity is beneficial to health and that children should be given opportunities to engage in a variety of activities (at varying intensities and durations) on a daily basis. Corbin, Pangrazi, and Welk's lifetime physical activity model (1994) is an example of this advice.

Physically literate people interact with sensitivity and ease with others in group situations, appreciating the expressive quality of movement in themselves and in others (Whitehead, 2001). Movement opportunities provide many of the first socialising experiences as children interact with others in their environment (Nichols, 1990).

The ability of a person to contribute positively, responsibly, and actively within the community is an outcome of positive social behaviour. Working in pairs and groups of different sizes, accepting individual differences, sharing in decision making, and taking on various roles are all necessary life skills. More specifically, social objectives manifest themselves in the preschool context. These might include controlling one's

behaviour, taking turns, using and respecting a range of equipment, listening to the teacher, sharing ideas and trying out those of others, taking responsibility for actions, fair play, and so on. The specific social environment (e.g., preschool, classroom, playground) dictates an expected norm for behaviour.

This social learning includes an understanding of appropriate behaviour, often within boundaries and frameworks determined by others. Observation of others, including members of a peer group, is a powerful means through which social learning takes place. Bandura (1969) discussed internalisation of behaviours, and more recent studies (Chartrand & Bargh, 1999) have highlighted the importance of copying and mimicking behaviours in fostering positive relationships.

The main philosophy of the Early Steps project was based on the main goal for education of the European Union, which is the improvement of the quality of educational systems (EE C 25 E of 29.1.2002, p. 531). Under the framework of this goal, the European Transnational Program for Early Childhood Education, which was financed by the Education and Training Department of the European Union (Socrates programme, Comenius 2.1 Action), was Early Steps: Promoting Healthy Lifestyle and Social Interaction Through Physical Education Activities During Preschool Years and refers to the improvement of early childhood education.

The goals and the objectives of the Early Steps project were in accordance with the aims of the European Year of Education Through Sport, as 2004 was designated by the European Commission and the Council of the European Union. These aims were summarised as follows: in the sensitivity of the educational institutions to use sport as a pedagogical tool, in the use of values that are conveyed through physical activities, in the development of physical and social abilities (teamwork, emulation), and in the attainment of a good balance between cognitive and motor activities through school life.

Activities of the Early Steps Project

The Early Steps project (2004-2007) is an alternative physical education curriculum designed to improve the quality of education for preschool children. The project was supported by a grant from the EU Socrates programme, Comenius 2.1 Action (project number: 118192-CP-1-2004-1-GR-COMENIUS-C2.1).

The Early Steps project had two major goals: to develop an innovative physical education curriculum for early childhood, and to provide an in-service training programme to help early childhood educators implement the curriculum in their schools. The total duration of the project was 3 years (October 2004 through September 2007), and the activities for each year are shown in table appendix.1.

The Early Steps activities of the first year were focused on the preparation of the phases of the project. The academic team had to answer the following questions:

- What were they going to achieve?
- How were they going to reach their goals?
- When did they have to go from one step to the next step?
- Who was going to participate in each activity of the project, and what were they going to do?

The first year included the two major phases of the project—the writing phase and the training phase. The writing phase included the design, preparation, and writing of the educational materials, which consisted of the Early Steps Physical Education Curriculum (ESPEC) and the training materials for the educators who were going to implement the curriculum. The aim of the training phase was to help the participating early childhood educators successfully implement the curriculum. After the completion of the first two phases of the project, the implementation phase began. This was the crucial phase of the project, during which the theory had to be converted to practice. The educators started to implement

ESPEC in the school setting. Additionally, the evaluation procedure took place before, during, and after the implementation phase. The third year of the Early Steps project covered two activities: the production of the revised ESPEC based on the results of the evaluation, and the dissemination of the results of the project.

Participants in the Early Steps Project

The Early Steps project lasted a total of 3 years, and the coordinating institute was the Department of Early Childhood Care and Education of the Alexander Technological Educational Institute (ATEI) of Thessaloniki (Greece). Fourteen educational institutes were partners in this project.

Four of the institutes were universities:

- ATEI of Thessaloniki, Department of Early Childhood Care and Education, Greece
- University of Jyväskylä, Department of Physical Education, Finland
- Roehampton University, School of Education, United Kingdom
- University of Cyprus, Department of Education, Cyprus

The other 10 institutes were preschool centres from five European countries. Two preschool centres from each country participated in the project. Four early childhood educators from every participating country were involved in the Early Steps project, which resulted in a total of 20 participants from five European countries. Moreover, from these countries, 458 children aged 4 to 5 years participated in the project activities.

Table Appendix.1 Activities of the Early Steps Project

Time	Activities
1st year (October 2004-August 2005)	• Designing and writing ESPEC—writing phase • Training of school education staff—training phase
2nd year (September 2005-July 2006)	• Implementation of ESPEC—implementation phase • Initial, middle, and final evaluation of ESPEC implementation
3rd year (August 2006-September 2007)	• Production of the revised ESPEC based on the results of the evaluation • Dissemination of the results of the Early Steps project

Early Steps Physical Education Curriculum

The academics of the Early Steps main team designed the curriculum collaboratively. ESPEC was based on developmentally appropriate practice that allows preschoolers to participate actively in learning procedures. This means that ESPEC incorporates a variety of learning experiences, materials, equipment, and learning strategies suitable for preschoolers with individual differences. More specifically, it takes into consideration the previous experiences, pace of development, types of learning, and needs and interests of the children. The key points of this approach are construction of physical knowledge through experimentation, knowledge of developmental sequences, systematic records of progress for each child, systematic records of planning and activity objectives, encouragement of interactive learning among children, consideration of children's interests and experiences, and encouragement of children's independence and responsibility.

Interdisciplinary teaching was behind the planning of ESPEC. This innovative teaching method is an educational process in which two or more subject areas are integrated with the goal of enhancing learning in each subject area. The concept of interdisciplinary teaching acknowledges the integrity and uniqueness of each subject area, yet it also recognises the interrelationships among subjects. Teachers can organise physical activities where movement can be used to explore concepts relevant to the content areas of art, language arts, mathematics, science, and social studies.

ESPEC includes 48 lesson plans, and the duration of each lesson plan is 40 to 45 minutes. This curriculum is based on two standards:

1. *Acceptance of and respect for individual differences.* During the preschool years, children begin to understand their relations with others. This means that the foundation for their social development is laid during this stage, and they begin to recognise the diversity among children. This diversity can concern abilities, gender, or ethnicity. Through participation in physical activities, young children learn to play and form pairs with all children of the group and to participate in physical activities within groups of various sizes. Participation in group physical activities leads children to respond easily to others' approaches during play, to accept others' ideas and to share their own, to assume leadership roles, and to follow other leaders when playing.

2. *Familiarity with healthy lifestyle issues.* The main mechanism for health maintenance is participation in physical activities (Corbin & Pangrazi, 1999). Unfortunately, the modern lifestyle leads to an inactive everyday life, lack of participation in physical activities, systematic watching of TV, and unhealthy nutrition. Most current health problems are based on habits that are acquired during the preschool and school ages. An indicator of these problems is the continually increasing number of children who are classified as obese. A programme of physical activities can help children

- understand the importance of exercise for health,
- estimate the need to maintain physical condition through daily participation in moderate physical activities,
- learn the importance of healthy nutrition, and
- recognise healthy foods.

Table appendix.2 describes these standards with their goals, which indicate what children should have learned after the implementation of ESPEC.

These two standards of ESPEC (social interaction and healthy lifestyle) are achieved using movement and physical education activities. The activities included in ESPEC provide children with opportunities to practise their skills, express their capabilities, and develop their abilities.

Training Phase of the Early Steps Project

ESPEC was implemented by the 20 early childhood educators from five European countries who took part in two in-service training seminars. Professional development of teachers is widely recognised as a key ingredient of school improvement (Guskey, 2000). In an age of accountability and educational reform, we want all students who participate in physical education classes to receive quality instruction through a well-designed curriculum taught by dedicated teachers. A major goal of the Early Steps project was to enhance the pedagogical knowledge of the early childhood educators as well as to help them learn ESPEC.

Each seminar lasted 3 days and was based on theoretical and practical experiences. The seminars included lectures and short workshops in the form of group discussion. The topics of the two seminars are shown in table appendix.3.

Evaluation of the Early Steps Project

Vasilis Grammatikopoulos

University of Thessaly, Greece

Chen (2005) reported two general points of views about selecting the approach or method for programme evaluation: universalist and contingency. The universalist view argues that there is always a best method and insists on the superiority of certain methods over others. On the other hand, the contingency view postulates that there is no single best way to conduct programme evaluation and the method choice should be situational.

Over the years, the evaluator's toolbox has been expanding and the options are multiple. It is argued that the dynamic nature of educational procedures is better evaluated using a method with a similar dynamic structure. Thus, our choice for the evaluation of the Early Steps project was a newly proposed evaluation method that is relied on by systems theory and cybernetics—dynamic evaluation.

Dimitropoulos (1998) first presented the structure of this evaluation procedure, which has been developed further and modified during its implementation in a major education programme (Grammatikopoulos, Koustelios, Tsigilis, & Theodorakis, 2004). The structure of the approach is based on eclecticism and dynamism. Eclecticism is characterised by contingency, which postulates that there is not a single best way to conduct evaluation. Nowadays, practitioners often apply an eclectic mix, borrowing from several evaluation approaches, techniques, and methodologies (Christie, 2003). Dynamism, the second component, is being borrowed by cybernetics, where the basic idea is feedback (Midgley, 2007). Dynamism refers to the revision of evaluation plans and the modification of data collection instruments, which are ongoing components of the evaluation.

Dynamic evaluation is a procedure that is continuous, part of the process under evaluation,

Table Appendix.2   Standards and Goals of the Early Steps Physical Education Curriculum

ESPEC	
Social behaviour	Healthy lifestyle
Standard 1 Be able to cooperate with others and respect individual differences.	**Standard 2** Through the acquisition and the development of motor skills, preschool children will have a desire to be involved in a healthy lifestyle.
Goal 1. Interact positively with group members. **Goal 2.** Recognise and respect individual differences.	**Goal 1.** Be involved in a variety of physical activities. **Goal 2.** Recognise changes in body functions during physical activities. **Goal 3.** Become aware of healthy lifestyle activities.

Table Appendix.3   Topics of the In-Service Training Seminars for Early Childhood Educators

1st training seminar (Finland, April 2005)	2nd training seminar (Greece, May 2005)
• Project presentation • Importance of physical education during early childhood • Importance of healthy lifestyle and social interaction • Definition and analysis of the standards, goals, and objectives for preschool children • Planning in physical education: structure of lesson plans	• Assessment procedure • Effective teaching • Teaching styles: guided discovery and cooperative learning • Teacher's role in enhancing children's intrinsic motivation towards physical activity • Evaluation

flexible, self-controlled, and self-corrected. More-over, dynamic evaluation constitutes an integral part of the evaluation procedure. Self-control and self-correction are also outstanding elements of dynamic evaluation. Self-control of the units is ensured with additional monitoring, whereas feedback meets the condition of self-correction as a fifth essential function. Thus, dynamic evaluation is a control mechanism of an evaluating procedure, the thermostat of the procedure that provides feedback.

The core idea is that shifting environments, such as the 3-year Early Steps project, require reassessment and modification; thus an evaluation method with a dynamic nature is considered ideal. The evaluation system for the Early Steps project is presented in figure appendix.1.

The significance of dynamic evaluation is that it aspires to secure the success of the evaluating process during its implementation. The input unit of the Early Steps procedure contained the evaluation of the initial programme plan and design, as well as the training of the early childhood educators. In the transformation unit, implementation

of the programme was the evaluation object, and in the output unit, estimation of the goal achievement was the main duty.

A detailed presentation of all procedures applied during the evaluation appears in table appendix.4. The temporal information about the application of the evaluation procedures demonstrates the dynamic design of the evaluation. To see all of the reports and questionnaires used as a part of the evaluation process, see pages 203-218.

The evaluation presented in table appendix.4 meets the required criteria for being a dynamic approach. First, it was a continuous process functioning as a part of the Early Steps project. Second, it was flexible because new evaluation activities were easily adopted during the implementation of the project. One example of this is the evaluation of the training provided to early childhood educators three times during the project. Two times immediately after the end of each seminar, the questionnaire used (see Early Steps Training Evaluation Questionnaire for Early Childhood Educators on page 203) was an adaptation of the Professional Development

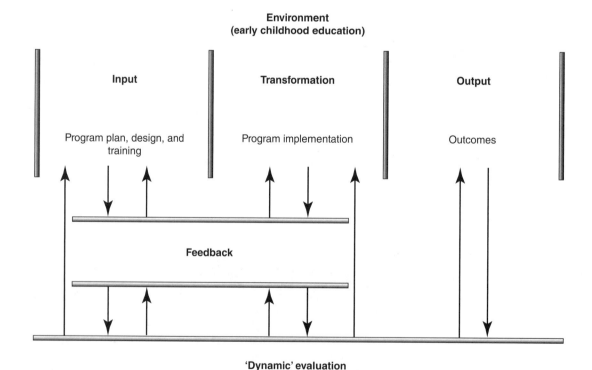

FIGURE APPENDIX.1   Dynamic evaluation for the Early Steps project.

Table Appendix.4   Evaluation Procedures Adopted for the Early Steps Project

System components		Evaluation object	Data source	When	Data collection method	System components
Environment	Input (design and training)	Program design	Independent expert	Before initial meeting	Report	Feedback
			Program producers	During initial meeting	Report	
		Training (first seminar)	Independent expert	After first seminar	Report	
			Training lecturers		Interviews	
			Training participants		Questionnaire	
		Training (second seminar)	Independent expert	After second seminar	Report	
			Training lecturers		Interviews	
			Training participants		Questionnaire	
		Training (whole training)	Training participants	After implementation of social behaviour curriculum	Questionnaire	
	Transformation	Implementation of ESPEC: social behaviour	Early educators	After implementation	Questionnaire	
			External observers	During implementation	Checklist	
		Implementation of ESPEC: healthy lifestyle	Early educators and parents	After implementation	Questionnaire	
			External observers	During implementation	Checklist	
	Output	Goal achievement of ESPEC: social behaviour	Early educators and parents	During and after ESPEC	Checklist	
			External observers	After ESPEC	Report	
			Children	During and after ESPEC	Questionnaires	
		Goal achievement of ESPEC: healthy lifestyle	Early educators and parents	During and after ESPEC	Checklist	
			External observers	After ESPEC	Report	
			Children	During and after ESPEC	Questionnaires	

Evaluation Form (PDEF), a newly designed tool for seminar evaluation (Grammatikopoulos et al., 2008). Additionally, after the implementation of the lesson plans, a follow-up evaluation of the training was conducted (see Follow-Up Seminar Evaluation Questionnaire for Early Childhood Educators on page 204), a time considered to be ideal for estimating the value of the training provided (Guskey, 2000).

Furthermore, the evaluation was self-controlled and self-corrected—it influenced the project design in order to improve the role of monitoring and feedback provision. For example, the evaluation of the project design traced the need for two consecutive seminars in order to better control the educators' training, which was considered crucial for the successful implementation of the project. In addition, the evaluation procedure was able to provide useful feedback throughout the project. It is also apparent that eclecticism was a salient feature of the evaluation; mixed-method data collection techniques were combined with internal and external procedures.

Conclusively, dynamic evaluation aspires to add knowledge to the evaluation field as it aims at comprehensiveness, implementation, and outcome assessment. Systems concepts can offer more effective ways of dealing with complex situations. The approach also aims at responsiveness by responding to issues that emerge in the setting and to data collected during the course of the evaluation, as in the responsive evaluation approach (Stake, 2003).

REFERENCES

Bandura, A. (1969). Social learning theory of identificatory process. In D. Goslin (Ed.), *Handbook of socialization theory and research.* Chicago: Rand McNally.

Chartrand, T.L., & Bargh, J.A. (1999). The chameleon effect: The perception-behaviour link and social interaction. *Journal of Personality and Social Psychology, 76*(6), 893-910.

Chen, H-T. (2005). *Practical program evaluation: Assessing and improving planning, implementation and effectiveness.* Thousand Oaks, CA: Sage.

Christie, C.A. (2003). What guides evaluation? A study of how evaluation practice maps onto evaluation theory. *New Directions for Evaluation, 97,* 7-35.

Corbin, C., & Pangrazi, R. (1999). *Toward a better understanding of physical fitness and activity: Selected topics.* Scottsdale, AZ: Holcomb Hathaway.

Corbin, C., Pangrazi, R., & Welk, G. (1994). Toward an understanding of appropriate physical activity levels for youth. *Physical Activity and Fitness Research Digest, 1*(8).

Dimitropoulos, E. (1998). *Educational evaluation.* Athens: Grigori [in Greek].

Grammatikopoulos, V., Zachopoulou, E., Tsangaridou, N., Liukkonen, J., & Pickup, I. (2008). Applying a mixed method design to evaluate training seminars within an early childhood education project. *Evaluation and Research in Education, 21*(1), 4-17.

Grammatikopoulos, V., Koustelios, A., Tsigilis, N., & Theodorakis, Y. (2004). Applying dynamic evaluation approach in education. *Studies in Educational Evaluation, 30*(4), 255-263.

Guskey, T.R. (2000). *Evaluating Professional Development.* Thousand Oaks, California: Corwin Press.

Logsdon, B., Allenan, L., Straits, S., Belka, D., & Clark, D. (1997). *Physical education unit plans for preschool-kindergarten: Learning experiences in games, gymnastics, and dance.* Champaign, IL: Human Kinetics.

McKenzie, T. (2003). Health-related physical education: Physical activity, fitness, and wellness. In S. Silverman & C. Ennis (Eds.), *Student learning in physical education: Applying research to enhance instruction* (2nd ed., pp. 207-226). Champaign, IL: Human Kinetics.

Midgley, G. (2007). Systems thinking for evaluation. In B. Williams & I. Imam (Eds.), *Systems concepts in evaluation: An expert anthology* (pp.11-34). Point Reyes, CA: EdgePress.

Nichols, B. (1990). *Moving and learning: The elementary school physical education experience.* St. Louis: Times Mirror/Mosby College.

Siedentop, D. (1996). Physical education and school reform: The case of sport education. In S. Silverman & C. Ennis (Eds.), *Student learning in physical education: Applying research to enhance instruction* (pp. 247-267). Champaign, IL: Human Kinetics.

Stake, B. (2003). *Standard-based & Responsive Evaluation.* Thousand Oaks, CA: Sage.

Werner, P., & Burton, E. (1979). *Learning through movement.* St. Louis: Mosby.

Whitehead, M.E. (2001). Physical literacy: Opening the debate. *British Journal of Teaching PE, 32* (1): 6-8.

World Health Organization (WHO). (2000). The World *Health Report 2000 - Health Systems: Imrpoving Performance. Geneva, Switzerland: World Health Organization.*

Form 1: Early Steps Training Evaluation Questionnaire for Early Childhood Educators

1. Evaluate the following.	Very good	Good	Moderate	Bad	Very bad
Training's lectures were . . .	5	4	3	2	1
Group work was . . .	5	4	3	2	1

2. Evaluate the contents of the lectures.	Very good	Good	Moderate	Bad	Very bad
Contents on Saturday (1st day) were . . .	5	4	3	2	1
Contents on Sunday (2nd day) were . . .	5	4	3	2	1

3. Evaluate the lecturers.	Always	Often	Sometimes	Seldom	Never
They were prepared and educated.	5	4	3	2	1
They communicated enthusiasm for our work.	5	4	3	2	1
They encouraged creative thinking.	5	4	3	2	1
They presented the material in clear and comprehensive ways.	5	4	3	2	1
They used time effectively.	5	4	3	2	1

1. Evaluate the following.	Very good	Good	Moderate	Bad	Very bad
Seminar organisation was . . .	5	4	3	2	1
Distributed educational material was . . .	5	4	3	2	1
Hospitality and events were . . .	5	4	3	2	1

2. Answer the following.	Strongly agree	Agree	Not sure	Disagree	Strongly disagree
The acquired knowledge will help my work at school (for the programme).	5	4	3	2	1
My total impression of the seminar was very good.	5	4	3	2	1

Early Steps logo reprinted, by permission, from Evridiki Zachopoulou.

From E. Zachopoulou, J. Liukkonen, I. Pickup, and N. Tsangaridou, 2010, *Early Steps Physical Education Curriculum: Theory and Practice for Children Under 8* (Champaign, IL: Human Kinetics).

Form 2: Follow-Up Seminar Evaluation Questionnaire for Early Childhood Educators

Answer the following.	Strongly disagree	Disagree	Slightly disagree	Slightly agree	Agree	Strongly agree	Do not know
In the two seminars, it was clarified how the lessons plans should have been carried out.	1	2	3	4	5	6	0
During the seminars, I gained many good ideas about implementation of the lesson plans.	1	2	3	4	5	6	0
Following the seminars, I understood clearly the methods for implementing the lesson plans.	1	2	3	4	5	6	0
The knowledge I gained from the seminars supported me during the lesson plans.	1	2	3	4	5	6	0
In the two seminars, I gained a lot of good ideas about teaching in early childhood education.	1	2	3	4	5	6	0
My teaching skills were improved after the two seminars.	1	2	3	4	5	6	0

Comments: _____

_____

_____

_____

After the end of the first part of the programme, do you think that any important issues have been neglected during the two seminars that would have been helpful in the implementation of the programme? If so, please report these issues and how you think they should be incorporated in the seminars: _____

_____

_____

_____

Early Steps logo reprinted, by permission, from Evridiki Zachopoulou.

From E. Zachopoulou, J. Liukkonen, I. Pickup, and N. Tsangaridou, 2010, *Early Steps Physical Education Curriculum: Theory and Practice for Children Under 8* (Champaign, IL: Human Kinetics).

Form 3: Social Behaviour List

The educator should give one Social Behaviour answer sheet to each child and discuss the symbols on the sheet to make sure of the children's understanding.

Then, the educator should read the questions out loud while the children mark their answers on the answer sheets. The answers include cues to behaviours that describe children's knowledge of healthy behaviour. Each question has three answers. Only one answer is correct.

1. When I share things with the other children, I feel
   a. ☺
   b. 😐
   c. ☹

2. I can play safely (without injuring myself) and effectively (to have the result that I want) on my own.
   a. ☺
   b. 😐
   c. ☹

3. It doesn't bother me if I cooperate (play) with different children every time.
   a. ☺
   b. 😐
   c. ☹

4. When I cooperate with my classmates to reach a common goal, I feel
   a. ☺
   b. 😐
   c. ☹

5. Everyone can contribute and help a group succeed (e.g., win, accomplish game goals).
   a. true
   b. false
   c. don't know

6. When I express my ideas and opinions to the others, I feel
   a. ☺
   b. 😐
   c. ☹

7. When I work or play in teams, I feel
   a. ☺
   b. 😐
   c. ☹

8. When my team and I help a person who is having difficulty with a particular situation, I feel
   a. ☺
   b. 😐
   c. ☹

9. When I help the other children, I feel
   a. ☺
   b. 😐
   c. ☹

10. When I participate in activities (games), it's not good to disturb the others.
    a. true
    b. false
    c. don't know

Early Steps logo reprinted, by permission, from Evridiki Zachopoulou.

From E. Zachopoulou, J. Liukkonen, I. Pickup, and N. Tsangaridou, 2010, *Early Steps Physical Education Curriculum: Theory and Practice for Children Under 8* (Champaign, IL: Human Kinetics).

Form 4: Social Behaviour Answer Sheet for Children

Child's name _____ Date of birth _____

School _____ Teacher's name _____

1. ☺   😐   ☹

2. ☺   😐   ☹

3. ☺   😐   ☹

4. ☺   😐   ☹

5. ☺   😐   ☹

6. ☺   😐   ☹

7. ☺   😐   ☹

8. ☺   😐   ☹

9. ☺   😐   ☹

10. ☺   😐   ☹

Early Steps logo reprinted, by permission, from Evridiki Zachopoulou.

From E. Zachopoulou, J. Liukkonen, I. Pickup, and N. Tsangaridou, 2010, *Early Steps Physical Education Curriculum: Theory and Practice for Children Under 8* (Champaign, IL: Human Kinetics).

Form 5: Social Behaviour List for Early Childhood Educators

- The checklist provided includes attributes of a child's behaviour that should be adopted before and after the implementation of the programme.
- The educator has to pay attention to whether the attributes are typical.
- Any child can have one or two good or bad days.

Child's name _____   Date of birth _____

School _____   Teacher's name _____

_____ (child's name) usually . . .	Strongly disagree	Disagree	Slightly disagree	Slightly agree	Agree	Strongly agree	Don't know
Shares the space with other children.	1	2	3	4	5	6	0
Shares resources with other children.	1	2	3	4	5	6	0
Is able to work safely and effectively on own.	1	2	3	4	5	6	0
Is able to identify and work in own space.	1	2	3	4	5	6	0
Is able to work with different partners.	1	2	3	4	5	6	0
Is able to work in small groups.	1	2	3	4	5	6	0
Is able to respond to a range of verbal, auditory, and visual stimuli.	1	2	3	4	5	6	0
Understands own contribution to a common goal.	1	2	3	4	5	6	0
Recognises contributions of other group members to a common goal.	1	2	3	4	5	6	0
Has a sense of cooperation in helping other children.	1	2	3	4	5	6	0
Enjoys working in groups.	1	2	3	4	5	6	0
Enjoys sharing ideas.	1	2	3	4	5	6	0
Enjoys sharing roles.	1	2	3	4	5	6	0
Has developed a team spirit and cooperative skills.	1	2	3	4	5	6	0
Understands the basic meaning of the expression "All for one."	1	2	3	4	5	6	0
Participates in activities without disturbing others.	1	2	3	4	5	6	0
Appreciates (is able to describe and reflect on) own work.	1	2	3	4	5	6	0
Appreciates others' work.	1	2	3	4	5	6	0
Enjoys helping others.	1	2	3	4	5	6	0

Early Steps logo reprinted, by permission, from Evridiki Zachopoulou.

From E. Zachopoulou, J. Liukkonen, I. Pickup, and N. Tsangaridou, 2010, *Early Steps Physical Education Curriculum: Theory and Practice for Children Under 8* (Champaign, IL: Human Kinetics).

Form 6: Social Behaviour List for Parents

- The checklist provided includes attributes of a child's behaviour that should be adopted before and after the implementation of the programme.
- The parents have to pay attention to whether the attributes are typical.
- Any child can have one or two good or bad days.

Child's name _____ Date of birth _____

School _____ Teacher's name _____

My child usually . . .	Strongly disagree	Disagree	Slightly disagree	Slightly agree	Agree	Strongly agree	Don't know
Shares the space with other children.	1	2	3	4	5	6	0
Shares resources with other children.	1	2	3	4	5	6	0
Is able to work safely and effectively on own.	1	2	3	4	5	6	0
Is able to identify and work in own space.	1	2	3	4	5	6	0
Is able to work with different partners.	1	2	3	4	5	6	0
Is able to work in small groups.	1	2	3	4	5	6	0
Is able to respond to a range of verbal, auditory, and visual stimuli.	1	2	3	4	5	6	0
Understands own contribution to a common goal.	1	2	3	4	5	6	0
Recognises contributions of other group members to a common goal.	1	2	3	4	5	6	0
Has a sense of cooperation in helping other children.	1	2	3	4	5	6	0
Enjoys working in groups.	1	2	3	4	5	6	0
Enjoys sharing ideas.	1	2	3	4	5	6	0
Enjoys sharing roles.	1	2	3	4	5	6	0
Has developed a team spirit and cooperative skills.	1	2	3	4	5	6	0
Understands the basic meaning of the expression "All for one."	1	2	3	4	5	6	0
Participates in activities without disturbing others.	1	2	3	4	5	6	0
Appreciates (is able to describe and reflect on) own work.	1	2	3	4	5	6	0
Appreciates others' work.	1	2	3	4	5	6	0
Enjoys helping others.	1	2	3	4	5	6	0

Early Steps logo reprinted, by permission, from Evridiki Zachopoulou.

From E. Zachopoulou, J. Liukkonen, I. Pickup, and N. Tsangaridou, 2010, *Early Steps Physical Education Curriculum: Theory and Practice for Children Under 8* (Champaign, IL: Human Kinetics).

Form 7: Healthy Lifestyle List

The educator should give one Healthy Lifestyle answer sheet to each child and discuss the symbols on the sheet to make sure of the children's understanding.

Then, the educator should read the questions out loud while children mark the right answer on their answer sheet. Each question has multiple answers, but only one answer is correct.

1. I can travel in space in many ways.
   a. true
   b. false
   c. don't know

2. If you want to develop your balance, which practices are good for that purpose?
   a. walking
   b. sitting
   c. tiptoeing
   d. jumping on one leg

3. Which is the best way to hold your arms when you walk on a balance beam?
   a. next to my body
   b. extended out
   c. extended up

4. Which is the easiest way to roll a ball straight?
   a. with one hand
   b. with two hands
   c. with one foot

5. The more exercise I get, the healthier my heart will be.
   a. true
   b. false
   c. don't know

6. I can count my heart rate (HR) if I put my left thumb to
   a. the left side of my neck
   b. the left shoulder
   c. the left side of my chest (heart)

7. Which of the following activities needs the most oxygen?
   a. walking
   b. running
   c. painting

8. Which of the following activities causes you to breathe faster?
   a. playing with a ball
   b. sitting
   c. watching TV

9. When do you sweat more?
   a. while painting
   b. while dancing
   c. while watching TV

10. When I start exercising, my body temperature
    a. increases
    b. decreases
    c. doesn't change

11. Exercising is
    a. exciting
    b. boring
    c. nothing special

12. When I exercise and play games with others, I feel
    a. ☺
    b. ☻
    c. ☹

13. Which of the following foods helps build stronger bones?
    a. dairy products
    b. sweets
    c. potatoes

14. Which of the following sweets builds a healthier body?
    a. chocolates
    b. cookies
    c. yoghurt with fruit

15. Breathing, HR, and perspiration are three body functions that change between exercising and relaxing.
    a. true
    b. false
    c. don't know

16. When I have small breaks during exercise, I feel
    a. ☺
    b. ☻
    c. ☹

Early Steps logo reprinted, by permission, from Evridiki Zachopoulou.

From E. Zachopoulou, J. Liukkonen, I. Pickup, and N. Tsangaridou, 2010, *Early Steps Physical Education Curriculum: Theory and Practice for Children Under 8* (Champaign, IL: Human Kinetics).

Form 8: Healthy Lifestyle List Answer Sheet for Children

Child's name _____ Date of birth _____

School _____ Teacher's name _____

1.　　✓　　　　✗　　　　?

2.

3.

4.

5.　　✓　　　　✗　　　　?

Early Steps logo reprinted, by permission, from Evridiki Zachopoulou. Photos (rows 2, 3, and 4) courtesy of Elisavet Konstantinidou.

From E. Zachopoulou, J. Liukkonen, I. Pickup, and N. Tsangaridou, 2010, *Early Steps Physical Education Curriculum: Theory and Practice for Children Under 8* (Champaign, IL: Human Kinetics).

6.

7.

8.

9.

10.

11.

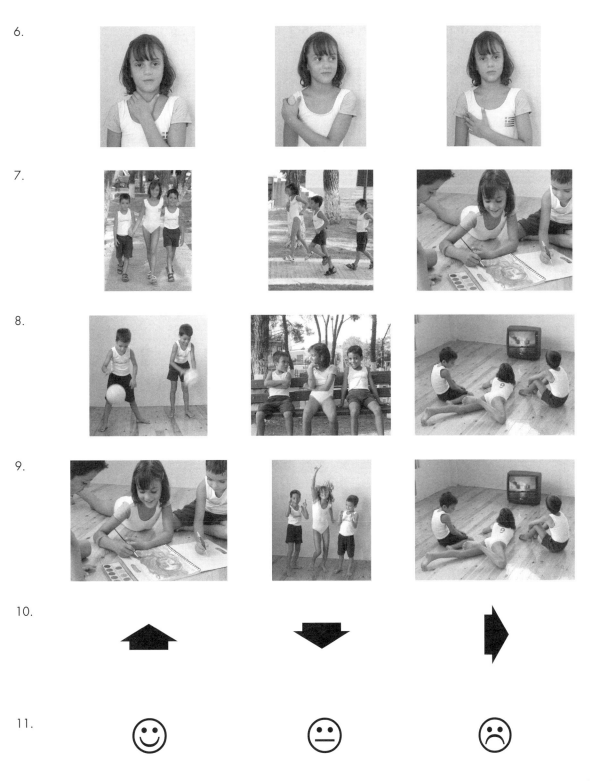

> continued

Photos (rows 6, 7, 8, and 9) courtesy of Elisavet Konstantinidou.

From E. Zachopoulou, J. Liukkonen, I. Pickup, and N. Tsangaridou, 2010, *Early Steps Physical Education Curriculum: Theory and Practice for Children Under 8* (Champaign, IL: Human Kinetics).

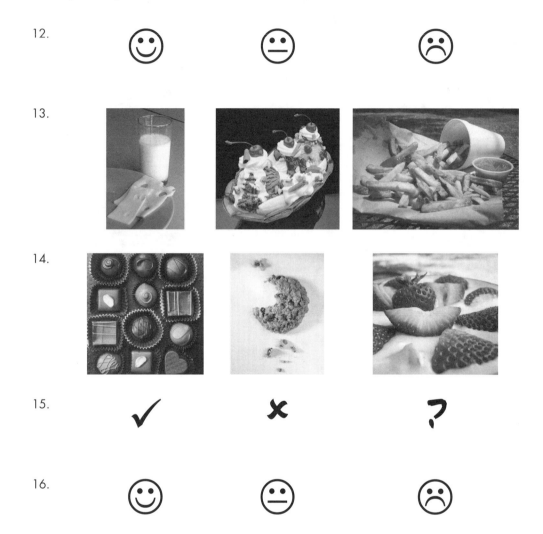

Form 9: Healthy Lifestyle List for Early Childhood Educators

- The checklist provided includes attributes of a child's behaviour that should be adopted before and after the implementation of the programme.
- The teacher has to pay attention to whether the attributes are typical.
- Any child can have one or two good or bad days.

Child's name _____   Date of birth _____

School _____   Teacher's name _____

_____ (child's name) usually . . .	Strongly disagree	Disagree	Slightly disagree	Slightly agree	Agree	Strongly agree	Don't know
Realises that more exercise means better health.	1	2	3	4	5	6	0
Understands that healthy activities increase heart rate (HR).	1	2	3	4	5	6	0
Identifies differences between activities that increase or do not increase HR.	1	2	3	4	5	6	0
Can distinguish activities that keep the heart healthy from those that do not (e.g., running versus sitting).	1	2	3	4	5	6	0
Identifies activities that increase the pace of breathing.	1	2	3	4	5	6	0
Recognises the relation between breathing and HR.	1	2	3	4	5	6	0
Identifies which activities affect body temperature.	1	2	3	4	5	6	0
Recognises the relationship between exercise and increasing body temperature.	1	2	3	4	5	6	0
Identifies the positive effect of exercise on health.	1	2	3	4	5	6	0
Enjoys participation in physical activities (e.g., play, games, exercise).	1	2	3	4	5	6	0
Recognises the value of healthy foods.	1	2	3	4	5	6	0
Discriminates healthy from unhealthy foods.	1	2	3	4	5	6	0
Understands the importance of and need for rest.	1	2	3	4	5	6	0

> continued

Early Steps logo reprinted, by permission, from Evridiki Zachopoulou.

From E. Zachopoulou, J. Liukkonen, I. Pickup, and N. Tsangaridou, 2010, *Early Steps Physical Education Curriculum: Theory and Practice for Children Under 8* (Champaign, IL: Human Kinetics).

Healthy Lifestyle List for Early Childhood Educators > *continued*

_____ (child's name) usually . . .	Strongly disagree	Disagree	Slightly disagree	Slightly agree	Agree	Strongly agree	Don't know
Recognises the changes in body function between exercising and relaxing (breathing, HR, perspiration).	1	2	3	4	5	6	0
Understands the importance and need for small breaks during exercise.	1	2	3	4	5	6	0
Prefers being outside to being inside.	1	2	3	4	5	6	0
Is able to receive a ball or other objects in three or more different ways.	1	2	3	4	5	6	0
Is able to travel in many ways.	1	2	3	4	5	6	0
Participates successfully in balancing activities.	1	2	3	4	5	6	0

From E. Zachopoulou, J. Liukkonen, I. Pickup, and N. Tsangaridou, 2010, *Early Steps Physical Education Curriculum: Theory and Practice for Children Under 8* (Champaign, IL: Human Kinetics).

Form 10: Healthy Lifestyle List for Parents

- The checklist provided includes attributes of a child's behaviour that should be adopted before and after the implementation of the programme.
- The parents have to pay attention to whether the attributes are typical.
- Any child can have one or two good or bad days.

Child's name _____ Date of birth _____

School _____ Teacher's name _____

My child usually . . .	Strongly disagree	Disagree	Slightly disagree	Slightly agree	Agree	Strongly agree	Don't know
Realises that more exercise means better health.	1	2	3	4	5	6	0
Can distinguish activities that keep the heart healthy from those that do not (e.g., running versus sitting).	1	2	3	4	5	6	0
Identifies activities that increase the pace of breathing.	1	2	3	4	5	6	0
Recognises the relation between breathing and heart rate (HR).	1	2	3	4	5	6	0
Identifies the positive effect of exercise on health.	1	2	3	4	5	6	0
Enjoys participation in physical activities (e.g., play, games, exercise).	1	2	3	4	5	6	0
Recognises the value of healthy foods.	1	2	3	4	5	6	0
Discriminates healthy from unhealthy foods.	1	2	3	4	5	6	0
Understands the importance of rest.	1	2	3	4	5	6	0
Understands the importance of small breaks during exercise.	1	2	3	4	5	6	0
Prefers playing to watching TV.	1	2	3	4	5	6	0
Prefers exercising to playing computer games.	1	2	3	4	5	6	0
Prefers being outside to being inside.	1	2	3	4	5	6	0
Is able to receive a ball or other objects in three or more ways.	1	2	3	4	5	6	0
Is able to travel in many ways.	1	2	3	4	5	6	0
Participates successfully in balancing activities.	1	2	3	4	5	6	0

Early Steps logo reprinted, by permission, from Evridiki Zachopoulou.

From E. Zachopoulou, J. Liukkonen, I. Pickup, and N. Tsangaridou, 2010, *Early Steps Physical Education Curriculum: Theory and Practice for Children Under 8* (Champaign, IL: Human Kinetics).

Form 11: Programme Evaluation Questionnaire for Early Childhood Educators

Answer the following.	Strongly disagree	Disagree	Slightly disagree	Slightly agree	Agree	Strongly agree	Don't know
School equipment adequately supported the needs of the programme.	1	2	3	4	5	6	0
The educational material provided gave me many good ideas for programme activities.	1	2	3	4	5	6	0
The seminars in which I participated clearly explained how the programme should be carried out.	1	2	3	4	5	6	0
The children appeared to have a desire to be involved in a healthy lifestyle.	1	2	3	4	5	6	0
The relationships between the teacher and the children helped the programme implementation.	1	2	3	4	5	6	0
The facilities of the school were adequate for the implementation of the programme.	1	2	3	4	5	6	0
The management of the school tried to solve any problems that appeared during the programme.	1	2	3	4	5	6	0
The knowledge I gained from the seminars was supportive during the programme implementation.	1	2	3	4	5	6	0
The activities proposed by the programme met the children's interests.	1	2	3	4	5	6	0
The school administrator helped with the programme implementation.	1	2	3	4	5	6	0
The educational material provided was easy to use.	1	2	3	4	5	6	0
Problems that appeared during the programme were faced by my colleagues collaboratively.	1	2	3	4	5	6	0
The children acquired and developed the skills taught during the programme.	1	2	3	4	5	6	0
The contents of the programme satisfied the children.	1	2	3	4	5	6	0

Early Steps logo reprinted, by permission, from Evridiki Zachopoulou.

From E. Zachopoulou, J. Liukkonen, I. Pickup, and N. Tsangaridou, 2010, *Early Steps Physical Education Curriculum: Theory and Practice for Children Under 8* (Champaign, IL: Human Kinetics).

Form 12: Supervision Sheet for Programme Implementation Evaluation

Institution: _____

Supervisor: _____

Preschool centre: _____

Early educator: _____

Date			Lesson plan	Minutes
Day	Month	Year		
			Number _____	
			Title _____	

_____ (educator's name) usually . . .	Strongly disagree	Disagree	Slightly disagree	Slightly agree	Agree	Strongly agree	Don't know
Was well prepared.	1	2	3	4	5	6	0
Used time effectively.	1	2	3	4	5	6	0
Was consistent with the time schedule.	1	2	3	4	5	6	0
Exhibited appropriate behaviour.	1	2	3	4	5	6	0

The children usually . . .	Strongly disagree	Disagree	Slightly disagree	Slightly agree	Agree	Strongly agree	Don't know
Participated actively.	1	2	3	4	5	6	0
Enjoyed their participation.	1	2	3	4	5	6	0
Found the innovations suitable.	1	2	3	4	5	6	0
Learned from the lesson.	1	2	3	4	5	6	0

> continued

Early Steps logo reprinted, by permission, from Evridiki Zachopoulou.

From E. Zachopoulou, J. Liukkonen, I. Pickup, and N. Tsangaridou, 2010, *Early Steps Physical Education Curriculum: Theory and Practice for Children Under 8* (Champaign, IL: Human Kinetics).

Supervision Sheet for Programme Implementation Evaluation > *continued*

_____ (lesson number) usually . . .	Strongly disagree	Disagree	Slightly disagree	Slightly agree	Agree	Strongly agree	Don't know
Was well designed and interesting.	1	2	3	4	5	6	0
Adopted innovations.	1	2	3	4	5	6	0
Was developmentally appropriate.	1	2	3	4	5	6	0
Achieved its goals.	1	2	3	4	5	6	0
Comments:							

_____

Supervisor's signature

_____

Educator's signature

From E. Zachopoulou, J. Liukkonen, I. Pickup, and N. Tsangaridou, 2010, *Early Steps Physical Education Curriculum: Theory and Practice for Children Under 8* (Champaign, IL: Human Kinetics).

Index

Note: Page numbers followed by *f* or *t* refer to the figure or table on that page, respectively.

A
academic learning time (ALT) 22
achievement
    and content covered 22
    and cooperation 18
    and learning time 22
    and routine 31
achievement goal theory 35
activities
    organisation of 25
    selection 24-25
Aim and Follow 95
Alphabet Soup 92
American Evaluation Association 190
Animal Gymnastics 135
Animal Hunt 99-100
animal-like movements 68, 102-103
Animal Magic 87
Animal Track 100
Art Activity 110
attention
    buffering from distractions distractions 15
    channeling 18
    and fine motor skills 4
authority principle 36*t*
Automobiles game 69

B
Back to Base 101
balancing activities 176
    beanbags 72
    difficult positions 106-107
    lesson plans 134-136, 137-138, 139-141, 142-143
    skill components 48
ball activities 147, 158
    bouncing through hoops 145
    carrying 145
    dribbling 62-63
    kicking 58
    relays with 65
    send and receive 144-145, 146-148, 149-150, 151-152
    travel with 144-145, 146-148, 149-150, 151-152
balloon activities 112, 161, 164
Ball School 147
Ball Tail 152
basketball 63
beanbag activities 72, 73, 79-80
Bear is Sleeping 136
Behavioral Risk Factor Surveillance System 49
behaviours
    altruistic 34

of effective teachers 22-23
    expectations of 26, 27
    helping 43
    managing students' 25
    praising 45
    prosocial 33-34, 44-45
Best Standing 78
Birds and Hawk 126-127
Blinds and Guides 117
body image 6, 49
body mastery 43
body temperature
    and clothing 166
    and drinking water 169
    lesson plans 165-167, 168-170
    objective 49
    perspiration 165-166, 168-170
bowling 175
breathing
    comparing 164
    facts 161
    feeling 161, 164
    and heart rate 163-164
    lesson plans 160-162, 163-164
    objective 49
    questions game 161-162
    and relaxation 187
Build and Animal Tower 172
Burning Ball 150
Busy Bees 95

C
Candle 123
cardiovascular system 153
Cat and Mouse 115
catching 72-73, 127
Catch the Puppy Tail 76
Caterpillar 109
Chase the Rabbit 98
chasing games 58, 62, 72, 98, 121
child-centred approach 1
    allowing for spontaneity 13
    need for 12-13
childhood, culture of 1
Child Says 83
class management 25. *See also* routines; rules
cognition
    and motor learning 46-47
    and socialisation 15
    and task-involving climates 35
command-style teaching 16
competition 18
concentration 50
convergent discovery 16-17
cooperation 43. *See also* helping others;

teamwork
cooperative learning 18
Crane and Frog 139-140
creative games 73, 81
critical-thinking skills 17
curriculum physical education 1

D
dance 184
    and breathe 185, 187
    and perspiration 167
developmental goals 1
diabetes 6
differentiation 16
discipline 17, 25
divergent production style 17
dribbling 62-63
dynamic systems approach 46

E
Eagles and Swallows 118
early childhood education 4
Early Steps Physical Education Curriculum (ESPEC) 43
    goals and objectives 43-46, 46-50
    lesson format 54-55
    standards 43, 46, 53-54
Early Steps Training Evaluation Questionnaire 193
eating habits 50
Education Reform Act (1988) 42
educator. *See* teachers
effort 16
ego-involving climate 35, 37
enjoyment 33
    lesson plans 171-173, 174, 176
    objective 50
    as predictor of sport commitment 33
environment 16
    forested 5, 6
    versatile 6
equipment
    for lesson plans 54
    playgrounds 5
    sharing 68-69
ESPEC. *See* Early Steps Physical Education Curriculum (ESPEC)
evaluand 191
evaluation
    considering age 191
    criteria 191-192
    definitions 190
    in early childhood education 190-191
    in education 190
    goals of 191-192
    objects of 191

evaluation *(continued)*
    principle 36*t*
    procedures 25, 190
    purposes of 190
Evaluation Scale 194
evaluee 191
exercise-play 4
expectations 22

F
feedback
    choosing to offer 14, 18
    giving to peers 45
    in guided-discovery 16
    and learning 23
    from peers 43
    self-control and correction 192
    specific vs general 27
    and teaching routines 26, 27
    verbal 16
fine motor skills 4
Follow the Leader 76
Follow-Up Seminar Evaluation Question-
    naire 193
foods, healthy 177-179, 180-182
Forest Trip 66-67
Four Countries 60
Fox and Hare 135
Freedom 121
free exploration 17
free play 4, 5
Frog Race 103
Frogs in a Pond 98
Fruit Play 133
Fruit Salad 133

G
gross motor skills 4
grouping principle 36*t*
group work
    cooperative learning 18
    goal 43-45
    lesson plans 58-59, 60-61, 62-63, 64-65
    objective 45
Growing and Moving 75
Guess the Change 110
guided-discovery teaching 16

H
Hail Melts 184-185
Happy Elephant 88
Head and Shoulders 79
healthy foods
    lesson plans 177-179, 180-182
    objective 50
healthy lifestyle 42, 46, 49-50
Healthy Lifestyle List
    for Early Childhood Educators 193
    for Parents 194
heart rate
    and breathing 163-164
    counting 156-158
    lesson plans 153-155, 156-159
    listening to 154
    objective 49

helping others
    lesson plans 114-116, 117-119, 120-
    121, 122-124
    objective 46
    specialized help 122-124
Hen and Chicks 118
Hidden Treasure 114-115
Hold and More 94
Hopping Mad 97-98
Hopping Race 187
hula-hoop activities 65, 70, 138
The Hunt 100-101
The Hunter 88-89

I
imagination 187
Incy Wincy Spider 91
individual accountability 18
indoor activities 5
Insects 91
instructional principles 23
intrinsic motivation 34-35

J
Jugglers 113
Jumping Track 143
Jump Rope with hoops 138
Jungle Adventure 86-87

K
kicking activities 58, 59, 61
kindergarten
    participation 4
    regulations by country 5*t*

L
learning
    constructivist view 17
    cooperative 18
    facilitating 12, 14
    and socialisation 15
    through experience 46
lesson plan components 25, 54-55
lesson plans
    balancing activities 134-136, 137-138,
    139-141, 142-143
    body temperature 165-167, 168-170
    breathing 160-162, 163-164
    on enjoyment 171-173, 174, 176
    flexibility 25
    on healthy foods 177-179, 180-182
    heart rate changes 153-155, 156-159
    helping others 114-116, 117-119, 120-
    121, 122-124
    need for rest 183-185, 186-188
    participation without disturbing
    others 74-77, 78-81, 82-85, 86-89
    send and receive objects 144-145,
    146-148, 149-150, 151-152
    sharing ideas and roles 90-92, 93-95,
    96-98, 99-101
    sharing space and resources 66-67,
    68-69, 70-71, 72-73
    team work 102-104, 105-107, 108-
    110, 111-113

    travel variations 126-127, 128-129,
    130-131, 132-133
    travel with balls 144-145, 146-148,
    149-150, 151-152
    work in groups 58-59, 60-61, 62-63,
    64-65
Life Belt 121
linear rational model of planning 24-25
locomotor skills 47, 64-65

M
Magician 130-131
Magic Spot 74-75
manipulative skills 48, 70-71
Marching Band 90-91
matching games 170, 178-179, 181
Maze Game 181
metabolic syndromes 6
Metamorphosis 92
Mosston, Muska 16
motionlessness 157-158, 183-185, 186-
    188
motivational climate 35, 37
motor learning 46, 47
motor skills development 5, 6, 15
Mountaineers 121
Mouse Tail 143
Move Like Me 75, 79
movement. *See also* travel variations
    accuracy 84, 95, 98, 131, 147
    adapting 126
    analysis 15
    animal-like 68
    creative expression 186
    mechanical 68
    propensity for 1
Musical Hats 172
musical hoops 137-138

N
Navigate the Ship 103
nonlocomotor skills 47, 48
Numbers Game 66
nutrition 50, 177-179, 180-182

O
obesity 6, 49-50
objectives, specifying 24
observation 13
    acting on 15-16
observation-interact-learn cycle 14*f*
obstacle-courses 4
On the Moon 129
outdoor activities 6

P
Pantomime 110, 115-116
parachute activities 126, 166-167
Paramedics 118
participation without disturbing others
    45, 74-77, 78-81, 82-85, 86-89
partners
    activities 59, 62, 71, 80, 113, 145
    choosing 27
peer evaluation 98

perceived autonomy 37
physical activity
    benefits of 6
    breaks in 50
    girls vs boys 6
    goal 46-47
    later in life 6
    learning in and through 42
    physiological responses 48-49
    and supervision 6
    variety 46
physical learning 15
planning 24-25
play
    informal 1
    structured vs free 5
    types of 4
playgrounds
    equipment 5
    safety 4
    surfaces 5, 6
positive independence 18
preschool
    special challenges 46
    variation by country 5t
preventive class management 25
process-product research 22
Professional Development Evaluation
        Form (PDEF) 193
professional organizations 42
programme evaluation 192
Programme Evaluation Questionnaire
        194
Puppy Moves 75-76
Puppy's Bedtime 77

R
Rabbits and Burrows 85
Rabbits and Kangaroos 154
Rabbits and Turtles 154
reaction skills 126
recovery 50. See also relaxation
relationships 43
relaxation 50, 138, 145
    and breathing 187
    and imagination 187
    lesson plans 183-185, 186-188
    and massage 147-148
relay games 64-65
respecting differences 43, 44f, 45
rest
    lesson plans 183-185, 186-188
    need for 50, 183-185
rewards principle 36t
Rhymes for Body Functions 169-170
Rhymes for Foods 178
rhythm 50
risk-taking 120-121
Robots 68, 174-175
Rob the Nest 84
Rocking and Standing 123
Rolls 106
rough-and-tumble play 4
routines 23, 26
    class events 27

teaching 26-27
rules 23, 26

S
safety 17
scaffolding theory 15
Sculptors 107
section places 68
sedentary lifestyles 1, 6
segmental movement analysis 15
self-determination 37
self-esteem 6, 18, 32, 150, 190
sensorimotor experiences 4
sequential movement analysis 15
Shaking 152
shape forming 112, 113
Shape Letters 107
Shapes 105-106
sharing
    equipment 68-69
    ideas and roles 90-92, 93-95, 96-98,
        99-101
    objectives 45
    space and resources 66-67, 68-69,
        70-71, 72-73
Shield and Ball 145
Ship and Lighthouse 115
Simon Says 82-83
skill acquisition 17
skills
    catching 72-73
    dribbling 62-63
    jumping 143
    kicking 58, 59, 61
    locomotor 47, 64-65
    manipulative 48, 64-65
    nonlocomotor skills 47, 48
    receiving objects 60-61, 62-63
    sending objects 60-61, 62-63
    spatial awareness 66
    stability 48
    stopping 68
    throwing 72-73
    traveling 66, 68-69
Sleeping Lions 101
Slow Motion 76-77
soccer 59
sociability 33
Social Behaviour List
    for Early Childhood Educators 193
    for Parents 193
social development 15, 33-34
socialisation 15, 32, 47
solidarity 117
Somersault 123-124
Space Travel 128-129
Spaghetti Dance 184
spatial awareness 50, 66
spectrum of teaching styles 16
Spiders 172-173
Spider's Web 92
stability 48. See also balancing activities
stations 154-155
Statue Balances 176
Statues and Dancers 171-172

Statues Game 64, 93-94
Sticky Hands 95, 97
Sticky Treacle 96-97
stimuli 74-75, 82-84, 88, 99
structured play 5
STTEP principle 16
students 16
    accountability 22
    active inventive role 18
Supervision Sheet 194

T
Tails 72
TARGET principles 35, 36t
Tar Pot 152
task-involving climate 35, 37
task principle 36t
tasks
    differentiation 16
    open-ended 81
teacher-effects research 22
teachers 16
    effectiveness 22-23
    existing knowledge 15
    indirect role 17
    instructional behaviours 23
    intervening 15
    as managers 22-23
    role in learning 15
    skillful observation 13, 14
    starting from the child 13-14
teaching styles 16-18
    choice of 16
    in combination 18
teamwork
    lesson plans 102-104, 105-107, 108-
        110, 111-113
throwing 72-73, 147
time principle 36t
The Tower 103-104
toxic childhood 1
Tracking the Elephant 87
Tracks 140
Traffic Police 151-152
Transportation 106
Trap Room 175-176
Traveling Ball 109
travel variations
    lesson plans 126-127, 128-129, 130-
        131, 132-133
Truck and Trailer 83
Trunk by Trunk 88
Tunnel 135-136
The Turtle 112

W
The Watchmaker 104
Wonder Person 142
Working Ants 91

Z
Zigzag Relay 64

About the Authors

Evridiki Zachopoulou, PhD, is an associate professor in the department of early childhood care and education at the Alexander Technological Educational Institution of Thessaloniki in Greece. She researches physical education for young children and teaches physical education to early educators. She has written numerous papers and research articles studying the effectiveness of physical education activities and movement programs on children's overall development. She has also published extensively in professional journals and magazines in the area of curriculum design. In her leisure time, she enjoys playing tennis and hiking.

Jarmo Liukkonen, PhD, is a professor in the department of sport sciences at the University of Jyvaskyla in Finland. He has conducted research on school physical education and teaches physical education to students and coaches. He has written numerous papers and research articles studying the pedagogical aspects of school physical education and youth sports. From 1991 to 2003, he was a member of the European Sport Psychology Association. In his spare time, he enjoys playing badminton, cross-country skiing, and gardening.

Tarja Vänskä-Kauhanen

Ian Pickup, who is completing his PhD, is director of sport and well-being at Roehampton University in London. He has extensive experience teaching physical education from the early years through the university level. He has led physical education teacher education teams at Roehampton and has written texts and chapters to support the development of non-specialist teachers. He is a member of the British Educational Research Association and a fellow of the Royal Society for the Encouragement of Arts and Commerce. He enjoys spending time with his children, playing club-standard squash, and keeping fit in the gym.

Niki Tsangaridou, PhD, is an associate professor in the department of education at the University of Cyprus in Nicosia, Cyprus. She has published extensively on teachin g and teacher education in physical education and has made numerous presentations on teacher education topics at international conferences and workshops. She is an editorial member of the *Journal of Teaching in Physical Education* and is a reviewer for other physical education research journals. She has also taught physical education methods courses and conducted workshops and seminars on teaching young children. In 2004, she received the Metzler-Freedman Exemplary Paper Award from the *Journal of Teaching in Physical Education*. Away from work, she enjoys sports, writing, and music.

Vasilis Grammatikopoulos, PhD, has a BEd in physical education and sport science and a MSc in school physical education from the Aristotle University of Thessaloniki, Greece, and a PhD in educational evaluation from the University of Thessaly, Greece. He is a lecturer in educational evaluation in the department of early years education at the University of Crete. Previously, he was at Liverpool Hope University as a postdoctoral teaching fellow and at the University of Thessaly, Greece, as an academic scholar. He has published over 20 research papers in peer reviewed international journals and is member of the American Evaluation Association and American Educational Research Association.

Arja Sääkslahti, PhD, graduated with an MSc from the University of Jyväskylä, Faculty of Sport Sciences in 1993. She worked as a physical education teacher in a teacher training school for kindergarten and primary school teachers and as a researcher in the University of Jyväskylä, Finland. She finished her PhD thesis in 2005 with the topic of "Effects of physical activity intervention on physical activity and motor skills and relationships between physical activity and coronary heart disease risk factors in 3- to 7-year-old children". Sääkslahti is a researcher and well-known lecturer among Finnish researchers and teachers. Most of her publications deal with preschool-aged children's physical activities, fundamental motor skill development, and children's health. She has also published physical education curriculums for preschool and for grades one and two.

You'll find other outstanding
physical education resources at
www.HumanKinetics.com